AMERICAN HISTORY BY ERA

The Age of Reform and Industrialization: 1896–1920

VOLUME 6

D1026884

Other titles in the
American History by Era series:

AMERICAN HISTORY BY ERA

The Age of Reform and Industrialization: 1896–1920

VOLUME 6

Roman Espejo, *Book Editor*

Daniel Leone, *President*
Bonnie Szumski, *Publisher*
Scott Barbour, *Managing Editor*

GREENHAVEN
PRESS®

THOMSON

™

GALE

San Diego • Detroit • New York • San Francisco • Cleveland
New Haven, Conn. • Waterville, Maine • London • Munich

© 2003 by Greenhaven Press. Greenhaven Press is an imprint of The Gale Group, Inc., a division of Thomson Learning, Inc.

Greenhaven® and Thomson Learning™ are trademarks used herein under license.

For more information, contact
Greenhaven Press
27500 Drake Rd.
Farmington Hills, MI 48331-3535
Or you can visit our Internet site at http://www.gale.com

Cover credit: © Hulton/Archive by Getty Images

Dover Publications, 74, 131
Library of Congress, 92, 126, 158, 179
National Archives, 34

Cover inset photo credits (from left): Planet Art; Corel; Digital Stock; Corel; Library of Congress; Library of Congress; Digital Stock; Painet/Garry Rissman

LIBRARY OF CONGRESS CATALOGING-IN-PUBLICATION DATA
The age of reform and industrialization: 1896–1920 / Roman Espejo, book editor. p. cm. — (American history by era; vol. 6) Includes bibliographical references and index. ISBN 0-7377-1142-6 (lib. : alk. paper) — ISBN 0-7377-1141-8 (pbk. : alk. paper) 1. United States—History—1896–1920—Juvenile literature. 2. United States—History—1896–1920—Sources—Juvenile literature. [1. United States—History—1896–1920. 2. United States—History—1896–1920—Sources.] I. Espejo, Roman, 1977– . II. Series. E661 .A525 2003 973.91—dc21   2002034723

Printed in the United States of America

CONTENTS

Baldwin recalled the natural disaster with eerie detail.

Chapter 3: 1913–1917: America Watches the World Go to War

neutrality could not mask the growing friction between pro-Ally and pro-German Americans.

Chapter 4: 1918–1919: The War Changes America

During the sixteenth century, events occurred in North America that would change the course of American history. In 1512, Spanish explorer Juan Ponce de León led the first European expedition to Florida. French navigator Jean Ribault established the first French colony in America at Fort Caroline in 1564. Over a decade later, in 1579, English pirate Francis Drake landed near San Francisco and claimed the country for England.

These three seemingly random events happened in different decades, occurred in various regions of America, and involved three different European nations. However, each discrete occurrence was part of a larger movement for European dominance over the New World. During the sixteenth century, Spain, France, and England vied for control of what was later to become the United States. Each nation was to leave behind a legacy that would shape the political structure, language, culture, and customs of the American people.

Examining such seemingly disparate events in tandem can help to emphasize the connections between them and generate an appreciation for the larger global forces of which they were a part. Greenhaven Press's American History by Era series provides students with a unique tool for examining American history in a way that allows them to see such connections. This series divides American history—from the time that the first people arrived in the New World from Asia to the September 11, 2001, terrorist attacks—into nine discrete periods. Each volume then presents a collection of both primary and secondary documents that describe the major events of the period in chronological order. This structure provides students with a snapshot of events occurring simultaneously in all parts of America. The reader can then gain an appreciation for the political, social, and cultural movements and trends that shaped the nation. Students reading about the adventures of individual European explorers, for instance, are invited to consider how such expeditions compared in purpose and consequence to earlier and later expeditions. Rather than simply learning that Ponce de León was the first Spaniard to try to colonize Florida, for example, students can begin to understand his expedition in a larger context. Indeed, Ponce's voyage was an extension of Spain's desire to conquer the Caribbean and Mexico, and his expedition was to inspire other Spanish explorers to head north from Hispaniola and New Spain in search of rich empires to conquer.

Another benefit of studying eras is that students can view a "snapshot" of America at any given moment of time and see the various social, cultural, and political events that occurred simultaneously. For example, during the period between 1920 and 1945, Charles Lindbergh became the first to make a solo transatlantic flight, Babe Ruth broke the record for the most home runs in one season, and the United States dropped the atomic bomb on Hiroshima. Random events occurring in post–Cold War America included the torching of the Branch Davidian compound in Waco, Texas, the emergence of the World Wide Web, and the 2000 presidential election debacle in which ballot miscounts in Florida held up election results for weeks.

Each volume in this series offers features to enhance students' understanding of the era of American history under discussion. An introductory essay provides an overview of the period, supplying essential context for the readings that follow. An annotated table of contents highlights the main point of each selection. A more in-depth introduction precedes each document, placing it in its particular historical context and offering biographical information about the author. A thorough chronology and index allow students to quickly reference specific events and dates. Finally, a bibliography opens up additional avenues of research. These features help to make the American History by Era series an extremely valuable tool for students researching the political upheavals, wars, cultural movements, scientific and technological advancements, and other events that mark the unfolding of American history.

INTRODUCTION

The United States emerged from World War I a more powerful nation. Having lived through those tumultuous years, noted American journalist Lincoln Steffens claimed that "we went into the war a conceited, but secretly rather humble, second-rate country; we came out self-assured. Our soldiers, our engineers, our organizers and managers, our industrialists and financiers—we had measured ourselves with our European competitors. . . . We were a first rate people, 'the' world's first power!" Echoing Steffens's view, American author John Lukacs contends that "by Armistice Day the United States was more than a World Power; it was the greatest power in the world."

America's emergence as a world power at the end of World War I was the culmination of a trend dating back to the Spanish-American War of 1898. That victory began an era that propelled America to a world-leader status. In the period between these two victories, the nation underwent dramatic economic growth and industrialization. Technological innovations introduced new, more efficient industrial processes. The populations of cities swelled to meet new demands for labor. The burgeoning immigrant population also enhanced this growth by bringing their ambition, labor, and vitality to the American economy. American corporations flourished in this new efficiency of labor. Furthermore, to compete with European powers, America increased its involvement in international affairs, gaining global dominance and giving rise to American imperialism; it vigorously pursued economic opportunities abroad and annexed foreign nations. By the time Congress declared war on Germany in 1917, the United States had gained the resources to influence the outcome of World War I. Thus, the era from 1896 to 1920 was a period of dramatic growth in America's domestic economy and international power.

THE INDUSTRIAL REVOLUTION AND THE MODERN CORPORATION

The United States experienced a rush of astonishing changes that turned it into the world's leading economic power. The industrial revolution, which gained momentum after the Civil War, was in full swing by the turn of the twentieth century. For instance, the capital that was invested into American manufacturing by 1900 reached a staggering figure of $10 billion, a tenfold increase since 1860. This dramatic shift in capital investment helped transform the United States into the top industrial nation of the world; during that same period, the value of manufactured American goods rose from $2 billion to $13 billion.

At the heart of the industrial revolution were technological innovations. For instance, the ability to convert iron into steel contributed significantly to the metamorphosis of the United States from an agrarian to an industrial nation. Steel lent itself to a variety of life-changing applications and was used to build automobiles, skyscrapers, railroad tracks, and bridges, changing the American landscape. For example, the miles of railroad in the United States rose from 79,082 in 1877 to a sprawling national network of 200,000 miles of railroad by 1900. The railroad brought the United States closer economically, drastically improving industries' access to untapped natural resources and opening businesses to nationwide trade and commerce. Also, automobile manufacturer Henry Ford pioneered the concept of mass production and achieved new levels of industrial efficiency: He reduced the assembly time of his Model T from fourteen hours to an hour and a half with highly economical approaches to production, significantly increasing production and reducing costs. Ford's ingenuity is largely responsible for today's mass production of standardized goods.

American enterprise at the turn of the twentieth century was dictated by a laissez-faire attitude, which is marked by the lack of federal regulation of business. Tycoons such as steel giant Andrew Carnegie and oil entrepreneur John D. Rockefeller dominated their respective markets and gained immense wealth through big business mergers, or corporations. One of the largest corporations resulted when one hundred fifty-eight companies totaling $1.4 billion in capital were merged to form the United States Steel Corporation in 1901. Corporations stifled competition and were responsible for two-thirds of all manufacturing in the United States by 1900. Under this system, a few businessmen had become extraordinarily rich; by 1910, seventy Americans controlled one-sixteenth of the nation's wealth. These corporations and the laissez-faire economic system became the targets of a reform movement and President Theodore Roosevelt stepped in to break up some combinations. Undeniably, however, the forces of industry and capitalism transformed the United States into the world's premier industrial nation. Senator Albert Beveridge best expressed the idea that the United States was poised for economic domination: "American factories are making more than the American people can use; American soil is producing more than they can consume. Fate has written our policy for us; the trade of the world must and shall be ours."

THE NEW IMMIGRANTS

The knock of opportunity in the United States, amplified by the industrial revolution, could be heard worldwide and spurred westward migration. Between 1890 and 1910, immigration to the United States peaked. Nearly 12 million people arrived during those two decades alone. Unlike the influx of Irish, British, German, and Scandinavian immigrants to the United States in the mid-1800s, immigrants in the early twentieth century came predominantly from southern and eastern Europe, Asia, and Latin America, bringing with them cultural and religious differences that would shape American society. They were known as the "new" immigrants. Many of these immigrants were fleeing problems plaguing Europe. For example, sudden increases in birthrates and declines in death rates pushed some populations in southern and eastern Europe to the brink of starvation. Other immigrants came to the United States to pursue religious and individual freedom.

However, most immigrants flocked to the United States for economic reasons. The level of educational and professional experience among these immigrants spanned the spectrum, but most of them were ambitious and hardworking, eager to better their lives and seek opportunity. This wave of immigration energized the American workforce. The newcomers arrived at a crucial time, offering American industrial development an abundance of labor. Many immigrants labored tirelessly to construct railroads, mine coal, and assemble mass-produced goods. Oftentimes, immigrants' willingness to work was exploited. Many of them took grueling, sometimes perilous jobs in factories, sweatshops, and coal mines. Other immigrants fared better, and the United States offered them the opportunities they were seeking.

THE SPANISH-AMERICAN WAR

During the nineteenth century, westward expansion was at the forefront of U.S. priorities; the nation did not engage in international affairs to a large extent. However, the call for the United States to enter the global arena echoed in 1898. Friction between Spain and the United States began with a disagreement over Spain's treatment of rebels in Cuba who were revolting against Spanish colonial rule. Although the United States initially did not support the Cuban rebels, the American press circulated sensationalistic stories of atrocities committed by the Spanish against Cubans that shocked the American public. Also, the United States was concerned about the safety of its citizens in Cuba. In February 1898, the battleship USS *Maine* was dispatched to Havana to deal with any crises arising from the rebellion. On February 15, while docked at a Havana harbor, the *Maine* mysteriously exploded and sank, killing 262 American navy personnel. Many theories explaining the explosion abound, but the Spanish could not be linked to the *Maine*'s tragic fate. Nonetheless, the American press named Spain as the cowardly perpetrator of the explosion, inflaming the public's anti-Spanish sentiments. On April 25, 1898, the United States declared war on Spain, and President William McKinley resorted to military action to end the conflict in Cuba.

The United States swiftly won the Spanish-American War, defeating Spain in four months. In the armistice, Spain agreed to give complete independence to Cuba and to surrender its colonies Guam, Puerto Rico, and the Philippine Islands. The United States, emboldened by the doctrine of manifest destiny that guided the country's expansion during the mid-1800s, annexed these colonies and paid Spain $20 million for possession of the Philippines. The United States wanted the Philippines because it provided strategic ports of trade with Asia.

Many called the annexation of these lands an act of imperialism and viewed it as contradictory to the principles on which the United States was founded (since it had divorced itself from colonial powers). American author Mark Twain was one of the most outspoken opponents of the U.S. annexation of the Philippines. In a letter to his lifelong friend Reverend Joseph H. Twichell, Twain wrote, "Apparently we are not proposing to set the Filipinos free and give their islands to them; and apparently we are not proposing to hang the priests and confiscate their property. If these things are so, the war out there has no interest for me." Furthermore, the annexation greatly angered the natives of the Philippines, who believed that their country would be granted independence. The United States, however, felt that the Philippines were not yet ready for self-government and viewed the annexation as a duty of democracy. When Filipinos rebelled, the United States asserted its dominion over the Philippines in the form of a military government. Led by Emilio Aguinaldo, a self-described "George Washington of the Philippines," many Filipinos rebelled against the United States, leading to the Philippine-American War in 1899. The war lasted for three years, with both countries committing atrocities against each other, until American forces subjugated the Philippine rebels. The United States did not grant the Philippines independence until 1946.

THE OPEN DOOR POLICY

Now strategically stationed in the Philippines, the United States was eager to gain access to nearby China, whose ancient empire had begun to disintegrate. In the late 1800s, the major world powers—Russia, France, Italy, Great Britain, Germany, and Japan—were scrambling to establish "spheres of influence" in China's vast and rich territories. Because the United States had yet to carve its own sphere of influence in China, U.S. secretary of state John Hay advocated the "Open Door" policy, based on a rejected British proposal. In the Open Door letters to each power, Hay requested that every nation agree to equal trading rights in China and within the spheres of influence. Furthermore, he asked that China's territorial integrity be preserved. The world powers responded to the letters and contended that, although each favored the Open Door in principle, they would accept it only after the other nations complied. In March 1900, Hay declared that the nations had reached a "final and definitive" conclusion that the Open Door policy should be enforced. Despite protest from Japan, Hay's declaration was honored—but not for long. Two years later, Russia gained industrial advantages in the Chinese province of Manchuria, violating the Open Door. Hay tried to counter Russia's actions by extending the Open Door to cover equality for each country in industrial development. However, regard for the policy decreased throughout the years and ceased to exist after the Second World

War, when China was declared a sovereign state.

The Open Door policy exhibited America's sharpening inclination to act as a mediator of international affairs while attending to the propagation of its own interests. According to historian Henry Bamford Parkes, "In theory the Open Door policy . . . represented an admirable combination of idealism and self-interest. It would benefit the Chinese by protecting them from foreign conquest; it would benefit the Americans by enabling them to share in the commercial and industrial development in the Far East; and it would check the growth of imperialistic rivalries and hostilities by preventing the European powers from excluding one another from any part of China."

THE PANAMA CANAL

In addition to its efforts to secure its interests in Asia, the United States also looked to expand its influence to the south by constructing a canal through the Isthmus of Panama. Building a canal through Central America had been a goal of the United States since the late 1800s.

Initially, the herculean project belonged to the French, but a lack of funding, engineering problems, and tropical illnesses brought construction to a halt. Hoping to enhance U.S. power, President Theodore Roosevelt purchased the rights to the project from France for $40 million and took over the effort in Panama.

Roosevelt relentlessly advocated the building of such a canal because it offered important naval advantages. If ships could cross the oceans without having to travel around South America, the U.S. Navy would not have to maintain separate Atlantic and Pacific fleets. In addition, a canal through Central America would shorten the oceanic route between America's East and West Coasts by thousands of miles, thus reducing shipping costs.

The United States had to overcome obstacles arising from foreign relations before recommencing the construction of the canal. Panama belonged to the republic of Colombia, and France had gained Colombia's concessions to build a canal in Panama. However, when Americans gained control of the project, the Colombian congress rejected its earlier decision to grant the United States similar concessions. Aided by the United States, Panama declared its independence from Colombia and prepared for a revolution. Roosevelt was angered by Colombia's actions and supported Panama's rebellion, remarking that "irresponsible bandits" ran Colombia's government. He sent battleships and marines to South America to support Panama's new government and defend America's interests. In 1903, Panama was declared a republic. It gave the United States complete control of the canal zone for a payment of $10 million. Construction of the canal, under the command of the United States, resumed the following year. In 1914, Colombia finally recognized Panama's independence in exchange for rights to the Panama Canal, which was completed in August of that year.

American support of Panama's movement for independence was clearly influenced by the interest to extend U.S. power. Roosevelt himself said that he was prepared to "occupy the Isthmus anyhow, and proceed to dig the canal. But I deemed it likely that there would be a revolution in Panama soon." However, many believe that the creation of the canal had much greater implications for the world than it did for the U.S. Navy. In his highly acclaimed book about the Panama Canal, *The Path Between the Seas*, David McCullough wrote, "Primarily the canal is an expression of that old and noble desire to bridge the divide, to bring people together. It is a work of civilization." Approximately 268 million cubic yards of earth were excavated in bridging the "divide" between the hemispheres.

THE UNITED STATES ENTERS WORLD WAR I

The outbreak of World War I in 1914 cast a shadow over the triumphant completion of the Panama Canal. Hopes that the canal was a precursor to global unity were quickly dashed. As the lone superpower in the Western Hemisphere, America viewed the war at a safe distance from the devastation and strife that entrenched Europe. This distance was not only geographical; it seemed political as well.

However, to cut supplies off from Great Britain, German submarines sank neutral American vessels around the waters of Great Britain without warning. In addition, it was revealed that German officials were secretly plotting to lure Mexico into a German-Mexican alliance against the United States. Although President Woodrow Wilson struggled to maintain America's neutrality after the outbreak of the war, these acts against America spurred him to ask Congress to give him the authority to declare war on Germany. With his powerful "war message" condemning Germany's acts, Wilson successfully persuaded Congress to enter into the war in the spring of 1917. Shifting gears from unsteady neutrality to war preparedness, the United States hurriedly built up and mobilized its military and assisted Allied forces on the western front, where the battle was locked in attrition.

The involvement of the United States in World War I gave the Allies an edge over the Central Powers. For instance, American Expeditionary Forces played a major role in halting the German offensive at Château-Thierry, France, which threatened to seize Paris if it was not stopped. In addition, the deployment of the U.S. Navy into the war zone around British waters helped to counter German submarine warfare, greatly reducing the amount of food and supplies sunk by German U-boats in an attempt to subdue Great Britain by starving its people. While some historians argue that the military and naval contributions of the United States were not decisive in winning the war for the Allies, others contend that Germany surrendered because it could not perceive a victory for the Central Powers with the flood of American reinforcements fighting on the side of the Allies. On November 11, 1918, World War I came to an end. The Central Powers surrendered and signed an armistice for peace.

During the war, the United States experienced new degrees of prosperity. U.S. trade with the Allies increased from $824 million in 1914 to $3.2 billion in 1916. Also, the mobilization of the nation's industries to produce the supplies and munitions for the war, overseen by the War Industries Board, resulted in rapid economic growth. Between 1917 and 1921, the gross national product averaged $80 billion, compared to $39 billion between 1912 and 1915. The average American benefited from the nation's involvement in the war as well. Annual salaries jumped dramatically, from six hundred twenty-eight dollars in 1915 to six hundred seventy-two dollars in 1920. Job opportunities improved, especially for women because they were needed to fill the shoes of the millions of men who were drafted. After the war, entire European economies collapsed, but the U.S. economy was fortified; it controlled most of the world's gold stock and acted as a creditor to European countries that had been economically weakened due to the war.

The United States also became a major force in global politics, straying from its tradition of isolationism. After experiencing a war of unmatched carnage, destruction, and oppression, President Wilson imagined that the United States would into lead the world an era of lasting peace. He elucidatd his goals—"the programme of the world's peace"—in his Fourteen Points. They called for "open covenants of peace" established through diplomacy, "absolute freedom of navigation upon the seas," "equality of trade," more self-determination for countries freed from imperial rule, and the formation of "a general association of nations" that would protect "political dependence and territorial integrity." The achievement of these goals would require an unprecedented level of American participation in world affairs. Bearing the idealistic aims of his Fourteen Points, Wilson toured Europe in December 1918 with the intent to attend the peace conferences in Paris. The people of Europe showered the American president with admiration. According to historian Frederick Lewis Allen, "His progress through the streets of London could be likened only to a Coronation procession. In Italy the streets were black with people come to do him honor." They looked to him and his country to erect a new world order of peace. In a letter to Wilson, one woman claimed, "You have given back the father to his home. . . . Glory to you, who, like Jesus, have said: Peace on Earth and Good Will to Men." By demonstrating America's economic and military might to the rest of the world, other nations believed that the United States and its president could establish and maintain a peaceful social order.

THE LEAGUE OF NATIONS

The power that the United States gained at the turn of the twentieth century gave Americans faith in the political and economic system that governed their nation. As the leader of the premier democratic nation of the world, President Wilson viewed it as his duty to help other nations gain prosperity through liberty and peace. He attended the 1919 peace conferences in Paris and led the American peace delegation, delivering his proposal for the League of Nations Covenant based on his Fourteen Points. To prevent future wars, Wilson proposed that an international organization, the League of Nations, should be established to settle conflicts between nations openly and peacefully. The proposal was supported by the Allies at the peace conferences and incorporated in the Treaty of Versailles.

However, before the United States could join the League of Nations, the Treaty of Versailles had to be ratified by the U.S. Senate, where Wilson and the League of Nations Covenant faced considerable opposition from the Republican Party. (Wilson had made the mistake of not electing any prominent Republicans to the American peace delegation.) Massachusetts senator and Republican majority leader Henry Cabot Lodge led the opposition. Lodge objected to Article X of the League of Nations Covenant, under which the United States would be committed to resolving international conflict through military intervention. In his first major speech to the Senate criticizing the League, Lodge contended that "the broad fact remains that if any member of the league suffering from external aggression should appeal directly to the United States for support the United States would be bound to give that support in its own capacity and without reference to the action of other powers." Lodge offered a compromise to the League that would limit American obligations required under Article X and reserve Congress's power to declare war and deploy troops. Wilson refused these compromises, ultimately resulting in the Senate's failure to ratify the treaty.

In January 1920, the Treaty of Versailles took effect and the League of Nations commenced operations in Geneva, Switzerland, albeit without the participation of the United States. Many historians conclude that the absence of American membership in the League gravely limited its efficacy in deterring future international conflict. It also marked the nation's shift toward isolationism.

THE ARRIVAL OF A WORLD POWER

After World War I ended, Henry Cabot Lodge stated, "The Spanish war marked the entrance of the United States into world affairs to a degree which had never been obtained before. It was both an inevitable and irrevocable step and our entrance into the war with Germany certainly showed once and for all that the United States was not unmindful of its world responsibilities." Indeed, the events that took place in early-twentieth-century America announced the arrival of the United States as a leading power in the global arena. The trend of remarkable economic prosperity and growing global dominance that began after the war with Spain positioned America to emerge victorious from the First World War. Against this backdrop of economic and political changes, the nation witnessed social, scientific, and cultural developments as well, including the Wright Brothers' first flight, the rise of muckraking journalism, and a major influenza epidemic. All of these topics are among the events and issues discussed in the following anthology.

1896–1904: America Ascends to Power

CHAPTER 1

THE *PLESSY V. FERGUSON* SUPREME COURT CASE

John Marshall Harlan

Although the Thirteenth and Fourteenth Amendments granted former slaves equal civil rights, black Americans entered the twentieth century nearly as oppressed as their enslaved predecessors due to racial segregation. In 1892, Louisianan Homer Adolph Plessy attempted to challenge a segregation law, the Separate Car Act, when he refused to leave a car of a train reserved for whites. Plessy was one-eighth black and seven-eighths white—considered black under Louisiana law—and was arrested and jailed for sitting in a "white" car. Plessy took his case to a Louisiana court, arguing that the Separate Car Act violated the Thirteen and Fourteenth Amendments. But John Howard Ferguson, the judge who presided over the case, found Plessy guilty on the basis that the state of Louisiana had the right to regulate railroads operating within its boundaries. After unsuccessfully appealing his case to the Supreme Court of Louisiana, Plessy took his case to the Supreme Court of the United States in 1896, contending that enforcing segregation by establishing "separate" facilities for blacks and whites maintained racial inequality. Nonetheless, a seven-to-one majority found Plessy guilty and decided that racial segregation did not breach the Fourteenth Amendment so long as these separate facilities were "equal."

Supreme Court Justice John Marshall Harlan was the only member of the U.S. Supreme Court to vote in favor of Plessy's

Excerpted from John Marshall Harlan's dissent of *Plessy v. Ferguson*, 1896.

claims. In his dissenting argument, Harlan insists that social equality for blacks cannot be achieved by establishing separate but equal accommodations. In addition, he insists that racially segregating the American people would deepen feelings of racial hatred.

Harlan served as attorney general of Kentucky from 1863 to 1867 and as a U.S. Supreme Court justice from 1877 to 1911. Later, he taught constitutional law at the George Washington University.

T he white race deems itself to be the dominant race in this country. And so it is, in prestige, in achievements, in education, in wealth, and in power. So, I doubt not, it will continue to be for all time if it remains true to its great heritage and holds fast to the principles of constitutional liberty. But in view of the Constitution, in the eye of the law, there is in this country no superior, dominant, ruling class of citizens. There is no caste here. Our Constitution is colorblind and neither knows nor tolerates classes among citizens.

ALL EQUAL BEFORE THE LAW

In respect of civil rights, all citizens are equal before the law. The humblest is the peer of the most powerful. The law regards man as man and takes no account of his surroundings or of his color when his civil rights as guaranteed by the supreme law of the land are involved. It is therefore to be regretted that this high tribunal, the final expositor of the fundamental law of the land, has reached the conclusion that it is competent for a state to regulate the enjoyment by citizens of their civil rights solely upon the basis of race.

In my opinion, the judgment this day rendered will, in time, prove to be quite as pernicious as the decision made by this tribunal in the *Dred Scott Case*. It was adjudged in that case that the descendants of Africans who were imported into this country and sold as slaves were not included nor intended to be included under the word "citizens" in the Constitution and could not claim any of the rights and privileges which that instrument provided for and secured to citizens of the United States; that at the time of the adoption of the Constitution they were "considered as a subordinate and inferior class of beings who had been subjugated by the dominant race, and, emancipated or not, yet remained subject to their authority, and had no rights or privileges but such as those who held the power and the government might choose to grant them . . ."

The recent amendments of the Constitution, it was supposed, had eradicated these principles from our institutions. But it seems that we have yet, in some of the states, a dominant race—a superior class of citizens, which assumes to regulate the enjoyment of civil rights, common to all citizens, upon the basis of race. The present decision, it may well be apprehended, will not only stimulate aggressions, more or less brutal and irritating, upon the admitted rights of colored citizens, but will encourage the belief that it is possible, by means of state enactments, to defeat the beneficent purposes which the people of the United States had in view when they adopted the recent amendments of the Constitution, by one of which the blacks of this country were made citizens of the United States and of the states in which they respectively reside, and whose privileges and immunities as citizens the states are forbidden to abridge.

AROUSING RACE HATE

Sixty millions of whites are in no danger from the presence here of 8 million blacks. The destinies of the two races in this country are indissolubly linked together, and the interests of both require that the common government of all shall not permit the seeds of race hate to be planted under the sanction of law. What can more certainly arouse race hate, what more certainly create and perpetuate a feeling of distrust between these races than state enactments, which, in fact, proceed on the ground that colored citizens are so inferior and degraded that they cannot be allowed to sit in public coaches occupied by white citizens? That, as all will admit, is the real meaning of such legislation as was enacted in Louisiana.

The sure guarantee of the peace and serenity of each race is the clear, distinct, unconditional recognition by our governments, national and state, of every right that inheres in civil freedom and of the equality before the law of all citizens of the United States without regard to race, State enactments regulating the enjoyment of rights upon the basis of race, and cunningly devised to defeat legitimate results of the war under the pretense of recognizing equality of rights, can have no other result than to render permanent peace impossible and to keep alive a conflict of races, the continuance of which must do harm to all concerned.

This question is not met by the suggestion that social equality cannot exist between the white and black races in this country. That argument, if it can be properly regarded as one, is scarcely worthy of consideration; for social equality no more exists between two races when traveling in a passenger coach or a public highway than when members of the same races sit by each other in a streetcar or in the jury box, or stand or sit with each other in a political assembly, or when they use in common the streets of a city or town, or when they are in the same room for the purpose of having their names placed on the registry of voters, or when they approach the ballot box in order to exercise the high privilege of voting.

There is a race so different from our own that we do not permit those belonging to it to become citizens of the United States. Persons belonging to it are, with few exceptions, absolutely excluded from our country, I allude to the Chinese race. But by the statute in question, a Chinaman can ride in the same passenger coach with white citizens of the United States, while citizens of the black race in Louisiana, many of whom, perhaps, risked their lives for the preservation of the Union, who are entitled, by law, to participate in the political control of the state and nation, who are not excluded, by law or by reason of their race, from public stations of any kind, and who have all the legal rights that belong to white citizens, are yet declared to be criminals, liable to imprisonment, if they ride in a public coach occupied by citizens of the white race.

THE THIN DISGUISE OF EQUALITY

It is scarcely just to say that a colored citizen should not object to occupying a public coach assigned to his own race. He does not object, nor, perhaps, would he object to separate coaches for his race, if his rights under the law were recognized. But he objects, and ought never to cease objecting to the proposition that citizens of the white and black races can be adjudged criminals because they sit, or claim the right to sit, in the same public coach on a public highway.

The arbitrary separation of citizens, on the basis of race, while they are on a public highway, is a badge of servitude wholly inconsistent with the civil freedom and the equality before the law established by the Constitution. It cannot be justified upon any legal grounds.

If evils will result from the commingling of the two races

upon public highways established for the benefit of all, they will be infinitely less than those that will surely come from state legislation regulating the enjoyment of civil rights upon the basis of race. We boast of the freedom enjoyed by our people above all other peoples. But it is difficult to reconcile that boast with a state of law which, practically, puts the brand of servitude and degradation upon a large class of our fellow citizens, our equals before the law. The thin disguise of "equal" accommodations for passengers in railroad coaches will not mislead anyone, nor atone for the wrong this day done.

THE TRIUMPH OF AMERICA IN THE SPANISH-AMERICAN WAR

HENRY WATTERSON

The Spanish-American War began on April 25, 1898, after the U.S.S. *Maine* exploded and sank in a harbor near Havana, Cuba, two and a half months earlier, killing 260 personnel on board. The *Maine* had been sent to Cuba on an observation visit in the midst of a Cuban revolt against Spanish colonial rule. An investigation conducted by the United States revealed that a mine may have caused the explosion, but the perpetrator could not be determined. The *Maine* disaster, coupled with America's disapproval of Spain's harsh treatment of Cuban rebels, compelled the United States to declare war against Spain.

The war was a quick and victorious one for the United States—to Vice President Theodore Roosevelt it was nothing short of "splendid." It ended on December 10, 1898, when Spain's defeat, Cuba's independence, and the United States' acquisition of the remaining Spanish colonies were finalized at the signing of the Treaty of Paris.

The late historian and prominent American journalist Henry Watterson, in the following selection, asserts that the United States declared war on Spain because it ultimately viewed the Spanish Empire as barbaric, cruel, and oppressive. He contends that the Spanish exploration and colonization of the Western hemisphere was motivated by greed, that the "demon of gold"

Excerpted from *The History of the Spanish-American War*, by Henry Watterson (New York: Werner, 1898).

had corrupted the once-noble Spaniards. Watterson asserts that the United States, having toppled the Spanish Empire, came out of the war as a world power.

T he war between the United States and Spain was like no other war of ancient or modern times. Begun at once as a protest of civilization and as a plea for humanity, it ended as an act of unpremeditated national expansion; and, from first to last, it abounded in surprises. In its inception, the public men of America were generally opposed to it, as they are apt to be opposed to everything either very original or very decisive; and, if the controlling members of the cabinet at Madrid favored it— as there are some reasons for believing that they did—theirs was rather a choice between two dangers, foreign and domestic, which menaced them, than any deliberate preference for war. In Spain all popular impulse seems to have been wanting. In the United States the declaration of war was forced upon the President and the Congress by the people.

A PEOPLE'S WAR

Thus, the war with Spain was essentially a people's war. The destruction of the battleship *Maine* in the harbor of Havana undoubtedly quickened the pulse of the nation and hurried the action of its official representatives. But, long before, the patience of public opinion in the United States had been exhausted by Spanish misrule in Cuba. The time was come to make an end of an intolerable situation. When we consider not merely the oppression and corruption which had marked a cruel despotism existing in sight of us, and exploiting itself in spite of us, but its actual cost to us in the treaty obligation of policing our coasts against the filibusters and in its consequent and constant injury to our commerce, it seems a matter of wonder that the day of reckoning should have been delayed so long.

From the coming of Spanish explorers Hernando Cortes and Francisco Pizarro to the going of Spanish general Valeriano Weyler, the flag of the Spaniard in the Western Hemisphere was the emblem solely of rapine and pillage. The discovery of Columbus seemed to act upon the Spanish imagination as a magic philter, distorting all its evil propensities and filling it with desires impossible of fulfillment. Under its spell the phantoms of the soothsayer and the fancies of the poet took definite shape. With some it was the dream of eternal life; with others a vision of untold riches; but, with all, the perversion of nature. Cut loose from the moorings of common sense, the standards of morality were lost. Incalculable rapacity begot inconceivable brutality, and, as a result, Spain, from the first, became the last of the great European powers. The demon of gold had taken hold of the greatest and noblest of the nations by its very vitals. The craze for lucre, which so often makes of good men bad men, under the most civilizing influences, had, under the most barbaric, diverted the courageous and enlightened Spaniard from the love of poetry and art to the love of money; and, after Columbus and his wondrous New World, Cortes and Pizarro, and the other minor tyrants and robbers, down to Weyler, came in a kind of geometric progression, as simple matters of course.

The flag, as the saying is, had finally dropped upon the dominion of the Spaniard in America. One after another, Spain had been despoiled of her American possessions. It was the moderation of the Great Republic which saved her Cuba and Porto Rico so long. If any other power except the United States had been concerned, she would have lost them fifty years earlier.

A SACRIFICE OF SENSIBILITIES

In the nature of the case, there could be no spirit of territorial aggrandizement disturbing the serenity of the people of the United States. With the vast area of unoccupied land in the west of their continent, the Americans took little, if any, account of Cuba, whilst Porto Rico was undreamed of. They had no quarrel with Spain. On the contrary, there was a sentimental regard for the Spaniard, an honorable gratitude, as it were, manifested during our great Fair[1] by the honors paid the Duke of Veragua, and the cordial reception given to the Princess Infanta Eulalia of Spain; and the idea of going to war with a nation so weak as we knew Spain to be, was repugnant to every brave and honorable man. There were two circumstances that, among intelligent Americans, weighed far more than the world will ever give us credit even for conceiving. As no orator since Patrick Henry, not excepting French republican leader Léon Gambetta, first President of Spain Señor Emilio Castelar had delivered those principles of civil liberty which are dear to all our hearts. That meant a great deal. It alternately appealed to our republicanism and stirred our

1. World's Columbian Exposition of 1893 in Chicago, Illinois.

enthusiastic admiration. Then there was set before our eyes the figure of a noble woman, with her boy king, in spite of our republicanism, appealing to our manhood. All in all, it cost us a great sacrifice of sensibilities to go to war with Spain.

American soldiers celebrate when they hear the news of the American victory.

But what could we do? The situation was inexorable. It was either ruthlessly to beat down, or be ignominiously humiliated. When nations can do nothing else they can fight, and fight we did. And so did the Spaniard. But centuries of moral poison, percolating through the veins of the body politic of Spain, had done their work. The obsolete Spaniard was no match for the alert and enterprising American. The war was quickly over. It might not have been so quickly over in the case of Germany and France; but its end would have been the same. Spain has no reason to be ashamed of her part in it. Throughout the United States, at least, the Spanish character stands higher to-day than it did before the war, though the Spaniards have Admirals Patricio Montojo and Pasval Cervera and General José Toral to thank for the maintenance of the national credit.

On our own side, the war has surely paid us back far more than it cost us, at the same time that it has brought us many things not contemplated in the beginning.

THE RISING GENERATION OF AMERICA

It annihilated sectional lines and solidified the Union. It proclaimed us a nation among the nations of the earth; no longer a huddle of petty sovereignties held together by a rope of sand. It dissipated at once and forever the notion that we are a race of mercenary shopkeepers, worshipping rather the brand upon the dollar than the eagle on the shield. It announced the arrival upon the scene of the world's action of a power which would have to be reckoned with by the older powers in determining the future of civilization. It rescued us from the turbulent discussion of many misleading questions of domestic economy, uplifting and enlarging all our national perspectives. Above all, it elevated, broadened, and vitalized the manhood of the rising generation of Americans. In the heroes who fell in battle, as in those who survived to tell the tale of surpassing endurance and valor, examples of priceless value were set before it; and in such illustrations as Admiral George Dewey and Constructor Richard Pearson Hobson, Major Generals William Shafter and Joseph Wheeler [heroes of the Spanish-American War], coming from extremes of North and South, notice was served upon Christendom of the existence of a homogeneous race of soldiers and sailors destined to carry the flag of the Great Republic to lands perhaps as yet unknown, and certainly able to hold it against all who might dispute its right of way.

The United States engaged in the war with Spain under many disadvantages. It was supposed that the Spanish navy outclassed our navy. It was known that we had no organized army. Europe was rife with evil prognostications. Although the continental nations officially declared their neutrality, the ruling elements, social and political, were all against us. In spite of the millions of Germans among us, the trend of German opinion as delivered by the newspapers of Berlin and Frankfurt and Köln was surprisingly hostile. Though France is a Republic, and our ancient ally besides, the Parisian journals, reflecting on the one hand the interests of the Spanish bondholders and on the other hand the prejudices of polite society,—perhaps also goaded by the avowed friendship of the English,—made haste to open upon us a cross-fire of the most fantastic billingsgate. It was on all sides freely predicted that the raw militia of America could not stand against the trained veterans of Europe, and that the American navy, overmatched in ships by the navy of Spain, and manned by a riff-raff of foreign adventurers, would become the easy prey of such Admirals as Cervera, Montojo, and Manuel de la Camara. There were admissions in some quarters that the superior resources and power of the United States would in the end prevail; but nothing was allowed the Yankees except grudgingly, and even then rendered in a tone of apology. In Spain it was given out that the South, still mourning the loss of the Southern Confederacy, was ripe for revolt, and that the landing of a Spanish army somewhere on the Gulf coast was only necessary to draw to it a host of rebels waiting for a chance to rise and eager for revenge.

DISPELLING ILLUSIONS

The war dispelled all these illusions. The United States went into it even in its own eyes something of a riddle as to the matter of martial equipment, resources, and capacity. It came out of it a conceded, self-confident world power. The victories of Dewey and Rear Admiral William T. Sampson settled forever all question as to the navy. The rapid mobilization of the army proved the wonder of mankind; and, although the army had less opportunity than the navy to show the stuff it was made of, the operations in front of Santiago were sufficient to establish its claim to the respect of the military establishments of Europe and to earn for it and its leaders the admiration of their own countrymen. From Nelson Appleton Miles, the able and gallant commanding General, to the humblest subaltern, the exhibitions of intrepidity and fortitude and skill were never exceeded by any band of officers or any body of troops of which the history of warfare gives us an account.

THE UNITED STATES ANNEXES THE PHILIPPINES

WILLIAM JENNINGS BRYAN

In 1898, when Spain and the United States signed the Treaty of Paris to end the Spanish-American War, Spain relinquished control of Puerto Rico, Guam, and the Philippine Islands to the United States. Eager to annex the Philippines, the United States paid Spain $20 million for possession of the Pacific archipelago.

The United States was strongly motivated to annex the Philippines. The country's location offered the United States a unique opportunity to engage in commerce with Asian and Pacific markets. In addition, many Americans believed that it was the United States' obligation to educate, elevate, and civilize the Filipino people. It was widely thought that the Malay inhabitants of the islands, newly liberated from the dominion of Spain, were not yet capable of self-government.

Detractors decried the U.S. acquisition of the Philippines and viewed it as an act of imperialism. In the following selection, excerpts from a speech delivered in 1899, anti-imperialist activist William Jennings Bryan asserts that the annexation of the Philippines will result in the subjugation of its people and will deeply contradict America's own principles of liberty and democracy. Despite such protests, the Philippines were annexed and remained under American control until 1946.

Bryan was a lawyer, politician, and three-time presidential candidate who served as U.S. secretary of state during the Woodrow Wilson presidential administration from 1913 to 1915.

Excerpted from William Jennings Bryan's speech delivered at the Washington Day Banquet hosted by the Virginia Democratic Association, February 22, 1899.

W hen the advocates of imperialism find it impossible to reconcile a colonial policy with the principles of our government or with the canons of morality; when they are unable to defend it upon the ground of religious duty or pecuniary profit, they fall back in helpless despair upon the assertion that it is destiny. "Suppose it does violate the constitution," they say; "suppose it does break all the commandments; suppose it does entail upon the nation an incalculable expenditure of blood and money; it is destiny and we must submit."

The people have not voted for imperialism; no national convention has declared for it; no Congress has passed upon it. To whom, then, has the future been revealed? Whence this voice of authority? We can all prophesy, but our prophesies are merely guesses, colored by our hopes and our surroundings. Man's opinion of what is to be is half wish and half environment. Avarice paints destiny with a dollar mark before it, militarism equips it with a sword.

He is the best prophet who, recognizing the omnipotence of truth, comprehends most clearly the great forces which are working out the progress, not of one party, not of one nation, but of the human race. . . .

A WAR FOR LIBERTY OR A WAR OF CONQUEST?

We have reached [a] crisis. The ancient doctrine of imperialism, banished from our land more than a century ago, has recrossed the Atlantic and challenged democracy to mortal combat upon American soil.

Whether the Spanish war shall be known in history as a war for liberty or as a war of conquest; whether the principles of self-government shall be strengthened or abandoned; whether this nation shall remain a homogeneous republic or become a heterogeneous empire—these questions must be answered by the American people—when they speak, and not until then, will destiny be revealed.

Destiny is not a matter of chance, it is a matter of choice; it is not a thing to be waited for, it is a thing to be achieved.

No one can see the end from the beginning, but every one can make his course an honorable one from beginning to end, by adhering to the right under all circumstances. Whether a man steals much or little may depend upon his opportunities, but whether he steals at all depends upon his own volition.

So with our nation. If we embark upon a career of conquest

no one can tell how many islands we may be able to seize, or how many races we may be able to subjugate; neither can any one estimate the cost, immediate and remote, to the nation's purse and to the nation's character, but whether we shall enter upon such a career is a question which the people have a right to decide for themselves.

Unexpected events may retard or advance the nation's growth, but the nation's purpose determines its destiny.

THE NATION'S PURPOSE

What is the nation's purpose?

The main purpose of the founders of our government was to secure for themselves and for posterity the blessings of liberty, and that purpose has been faithfully followed up to this time. Our statesmen have opposed each other upon economic questions, but they have agreed in defending self-government as the controlling national idea. They have quarreled among themselves over tariff and finance, but they have been united in their opposition to an entangling alliance with any European power.

Under this policy our nation has grown in numbers and in strength. Under this policy its beneficent influence has encircled the globe. Under this policy the taxpayers have been spared the burden and the menace of a large military establishment and the young men have been taught the arts of peace rather than the science of war. On each returning Fourth of July our people have met to celebrate the signing of the Declaration of Independence; their hearts have renewed their vows to free institutions and their voices have praised the forefathers whose wisdom and courage and patriotism made it possible for each succeeding generation to repeat the words,

> "My country, 'tis of thee,
> Sweet land of liberty,
> Of thee I sing."

This sentiment was well-nigh universal until a year ago. It was to this sentiment that the Cuban insurgents appealed; it was this sentiment that impelled our people to enter into the war with Spain. Have the people so changed within a few short months that they are now willing to apologize for the War of the Revolution and force upon the Filipinos the same system of government against which the colonists protested with fire and sword?

The hour of temptation has come, but temptations do not destroy, they merely test the strength of individuals and nations; they are stumbling blocks or stepping-stones; they lead to infamy or fame, according to the use made of them.

Benedict Arnold and Ethan Allen served together in the Continental army and both were offered British gold. Arnold yielded to the temptation and made his name a synonym for treason; Allen resisted and lives in the affections of his countrymen.

Our nation is tempted to depart from its "standard of morality" and adopt a policy of "criminal aggression." But, will it yield?

If I mistake not the sentiment of the American people they will spurn the bribe of imperialism, and, by resisting temptation, win such a victory as has not been won since the battle of Yorktown. Let it be written of the United States: Behold a republic that took up arms to aid a neighboring people, struggling to be free; a republic that, in the progress of the war, helped distant races whose wrongs were not in contemplation when hostilities began; a republic that, when peace was restored, turned a deaf ear to the clamorous voice of greed and to those borne down by the weight of a foreign yoke, spoke the welcome words, Stand up; be free—let this be the record made on history's page and the silent example of this republic, true to its principles in the hour of trial, will do more to extend the area of self-government and civilization than could be done by all the wars of conquest that we could wage in a generation.

ANNEXATION NOT NECESSARY FOR WORLD POWER

The forcible annexation of the Philippine Islands is not necessary to make the United States a world power. For over ten decades our nation has been a world power. During its brief existence it has exerted upon the human race an influence more potent for good than all the other nations of the earth combined, and it has exerted that influence without the use of sword or Gatling gun. Mexico and the republics of Central and South America testify to the benign influence of our institutions, while Europe and Asia give evidence of the working of the leaven of self-government. In the growth of democracy we observe the triumphant march of an idea—an idea that would be weighted down rather than aided by the armor and weapons proffered by imperialism.

Much has been said of late about Anglo-Saxon civilization. Far be it from me to detract from the service rendered to the world by the sturdy race whose language we speak. The union of the Anglo and the Saxon formed a new and valuable type, but the process of race evolution was not completed when the Anglo and the Saxon met. A still later type has appeared which is superior to any which has existed heretofore; and with this new type will come a higher civilization than any which has preceded it. Great has been the Greek, the Latin, the Slav, the Celt, the Teuton and the Anglo-Saxon, but greater than any of these is the American, in whom are blended the virtues of them all.

Civil and religious liberty, universal education and the right to participate, directly or through representatives chosen by himself, in all the affairs of government—these give to the American citizen an opportunity and an inspiration which can be found nowhere else.

A GRANDER DESTINY

Standing upon the vantage ground already gained the American people can aspire to a grander destiny than has opened before any other race.

Anglo-Saxon civilization has taught the individual to protect his own rights; American civilization will teach him to respect the rights of others.

Anglo-Saxon civilization has taught the individual to take care of himself; American civilization, proclaiming the equality of all before the law, will teach him that his own highest good requires the observance of the commandment: "Thou shalt love thy neighbor as thyself."

Anglo-Saxon civilization has, by force of arms, applied the art of government to other races for the benefit of Anglo-Saxons; American civilization will, by the influence of example, excite in other races a desire for self-government and a determination to secure it.

Anglo-Saxon civilization has carried its flag to every clime and defended it with forts and garrisons. American civilization will imprint its flag upon the hearts of all who long for freedom.

To American civilization, all hail!

"Time's noblest offspring is the last!"

Urban Growth in the United States

Adna Ferrin Weber

The United States experienced an astonishing growth of its cities during the latter half of the nineteenth century. Between 1870 and 1900, the American urban population leapt from 9.9 million to 30.1 million. In the following selection, excerpted from his pioneering study of statistics and urban sociology, *The Growth of American Cities in the Nineteenth Century*, Adna Ferrin Weber asserts that the efficiency of industrial organization turned America into the "land of mushroom cities." Weber asserts that the industrialization of farming techniques greatly diminished the proportion of the population required to serve America's agricultural needs, allowing a great majority to depart wholly from the soil and congregate in the cities.

The late Weber was a noted scholar in statistics, economics, and social science and a senior fellow of the American Statistical Association.

I n a new country the rapid growth of cities is both natural and necessary, for no efficient industrial organization of a new settlement is possible without industrial centres to carry on the necessary work of assembling and distributing goods. A Mississippi Valley empire rising suddenly into being without its Chicago and its smaller centres of distribution is almost inconceivable to the nineteenth-century economist. That America is the "land of mushroom cities" is therefore not at all surprising.

But, on the other hand, it is astonishing that the development of the cities in a new country should outstrip that of the rural

Excerpted from *The Growth of Cities in the Nineteenth Century*, by Adna Ferrin Weber (New York: Macmillan, 1899).

districts which they serve. The natural presumption would be that so long as land remains open to settlement, the superfluous population of the older States or of Europe would seek the fundamental, or food-producing, industry of agriculture, and build up cities only in a corresponding degree. Yet in the great cereal regions of the West, the cities have grown entirely out of proportion to the rural parts, resulting there, as in the East and in Europe, in an increasing concentration of the population. The only States where the urban population has in recent years proportionately diminished or remained stationary are Louisiana, South Carolina, Vermont, Mississippi, and one or two others. These are the commonwealths where industry is less progressive and up-to-date than elsewhere; the population is not economically organized, or there would be a more pronounced growth of centres of industry and commerce. . . .

A DISTRIBUTION OF POPULATION

It is now clear that the growth of cities must be studied as a part of the question of distribution of population, which is always dependent upon the economic organization of society—upon the constant striving to maintain as many people as possible upon a given area. The ever-present problem is so to distribute and organize the masses of men that they can render such services as favor the maintenance of the nation and thereby accomplish their own preservation. Population follows the line of least resistance in its distribution, and will consequently be affected by changes in the methods of production. When the industrial organization demands the presence of laborers in particular localities in order to increase its efficiency, laborers will be found there; the means of attraction will have been "better living"—in other words, an appeal to the motive of self-interest. Economic forces are therefore the principal cause of concentration of population in cities. . . .

We may liken industrial society of to-day—embracing all countries within the circle of exchange of products—to a great organism composed of heterogeneous parts. This organism, however, is the product of ages of slow growth. Originally, in place of the one all-embracing social organism, there were myriads of small social units, each complete in itself and independent of the others, if not positively hostile to them. The history of civilization is simply the narrative description of the breaking down of the barriers that separated the primitive social units

—the original family group, clan, patriarchal family, the enlarged village community or the manorial group. And the most conspicuous and influential role in the process was played by the trader, working upon men's desires for what they did not possess or produce. Neither war (conquest) nor religion has been of so vital and far-reaching influence in the integration and amalgamation of isolated social groups as trade and commerce.

When, therefore, it is pointed out that towns owe their origin to trade, that the commercial metropolis of to-day is the successor of the primitive market-place established beside the boundary stone between hostile but avaricious tribal groups, that the extension of the market means the enlargement of the market-centre—then one will readily perceive the connection of the growth of industrial society to its present world-wide dimensions with our problem of the concentration of population. . . .

THE DIVORCE OF MEN FROM THE SOIL

If men were like other animals and had no further wants than bodily appetites and passions, there would be no large aggregations of people; for in order to produce food, men must live either in scattered habitations like American farmers, or in hamlets like the ancient family or tribal group, the village community, the Russian *mir*, and the modern agricultural village of Continental Europe. Even with a comparatively high grade of wants, men may live in these small groups, each of which is economically autonomous and self-sufficing, producing for itself and buying and selling little if anything. It is the period of the *Naturalwirthschaft*,[1] in which all payments are in kind. The principle of division of labor finally led to the disruption of the village community, but its triumph was long delayed. The principle was of course grasped only imperfectly by primitive man. At first the only division of labor was that based on sex, age, muscular power, or relation to the governing head of the group; in other respects there was no assignment of special tasks to particular individuals. Very gradually men discovered among themselves differences of natural aptitude. The members of a community at length realized that it was more economical to have their flour made in a village mill by one member who should give all his time to that particular work, than to have it made by bits in a score of individual mills. One by one other in-

1. *Naturalwirthschaft* refers to village communities that trade commodities without the use of money.

dustries have followed the mill—have departed from the separate households and taken up their abode in a central establishment. Clothing ceased to be made at home; there arose a village weaver and a village shoemaker. To this process of development there is almost no conceivable end. Only a few years ago the American farmer not only raised his own food, but furnished his own fuel and sometimes made his own clothing. Now [1899], however, he is a specialist, and thinks nothing of going to the market even for table supplies. Formerly, the farmer made his own tools; now he buys implements made in factories. But yesterday, and the men who reaped the fields of ripe grain were bound to the soil and compelled to dwell in isolated homes or small communities; to-day these men live in cities and make machinery to reap the grain.

Providing for the New Wants

Thus, it appears that agriculture, the industry that disperses men, has ever narrowed its scope. Formerly, when men's wants were few and simple, agriculture was the all-embracing occupation. The agriculturist produced the necessary sustenance, and in his idle moments made whatever else he needed. But human wants have greatly multiplied and can no longer be satiated with food-products alone. Moreover, the business of providing for the new wants has been separated from agriculture. The total result is that the proportion of people who must devote themselves to the satisfaction of the elementary wants of society has vastly diminished and is still diminishing.

And this result is attained not only by the diminishing importance of bread and butter in the realm of human wants, but also by the increased per-capita product which a specialized body of workers can win from the soil. By the use of fertilizers, by highly scientific methods of cultivation, by labor-saving machinery, and by the construction of transportation systems to open up distant and virgin fields, the present century has immensely reduced the relative number of workers who must remain attached to the soil to provide society's food-supply.

These facts are of fundamental importance in seeking the causes of urban growth. For cities are made up of persons who do not cultivate the soil; their existence presupposes a surplus food-supply, which in turn promises either great fertility of the soil or an advanced stage of the agricultural arts, and in either case convenient means of transportation.

Laissez-Faire and the Gospel of Wealth

Foster Rhea Dulles

The rise of trusts (large mergers of corporations and firms) in early twentieth-century America stifled competition from small businesses and placed immense wealth into the hands of a few tycoons. According to the late historian and author Foster Rhea Dulles, this monopolization of economic power was the outcome of the federal government's policy of laissez-faire, which calls for limited government interference in the economy in order to foster growth and competition in business. In defense of their massive fortunes and the right to free enterprise, Dulles asserts that business moguls like Andrew Carnegie supported the "Gospel of Wealth," a business philosophy based on the belief that it is unethical to restrict a man's pursuit of wealth as long as he uses it to serve the poor.

S upporting the movement which led to phenomenal industrial advance and to the new concentration of economic power was the prevailing philosophy of *laissez-faire*. Derived from the social doctrines of British philosopher Herbert Spencer, given further emphasis by the individualistic spirit born of the frontier, *laissez-faire* called for full freedom for the individual—and for the corporation in its legal status as a person—in every phase of economic activity. There should be no interference on the part of Government in the economic devel-

Excerpted from *Twentieth Century America*, by Foster Rhea Dulles (New York: Houghton Mifflin, 1945).

opment of the country, and no attempt whatsoever to regulate business or industry. National progress was believed to be largely dependent upon such a hands-off policy, and the rise of [big business] trusts and monopolies was considered the natural and beneficent working-out of economic laws.

Even the greatest foes of this system could not wholly deny its benefits. Author Edward Bellamy wrote in his socialistic novel, *Looking Backward*:

> Oppressive and intolerable as was the régime of the great consolidations of capital, even its victims, while they cursed it, were forced to admit the prodigious increase of efficiency which had been imparted to the national industries, the vast economies effected by concentration of management and unity of organization, and to confess that since the new system had taken the place of the old, the wealth of the world had increased at a rate before undreamed of. . . .

TWISTED INTO FOSTERING MONOPOLY

Nevertheless, certain of the manifestations of *laissez-faire* appeared to violate its own basic tenets. Monopoly tended to stifle the free competition which was the theoretical basis of nineteenth-century capitalism, and the rising trusts actually profited immensely from direct governmental aid. They secured important economic concessions often denied small business through grants of land, timber rights, and mining concessions from the public domain. They throve upon a currency policy generally devised in the interests of capitalist finance rather than of labor or agriculture. They flourished under the protection of customs duties effectively cutting off all foreign competition. The protective tariff was indeed attacked as "the mother of trusts." *Laissez-faire* was twisted into a program for fostering monopoly rather than promoting competition, its critics declared, and the only freedom it upheld was that of the large corporations to control both production and prices in their own interests.

If there was a certain inevitability in the growth of monopoly under the pressure of mass production and mass distribution, this entire process was also hastened by the driving force of as remarkable a group of men as America ever produced. Farsighted and ruthless, they sensed the opportunities which developing industrialism presented, and proceeded to take every advantage of them. Robber barons or industrial statesmen, they fashioned the image of modern America and eclipsed all other national leaders in the era in which they lived. John D. Rockefeller shrewdly building up the great monopoly of the Standard Oil Company; Andrew Carnegie skillfully bringing one steel company after another under his control; James J. Hill consolidating the railroads of the Northwest; J.P. Morgan establishing a new empire of finance—these were the men, unswerving and audacious in pursuit of their aims, who stamped upon their times the strong imprint of their domineering characters.

THE GOSPEL OF WEALTH

In justification of their attitude, the principles of *laissez-faire* were supplemented by an even simpler philosophy which Andrew Carnegie popularly designated as the "Gospel of Wealth." He stoutly maintained that it was the opportunities afforded by America for winning a fortune which had made it such a great nation, and that on these grounds alone there should be no restraints upon the freedom of individual or corporation. Any governmental restrictions would be a denial of the American heritage and a brake upon national progress. But the rich man, Carnegie further declared, not only promoted economic advance through the wealth he created and made available for the public welfare. He was destined to serve as a guardian for the poor. He could bring to their service "his superior wisdom, experience, and ability to administer, doing for them better than they would or could do for themselves. Thus is the problem of Rich and Poor solved. The laws of accumulation will be left free; the laws of distribution free. Individualism will continue, but the millionaire will be but a trustee for the poor."

THE LAW OF THE JUNGLE

Carnegie lived up to his theories. He had risen from bobbin boy to ironmaster, becoming one of the rich, the good, and the wise through his own character and ability, and at the peak of his career he gave over making money to distributing it for the public good. There were some few others who followed his example. But the idea of trusteeship was more generally ignored than observed. Despite all Carnegie might say, the creators of the new industrial order had for the most part only the slightest concern for the public interest. Any feeling of social responsibility was often submerged in the bitter economic struggle in which the law of the jungle, survival of the fittest, overshadowed more charitable considerations. Whereas democracy's doctrine of individualism had once meant the equal right of every person to life, liberty, and the pursuit of happiness, the buccaneers of industry and finance interpreted it as the right to trample underfoot all those who could not protect their own interests. "What do I care for the law?" that ruthless railroad baron, Commodore Cornelius Vanderbilt, is reputed to have exclaimed. "I got the power, ain't I?" Industry fully believed in its right to bend the Government and the courts to its own purposes. There could be no higher goal than consolidation and monopoly. Property rights held precedence over human rights, and the greedy exploitation of natural resources was matched by an almost equally wanton exploitation of labor.

For the middle class generally the example of their leaders, the opportunities for making money which the country afforded, and the underlying idea that nothing succeeds like success, placed a new emphasis upon wholly material standards of achievement. Many of the traditional ideals and social concepts of the American people appeared to be transformed under the influence of a pervasive attitude that placed the pursuit of riches above every other goal. With the heroes of the age, those industrialists, capitalists, or speculators whose wealth was accepted as unmistakable proof of their ability, the public cared little about whom they might have pushed aside or trodden underfoot in the mad scramble for financial rewards. Speculation in western lands, fraudulent purchase of government franchises, manipulations in stocks and bonds, the juggling of secret railway rebates, outright fraud and corruption—the end justified the means. "The dollar is the measure of every value," wrote author William Dean Howells; "the stamp of every success."

WEALTH AS HEAVENLY APPROVAL

Even the pulpit gave its benediction to the triumph of materialism in American life, the Church falling back upon old Puritan traditions to hold riches in the highest esteem as unquestionable proof of hard work, frugality, and righteousness. Wealth was a sign of heavenly as well as worldly approval. God might still love the poor, for certainly there were many of them in the America of 1900, but it was believed that he admired the rich. "In the long run," declared [prominent religious figure] Bishop Lawrence of Massachusetts, "it is only to the man of morality that wealth comes. . . . Material prosperity is helping to make the national character sweeter, more joyous, more un-selfish, more Christlike." The Church did not seek to impose any restraints on the methods by which a fortune was accumu-lated; it only requested that some part of it should be given away in charity. "Men should make money according to the laws of business," another religious leader stated, "and spend it according to the laws of God." John D. Rockefeller, who was undoubtedly sincere in saying "the good Lord gave me my money," was not disabused of this comforting thought by his church. It had hopes of largess for itself.

There were many other indications of the high repute in which business success and riches were held. Newspapers and magazines underscored the important rôle of the wealthy in our national life by widely publicizing everything they did. The success story, symbolized by author Horatio Alger's endless tales of the poor boy making good, came to its flowering. Even more significant, the urge to prove that one was among the elect led to extravagant spending as concrete evidence of the pos-session of wealth. What economist Thorstein Veblen called "conspicuous consumption" was widely in evidence in urban society and among those social climbers who sought to breathe its rarefied atmosphere.

The lavish expenditures of the new gold rush of millionaires especially dazzled a public which eagerly read all accounts of their spectacular lives. The homes of these newly rich were gaudy show places crowded with the loot of foraging expedi-tions to the Old World. Yachts, four-in-hand coaches, and polo ponies typified their recreational life. When they entertained, squadrons of butlers and footmen, in silk stockings and pow-dered hair, served epicurean feasts on massive gold plate. In-credible sums were spent upon the costumes for their elaborate fancy-dress balls. At one party described by the historian of New York's Four Hundred [the four hundred most important people in New York City], a miniature lake was built into the dinner table, surrounded by a network of golden wire, within which four swans swam placidly before the diners. Cages filled with singing birds hung from the ceiling; waterfalls splashed upon banks of flowers around the sides of the room. On another occa-sion such was the display of jewels and expensive Paris models at the new Metropolitan Opera House that a cynical critic found the air perfumed with the odor of crisp greenbacks while "the tiers of boxes looked like cages in a menagerie of monopolists."

LIFE IN SMALL-TOWN AND RURAL AMERICA

JOHN W. DODDS

The march of industry and flood of immigrants into America's cities gained unprecedented momentum at the turn of the twentieth century. The soaring skylines and cosmopolitan way of life in urban areas such as New York City, Chicago, and San Francisco captured the world's imagination and served as a testimony to the ascension of the United States as an economic and world power. However, John W. Dodds asserts that urban life was not the norm for the majority of Americans in the early 1900s. In the following selection, Dodds claims that most Americans still lived on farms or in small, self-contained towns, unfazed by the bustle and clamor of the nation's cities. He maintains that they led simple lives, attentive primarily to the clear-cut values of work, religion, community, and family.

Dodds is an author and scholar at Stanford University in Palo Alto, California.

L ife on the farm in the first year of the twentieth century was more like 1860 than 1940. In the first place, the majority of the people lived there. The population of the United States in 1901 was 77,585,000, and of this 60 percent was rural. The rhythms of daily life, set by the sun, had changed very little over the years, whether in the larger spaces of the great plains or on the smaller farms of the East and South. Horsepower and manpower were still the units of energy for the spring planting of the crops, the summer cultivating, the autumn harvesting, and for a multitude of other daily duties.

Excerpted from *Everyday Life in Twentieth Century America*, by John W. Dodds (New York: G.P. Putnam's Sons, 1965). Copyright © 1965 by G.P. Putnam's Sons. Reprinted with permission.

Some reaping of grain was still done by hand with the scythe or "cradle," though the horse-drawn McCormick reaper had changed all this in most communities.

The cows were milked by hand and the milk was put in large pans and placed in a cool structure. Sometimes the structure was called a "milk house," but if it could be located over or alongside a spring it was a "springhouse." There the cream would rise to the surface to be skimmed and churned—for all farmers made their own butter, or rather their wives and children did. Sometimes the more mechanically minded had a "dogpower" churn, turned by a set of gears activated by a dog walking on a treadmill. Farm families baked their own bread and of course raised their own fruits and vegetables and slaughtered their own meat. The occasional Saturday trips to the nearest general store were to get such staples as flour, navy beans (white kidney beans), molasses, oatmeal, and for the winter diet, dried prunes or peaches. And sometimes, for the children, candy—"jawbreakers," or long beltlike strips of licorice. Farmers had to be largely self-sufficient. Even as late as 1955 they had an average annual family income, from the farms themselves, of less than $1,000. In 1900 it would have been less than half of that.

MUCH LIKE THEIR FATHERS

People on the farms, then, lived much like their fathers and grandfathers before them. They rose before dawn most of the year and went to bed at night by kerosene lights and cooked their meals on wood or coal stoves. . . . There was no plumbing; they drew water from springs or wells, bathed in a washtub in the kitchen, and made treks to an outhouse which could hardly be called a sanitary "convenience." The roads connecting the scattered villages and farms were drifted with snow in the winter, bogged with mud in the spring, and deep with dust in the summer. Children walked to the one-room country schoolhouse . . . , where the teacher, if she represented the national norm, received an annual salary of $325.

Children had their own delights, of course: picking chestnuts or hunting in the woods on crisp October mornings, fishing and swimming in nearby "cricks," gathering wild blackberries or blueberries, finding the first trailing arbutus under the snow in the early spring, listening to sleigh bells on a tingling winter night.

Any community activity was largely a neighborhood one:

picking up the rare mail and the weekly paper at the village post office (farmers were not given to extensive correspondence); talking politics across the line fence with a neighbor; getting dressed up in store clothes to go to the rural Sunday school and church services. The local minister often had two parishes some miles apart, and often he did some farming during the week. Sometimes there were Sunday school picnics or "strawberry festivals" in the churchyard or evening "socials" at the schoolhouse, with orations, selected literary readings and even debates—both children and parents nodding sleepily in the hot little schoolroom after a hard day's work. There was a good deal of "neighboring" when larger tasks required joint effort, such as the raising of a rooftree for a new barn. At harvest time steam threshing machines made the rounds from farm to farm and "thrashing day," with the women preparing gargantuan meals for the hungry farmers, was always a great community event.

Occasionally families enjoyed something in the nature of a celebration. Sometimes a one-ring circus would visit the county seat, and everyone would pile into a wagon (or even at times take the "hack" that ran between towns) for a day's outing. The annual county fair was a great event, too—an exciting mélange of horse-cattle-pig exhibitions, prize-winning pies and canned fruits and vegetables, horse races, lots of popcorn and soda pop, and a sort of carnival sideshow which parents inspected critically before allowing the children to attend.

Pleasures were for the most part simple, and the life very close to the soil. People talk today about getting back to the land. Most of them have little idea of what it meant to be on the land in 1900, the really hard life it represented. . . .

THE ROUTINES OF SMALL-TOWN LIVING

If the rhythms of farm life in the early nineteen hundreds were different from today, those of urban life were even more different. Nearly half of all the people in towns and cities were in places of under 10,000. The small town was in many ways the heart of America. It has been written about, sung about, satirized, dramatized, and has become the symbol (sometimes even the sentimentalization) of the American way of life almost a century ago. The cities were growing, burgeoning—frequently with people who were fleeing the farms, and they in turn were becoming the focus of the new industrialization which was the hallmark of the U.S.A. But the industrial cities were still strange conglomerate masses of people, more and more foreign as they became swollen, after the 1870's, with the floods of immigrants from central and southern Europe who were manning the factories and mills. . . . The great continuities of the American tradition could be more easily identified in the smaller towns.

Life moved slowly in these places, and before World War I changes came slowly, too. To be sure, new motorcars came to town and snorted, smoky and smelly, up and down the brick or cobblestone streets. Many homes had gas, though not yet electricity, and except for the poorer districts, bathrooms and plumbing. Central heating was still something of a luxury; coal or gas stoves kept people warm, and many who were youngsters then can still remember the beautiful frost crystals inside the windowpanes on cold winter mornings. There were other remembered things, too: the rich smell of buckwheat cakes that came up the back stairs early in the morning; cutting and dragging in the tall Christmas tree from the nearest woods through the December snow and decking it with strings of popcorn and tinsel and puffs of white cotton; the long winter evenings when children did their homework around the dining-room table while mother darned socks and long black cotton stockings and father read the paper under the fishtail gaslight—or perhaps under a glaring Welsbach gas mantle which flooded the whole room with hissing brilliance.

EMINENTLY PREDICTABLE

No one thought of life then as being "stylized," but it was eminently predictable and its patterns rested upon a comfortable recurrence. Monday was always washday; Tuesday ironing day; Wednesday baking day; Friday cleaning day, and so on. Not infrequently the big sprawling kitchen was the center of much of the family life. People not only ate many of their meals there, but small children played there under the mother's eye. It was a kind of all-purpose room which architects and families of the later mid-century were to rediscover with delight.

Houses were set well back on roomy lots with lots of trees for youngsters to climb and with room for a sizable vegetable garden. Each house had its front porch where on summer evenings the adults would sit in porch swings and hold long conversations with friends and neighbors who came over to "visit." Everybody knew everybody else in the early-century American town; most of the families had lived there all their lives. The doctor was your friend as well as your physician. You knew the grocer and the dry-goods store owner and the schoolteacher, as well as the plumber and the carpenter—each of whom, incidentally, took pride in being a *good* plumber and a *good* carpenter. They shared the hymnbook with you in church and it never entered their heads that they weren't just as dignified—in the sight of man as well as in the sight of God—as anyone else.

A DAY OF REST

The American small-town Sunday was really a day of rest then, for the codes in many places were such that almost any non-pious activity was frowned on. It was not a day for picnics, sports, or frolic, or even for reading that was not edifying. Father might take a long afternoon snooze, but the children, before they were released to read *The Youth's Companion*, might well have to study the *Shorter Catechism* and read a chapter in Wayland's *Elements of Moral Science*. Some towns took pride in having persuaded the railroad not to run local trains on Sunday, and others even banished the Sunday papers from the newsstands. The Puritan Ethic made Sunday something to be endured even for those who did not question its premises. But no one returned to work Monday morning tired out!

THE SEARS, ROEBUCK CATALOG

Some of the best reading for one who wants to capture the tangibilities of life as it was lived in country and town during the first third of the century is in the pages of the Sears, Roebuck catalogs. Here is the record of what people actually bought and used, from farm machinery to clothes to books to household equipment—bought at a price which seems fantastically low today. At the turn of the century you could get oak well buckets for 36 cents each, potbelly stoves at $2.40, wood-or-coal kitchen ranges for $7.00; five-pound tubs of apple butter for 40 cents, maple syrup for 67 cents a five-gallon jug. A 30-volume set of the *Encyclopaedia Britannica* sold for $29.50. (It was true, of course, that the average hourly wage in industry was 29 cents. Farm laborers received a dollar a day.). . .

"SINCERITY" OF ARCHITECTURE

If you had been dropped into the residential section of an American town in the early part of the century you would have found most houses neither notably beautiful nor abysmally ugly. Most of them were squarish brick or wood boxes, set in a sizable yard and shrouded gratefully by trees which softened their harsher contours. Typically they had big front porches where the family could sit in rocking chairs on a warm summer's evening and watch the horses and buggies, and an occasional Ford, go by. Each had its own back porch and a big attic and cellar. These houses had no pretension to architectural style; they sprang from a book of plans or a builder's brain. There were, to be sure, various layers of architectural or regional differences. Some houses would be clean Colonial or Cape Cod, others would be architectural monstrosities surviving from the period after the Civil War when "Carpenter's Gothic" was the rage—a confusion of pointed towers, useless turrets, and eccentric dormer windows, all ornamented by jigsaw scrollwork and grotesque decoration, a sort of nightmare architecture. Sometimes you would find a surviving "Queen Anne" house, a relic of what the builder thought was "quaint" or "picturesque" in the later nineteenth century, dressed up with "ornamental" chimneys and swallowed by a rash of cornices and bulging excrescences.

Other sections of town might represent a hodgepodge of builders' choices in the *beaux-arts* style popularized by the Chicago World Fair of 1893—a mixed grill of Greek, Roman, and Renaissance. Any kind of purity of style was overwhelmed by a random eclecticism ranging from "Egyptian" to "Byzantine" cottages to "Italian" villas. People were trying to be comfortable, or stylish, in the surroundings of a past that never really existed. There was, however, one kind of organic architecture that came in, as it were, by the back door. Infiltrating the Middle West and the East was an importation from California called the "bungalow," a wooden cottage marked by big overhanging eaves, cobblestone chimneys, and big windows. Though it frequently became degraded in the builder's hands, it gave to the early century a new kind of freshness and honesty. As a matter of fact, though, the most eccentric creators of pseudo-Gothic or Queen Anne houses always prided themselves on the "sincerity" of their architecture—sincerity being a strangely ambiguous term.

IMMIGRATION AT THE TURN OF THE CENTURY

EDWARD LOWRY

In the early years of 1900, the United States was in the midst of the largest influx of immigration it had ever absorbed. While immigrants from Great Britain, Ireland, and Germany had been steadily streaming to the United States since the mid-1800s, the "new wave" of immigration was characterized by the arrival of people from Asia, Mexico, Scandinavia, and most notably, southern and eastern European countries, such as Italy, Poland, and Russia.

In the following selection first published in 1902, author Edward Lowry offers a detailed observation of what new immigrants experienced at their initial arrival in New York. From the lengthy, detailed census they must answer at Ellis Island, to their encounters with the customs inspectors, Lowry captures the exhausting challenges faced by those immigrating to the United States at the turn of the twentieth century.

I n an open ditch, red and raw under a broiling sun, sixty-five Italian immigrants, stripped to the necessities, toiled silently with shovel and pick. A hard-faced, red-necked man, their taskmaster, walked up and down the trench, and wherever he stopped the men worked with feverish speed. Temporarily, at least, this will be the fate of thousands of the other immigrants who flowed in through Ellis Island in this year's spring flood—the greatest in twenty years.

Excerpted from *The World's Work*, by Edward Lowry (New York: Doubleday, Page, & Company, 1902).

During the fiscal year ending June 30, 1901, there were landed at New York 388,931 immigrants; in May alone, 92,485, and on one day in May, 6,490. The highest previous monthly record in twenty years was in May, 1893—the flood is always heaviest in spring—when 73,000 were landed. Persons with contagious or incurable diseases are sent back, and a far greater number of others on the ground that they are likely to become public charges. The others give their occupations and enter, but not always to take up the occupation given, for many calling themselves musicians have been found later working as waiters in restaurants or toiling as laborers on public works.

A SEARCHING CENSUS

The Government assumes jurisdiction over the aliens as soon as their steamer has been passed at quarantine. Inspectors go aboard from the revenue cutters down the bay and obtain the manifests of alien passengers, which the steamship companies must supply. These manifests must show:

Full name—age—sex—whether married or single—calling or occupation—whether able to read or write—nationality—last residence—seaport for landing in the United States—final destination in the United States—whether having a ticket through to such destination—whether the immigrant has paid his own passage, or whether it has been paid by other persons, or by any corporation, society, municipality or government—whether in possession of money, and if so, whether upward of $30, and how much, if $30 or less—whether going to join a relative, and if so, what relative and his name and address—whether ever before in the United States, and if so, when and where— whether ever in prison or almshouse, or supported by charity— whether a polygamist—whether under contract, expressed or implied, to perform labor in the United States—the immigrant's condition of health, mentally and physically and whether deformed or crippled; and if so, from what cause. It is a searching census, indeed.

"PRIMARY INSPECTION"

When the steamship reaches her pier the inspectors discharge such immigrants as they may deem it unnecessary to examine (usually not over fifteen or twenty). All the others are transferred to barges and taken to Ellis Island. There on the main floor of the big immigration building they are divided into groups according to the manifests, and separated. Later, in lines set off by iron railings, they undergo "primary inspection." Each immigrant is questioned to see if his answers ally with the manifests. If they do, he is discharged; if they do not, he is detained for "special inquiry," by boards composed of four inspectors, who decide all questionable cases. Only the Secretary of the Treasury can overrule their decision. The immigrants are kept in the big detention room downstairs until the railway agents take them to board trains to their final destinations. While on the island they are lodged by the Government and fed by the steamship companies. . . .

ODD BAGGAGE OF THE IMMIGRANTS

I welcomed Florio Vincenzo when he came over to become one of us. He had no doubts of the future for he wooed the Goddess of Good Fortune boldly. Florio is fourteen; he came from Palermo. He traveled light. When he opened his cheap paper valise, it was apparently empty, save for a pair of discredited and disreputable old shoes. Florio bowed, cap in hand, and his white teeth flashed as he smiled suavely.

There was an odor that an old inspector knew. He picked up one of the shoes and extracted from it, after some manipulation, a creased and crumpled hunk of Bologna sausage. The other shoe was stuffed with a soft, sticky and aggressively fragrant mass of Italian cheese. These articles and a sum of Italian money equivalent to about $1.80, and the clothes he stood in, formed the basis on which Florio expected to rear his fortune.

Pietro Viarilli was gray-haired, round-shouldered, and weazened. He, too, had come to make his fortune. His impedimenta consisted of one padlocked canvas valise lined with paper and containing two striped cotton shirts, one neckerchief of yellow silk, blue flowers and edges, one black hat (soiled and worn), one waistcoat, two pairs of woolen hose of gay design, one suit of underwear, one pint of olive oil and about half a peck of hard bread biscuits. Until his arrival the list included a quart of Vesuvian wine of the rich purple hue one may buy in cheap cafes in Naples. Carelessly Pietro had slung his valise from his shoulder, and had smashed his bottle, drenching his store of biscuits. He and his companions had munched them greedily until the supply was exhausted.

The contents of the bags and boxes of the Scandinavians, English, Scotch and Irish are usually more diverse. These immigrants bring over articles of personal adornment or household ornaments of a sentimental interest. The Scandinavians bring more baggage than any others. Close behind come the English and the French. Roughly speaking, those from the North of Europe bring more personal effects than those from the South. The 2,000 immigrants who arrived on a Liverpool ship one morning this summer brought 1,185 pieces of checked baggage, exclusive of about 900 pieces of hand baggage. This is about two-thirds more than the same number of persons from Southern Europe would have brought. For this reason Hungarians, Slovaks, Greeks, Sicilians, and other South-of-Europe peoples, are called "walkers" by baggage men.

During one month this spring 21,367 pieces of baggage were received at Ellis Island, examined and sent to various parts of the country, frail and poorly made, and awkwardly shaped, much of it unmarked and the rest scrawled over with undecipherable hieroglyphics. The Government makes no charge for storage, and the immigrant, if he chooses, may leave his trunk or box on the island for a year, yet seldom a piece is lost.

It is said that the old customs inspectors tell at a glance from the contents of a bag what part of Europe its owner has come from. The Italians bring over wine, fruits, oil or nuts; the English and the Scotch will have a piece of tweed or heavy cloth, and the Irish bring frieze. In the main, however, these immigrants come away from their homes to a strange country bringing less clothing and fewer personal effects than the average American workingman would drag out of a burning house, and chosen about as wisely.

MONEY BROUGHT BY THE IMMIGRANTS

At the examination the immigrants are asked to show their money. Some craftily fail to show it all; others willingly display their whole petty hoardings. The money is carefully counted, and, after a record has been taken, restored to them. Later, they are asked if they wish any money changed. Many refuse for fear of being cheated; others stop before the busy money-changers' booth at the end of the long examination room.

Last year the 388,931 immigrants showed $5,490,080, an average of $14.12. The French led all the others with an average of $39.37. The Hebrews stood at the foot of the list bringing on an average $8.58. The Germans followed the French with an average of $31.14. The other nationalities stood in the list as follows:

Race	Average per Capita.
Italians (Northern)	$23.53
Bohemian and Moravian	$22.78
Scandinavian	$18.16
Irish	$17.10
Armenian	$15.75
Croation and Dalmation	$15.54
Greek	$15.10
Slovak	$12.31
Magyar	$10.96
Italian (Southern)	$8.67

A pleasant-faced little man with trustful blue eyes stood before the desk one afternoon. His wife, a typical German woman, and three children formed a patient, waiting group behind him. The man wore a suit of "copperas jeans," stained and worn, top-boots, and the high peaked cap of the German peasant. He was fumbling through his pockets and in hidden recesses of his garments and producing money. Thalers, marks, Imperial treasury notes and gold pieces fell from his dirty fingers until a tidy little heap was lying on the counter.

Some of the immigrant officers looked on in amazement. The little German had seemed peculiarly unproductive soil for such a harvest—which amounted to over $600 to be converted into United States treasury notes. He grinned cheerfully when the neat pile of crisp green bills was handed to him, and opening his shirt, stowed the roll where he could feel it next to his body. But he was an exceptionally wealthy immigrant.

The Assassination of President William McKinley

Aaron T. Haverin

President William McKinley was the second American president to be assassinated. He was shot twice, at point-blank range, by a lone gunman on September 6, 1901, at the Pan-American Exposition in Buffalo, New York. McKinley died eight days later due to his wounds and an unsuccessful surgery to remove a bullet lodged in his abdomen. His vice president, Theodore Roosevelt, succeeded him, becoming the twenty-sixth president of the United States. The gunman, twenty-eight-year-old Leon Czolgosz, was convicted of McKinley's murder nine days after the shooting. He was executed on October 29 that year.

In the following selection, Buffalo, New York, historian Aaron T. Haverin draws from the *Buffalo Courier*, the *Buffalo Evening News*, *Leslie's Illustrated Weekly*, *Harper's Weekly* and *The Illustrious Life of William McKinley* to retell the events of McKinley's assassination. According to Haverin, Czolgosz asserted that he was a follower of the notorious anarchist Emma Goldman and that "no man [the president] should have this power while others have none." No connection could be established between Czolgolz and Goldman, but the author insists that Goldman felt coldly indifferent to McKinley's death.

O n the morning of September 5, 1901, a slim man arrived at the gates of the Pan-American exposition. He blended in with the crowd nicely. No one would suspect that he was buying his ticket for any other purpose other than to enjoy what thousands were calling the Grandest of all the World's Fairs.

After passing through the gates, the man began a deliberate survey of the Exposition grounds paying close attention to certain details such as the layout of the walkways, the throngs of people, and the security guards. Suddenly he saw his objective. An enormous crowd had gathered to hear a speech delivered by President William McKinley—perhaps some would actually get the opportunity to greet him personally and shake his hand.

With a guarded determination, the man approached the huge throng of people waiting to catch a look at the President. After some time, the man found himself close enough to be able to hear McKinley's speech. He saw the President rise and mount to the stand. He forced his way down to the front row to stand with the cheering people, but he stood mute.

He listened to the President's speech with a deaf ear. He was determined to get closer to the President but as he made his attempt, a guard appeared in front of him blocking his chance. The man decided to wait for a better opportunity.

After the President's address, the man was among the hundreds of people who attempted to crowd up to the President's carriage, but he was forced back. He saw the President drive away and cursed his misfortune.

THE NEXT DAY

The next day, the man returned to the Pan-American Exposition and waited for President McKinley to return. In the early afternoon, the President was to greet people in the Temple of Music and the man was one of the first to enter. He got as close to the stage as possible and was there when the President entered the Temple through a side door. The man was one of the first to hurry forward when the President took his position and prepared to shake hands with the people.

One by one the President took their hands, and with a smile on his face, gave a sharp downward jerk to each person's hand as he greeted them. No one paid any attention to the man as he stood in the line that slowly approached the President. Perhaps it was a bit odd that his hand was wrapped in a handkerchief and held close to his chest, but maybe he was nursing an injury and was embarrassed by his wound. Best to keep it covered up.

Finally, the man reached the President. He did not look into

McKinley's face. As the smiling President reached out to take the man's right hand, he extended his left hand, pressed it against the President's chest and fired the gun he was concealing under the handkerchief. He fired twice, and would have fired again if not for the fact that he was tackled and drove to the ground.

Utter pandemonium rose up from the crowd in the Temple of Music. President McKinley, while gripping his chest, fell back into the arms of one of the security guards. A large pool of blood was forming on his white shirt. "Am I shot?" he exclaimed. After unbuttoning his vest and examining the President, the guard replied, "I'm afraid that you are, Mr. President."

It all happened in an instant. Almost before the noise of the second shot sounded, the assassin was tackled by secret service men and a squad of Exposition police seized the man and tore the weapon out of his hand. Soldiers of the U.S. artillery who were present at the reception set upon the assassin and began to brutally beat him. A soft yet determined voice spoke through the chaos, "Go easy on him boys." The words came from McKinley who was slumped on the floor in terrible pain. The President reached up for Pan-American President Milburn and said, "My wife, be careful about her. Don't let her know."

"LET NO ONE HURT HIM"

As word of the assassination attempt began to filter out of the Temple of Music, the thousands who were in attendance that day began what could only be described as a riot. People tried to shove their way into the Temple to see if what they were hearing was true, while others began an immediate cry for the death of the assassin at their hands. As the scene got more and more out of control, the military was called upon to try and restore some order while the Pan-American Exposition police attempted to get the assassin off the grounds.

The prostrate body of the assassin lay on the floor near where McKinley was dying. The man had received a terrific beating from the police, soldiers, and detectives. The President took a painful glance over at the scene. He raised his right hand, red with his own blood, and placed it on the hand of his secretary. "Let no one hurt him," he gasped, and sank back into a chair. The guards carried the assassin out of his sight.

At police headquarters, the assassin was interrogated by the District Attorney. "What is your name?" he asked bluntly.

"Leon Czolgosz," came the weak reply.

"Did you mean to kill the President?" asked the D.A.

"I did."

"What was the motive that induced you to commit this crime?"

"I am a disciple of Emma Goldman. I killed the President because I done my duty. I did not feel that one man should have all this power while others have none."

With these words, Czolgosz was led away to a cell to await his trial. Meanwhile, the City of Buffalo was anxiously awaiting the news on whether or not President McKinley would survive the assassin's deadly attack.

EVENING AT THE MILBURN HOUSE

For a little over a week, President William McKinley clung to life although he drifted in and out of consciousness. During the days following the operation that was hoped had saved his life, confidence was high that the President would recover fully. In this period of suspense, apprehension and hope, there were many troubled minds that felt a fully recovered President would result in the setting free of Leon Czolgosz. However, the President's death changed the scene for the murderer.

Perhaps the most tender scene of the entire tragedy was the parting of the President and his wife. It was early in the evening at the Milburn House, on September 13, 1901, that the administration of oxygen brought McKinley back from a comatose condition. He slowly opened his eyes and looked around the room with a kindly, gentle expression that brought feelings of admiration and love to all those present in the room with him. They saw that he was trying to speak so they bent over him to listen.

"Mrs. McKinley," he slowly whispered and then closed his eyes in pain. It was apparent to all that he knew that the end was near; the time had come to say his good-byes. Ida McKinley was helped into the room and saw that her husband had once again fallen into unconsciousness. After waiting for a few moments, she obeyed the suggestion of the doctors present that perhaps she should return to her room to wait.

It was not until 8 o'clock that McKinley regained consciousness again and once more he whispered Mrs. McKinley's name. Once more they brought her in and put a chair beside her husband's bed. All present in the room saw that the President was conscious and turned away—all except a nurse and one doctor.

When Mrs. McKinley was seated she took her husband's hand. A faint smile came to his lips. They sat in silence for a few moments before the President whispered, "Nearer, My God, to Thee." Then he seemed to drift out of consciousness.

The quietude in the room was almost deafening. Mrs. McKinley was trembling as she held on to her husband's pale hand. It was very obvious that as the moments passed, McKinley's breathing became very labored and shallow. Those present knew that the end was imminent. The white-robed nurses stepped back into the shadows of the dimly lit room, the physicians turned away and bowed their heads.

"THE PRESIDENT IS NO MORE"

After some time, the President regained consciousness again. His eyes fluttered and glanced around the room. When he saw his wife, he weakly smiled at her and clutched her hand. They gazed into each other's eyes and everyone knew that it was time for him to say good-bye to the woman he loved. McKinley opened his mouth as if to speak and his wife leaned over and put her ear to his quivering mouth.

"God's will, not ours, be done," he whispered.

"For his sake. For his sake," she whispered back to him. She took both his hands and smiled at him, tears flowing from her eyes.

"Good-bye, all; good-bye. It is God's way. His will be done." These were the last words William McKinley spoke.

Mrs. McKinley, sobbing pitifully, stood and slowly released her husband's hands and disappeared into her own room. As the evening continued, the President's pulse grew fainter and fainter. At 2:16 A.M., Dr. Rixey, McKinley's personal physician, put his finger on the President's neck—tears streaming down his face. He slowly raised his head and turned to face the others in the room.

"It is over," he said. "The President is no more."

President William McKinley was 58 years old. The official cause of death was listed as gangrene of both walls of the stomach and pancreas following a gunshot wound.

Meanwhile, in Chicago, another drama was taking place.

The middle-aged woman was sitting in Police Headquarters being carefully guarded by several prison Matrons. A cold and defiant look was on her slim face. A grim silence was gripping the room and it seemed that several moments had passed without anyone uttering a sound.

With a slow determination, the woman turned and spoke to one of the Matrons. "Suppose the President is dead. Thousands die on a daily basis yet no one cries for them. Why should anyone shed a tear over this man?"

For her comments, all she received were blank looks of disbelief. Suddenly, a patrolman burst into the room screaming, "The flags are being lowered! The President must be dead!"

The woman sat unmoved.

A Police Matron began to curse the woman. "The President is dead! President McKinley is dead!" The Matron shook a finger at the woman.

"Well, I don't care. Why should I? There are thousands of men dying every day. No fuss is made over them. Why should any fuss be made over the President?" Another Matron started for the woman with the intent to strike her but she was held back.

"Have you no heart? You have no sorrow for the man—his family?" the Matron screamed.

"I tell you, I don't care." The response was cold and flat.

"But as a woman you should at least show some feeling for the wife for whom he has always cared so dearly."

An icy glare left the woman's eyes and penetrated into those of the Matron's. "There are thousands of men dying every day," she repeated. "I do feel sorry for Mrs. McKinley. But there are other wives who receive no comfort."

This closed the conversation with Emma Goldman, the woman who was being held as the mastermind behind the assassination of President William McKinley. No evidence ever was found to connect her with Leon Czolgosz and the assassination of the President.

THE WRIGHT BROTHERS' FIRST FLIGHT

HENDRIK DE LEEUW

The quiet yet intense ambition that Ohio brothers Orville and Wilbur Wright shared is as remarkable as their invention of the airplane. From their childhood kite-flying experiments to the historical flight of their biplane the *Flyer* on December 17, 1903, at Kitty Hawk, the Wright brothers exercised persistence and patience to create the first heavier-than-air machine that could achieve and sustain flight. Hendrik de Leeuw, in the following selection, traces the progress the Wright brothers made to realize their dream. As amazing as the *Flyer*'s flight was, de Leeuw claims that the Wright brothers' astonishing feat on that cold day in Kitty Hawk went unnoticed.

De Leeuw is the author of several books, including *From Flying Horse to the Man in the Moon* and *Sinful Cities of the Western World*.

T he 17th of December, 1903, became a red letter day in the history of aviation. A most important event took place that was also to sway the history of the entire world: the crowning achievement of heavier-than-air flight. It was the work of Orville and Wilbur Wright, a devoted and highly religious-minded pair of ingenious and quietly confident workers.

A Fascinating Toy

However, the story of the miracle that took place on December 17, 1903, had actually begun long before that historic date. It had begun, in fact, twenty-five years earlier when the Wright Brothers' childhood interest in flying had been aroused by the gift of a toy helicopter. This small toy, the gift of a loving father to his two young sons, may have started it all. Their loving father was the United Brethren Bishop Milton Wright who, together with his daughter Katharine, lent his sons undivided support. The year was 1878.

Fourteen years had passed since Bishop Wright had presented his sons with the little helicopter model. The memory of this fascinating toy, supported by their kite-flying experiments, kept the boys' dream of flying alive. As they grew to young manhood the persistent vision shared by them grew even stronger. They felt that this must not be an idle dream, they must make it come true.

In these early nineties, America was in the midst of the bicycle craze. Everyone who could afford it owned a bicycle of some sort and belonged to a bicycle club. Since the bicycle craze was growing, the Wrights did the logical thing. They set up a bicycle shop next door to their home. This was December, 1892. Their reputation for straight dealing spread about town, and soon scores of cyclists began to pedal their way to the Wright bicycle shop.

Speed and Volume

While Orville and Wilbur were engaged in handling their ever-growing business, Chicago aeronautical engineer Octave Chanute was experimenting with his contraptions on the sand dunes at Lake Michigan. The Wrights read Chanute's *Progress of Flying Machines* with great interest, and it spurred their resolve to undertake actual flights of their own at an early date. Reading everything that had been written on the subject, they hastened the start of their own experiments. They began their own series of kite and glider tests, an approach to the construction of a man-carrying glider, in July, 1899. As a result of these tests, they concluded that the speed and volume of wind flowing around the wings of a glider were the key to sustained flight, and that further tests must be made in an area where the prevailing winds blew strong and steadily.

After a careful study of charts and metereological data sent to them by the U.S. Weather Bureau, they picked Kitty Hawk, in North Carolina, as the site for their glider tests. Then, after some correspondence with Joseph Dosher, in charge of the Kitty Hawk weather station, they decided to make a personal inspection. These boys never left anything to chance.

And so, on the bright early fall day of September 6, 1900, Wilbur left Dayton for his first visit to Kitty Hawk, a name that was to become as world-renowned as their own.

A KEY INVENTION

It might also be of interest to mention at this juncture that, after carefully observing the soaring flights of buzzards, Wilbur stumbled across what resulted in one of his key inventions. He noticed that when the birds were rocked to one side by a gust of wind, they would right themselves by increasing the angle of incidence of the dropped wing. This seemed to give them more lift and enabled them to level off. It was this experience that was responsible for the birth of the idea of the wing "warping" control or "ailerons." Patented by them afterwards, it became one of the essential controls of all aircraft to this very day.

But let's go back to their experience at Kitty Hawk, where the inhabitants welcomed them with neighborly kindness. Here the brothers set up housekeeping in a tent on the site that Wilbur picked as their testing ground. The one thing that amazed these young men from the lush farmlands of their own midwest was the sand—nothing but acres of sand—millions of tons of sand blown up in heaps from the sea.

The crude engine they constructed left much to be desired; its sputtering and coughing jogged the frail craft into sideslips on each succeeding flight. They continued to develop greater skill, however.

Their first flying attempt, undertaken on December 14, was unsuccessful because their machine jumped the greased rail from which they had intended to catapult into the sky. They repaired a broken wing in a jiffy and on the morning of December 17, while a small audience of neighboring fishermen and a Mr. A.D. Etheridge of the Kitty Hawk Coast Guard Station were watching, Orville stretched himself in prone position across the lower wing of the biplane.

It was a bitter-cold day. Incredulous until the last and shivering as they faced the biting wind from the bleak Kill Devil sand dunes, the spectators tried to follow the movements of the two pioneers, but all they could see was the frail-looking wooden biplane with its linen-covered wings. Then came the historic moment which would mean success or failure. Hoisting the signal once again, Orville waved to his brother to remove the blocks from the front of the skids. The noisy engine set the frail craft a-shuddering. Grabbing hold of the controls, Orville slipped the release wire, and off he went, as the *Flyer* rose eight to ten feet into the air. She wavered. She steadied, and then she rose, as John T. Daniels of the Coast Guard clicked the camera. And so the *Flyer* was airborne at last at thirty miles an hour, before she again plowed her wing into the sand, as Orville grunted from the shock of the landing.

There had been no fanfare, no feature story, no stir or comment from the papers except a short paragraph about this event. It would be some time before the American public would actually know what had taken place on that cold, wintery day at Kitty Hawk. As written by Orville later: "This flight lasted only 21 seconds, but it was nevertheless the first in the history of the world in which a machine carrying a man had raised itself by its own power into the air in full flight, had sailed forward without reduction of speed and finally landed at a point as high as that from which it started."

Opening Night at Coney Island

New York Times

By the turn of the twentieth century, the rapid changes brought by industrialization allowed employers to decrease the hours of work and offer days off for vacation, giving Americans more leisure time. Naturally, American workers spent this free time amusing themselves to escape the monotonous workweek.

Aware of the increased idle time of Americans, shrewd entrepreneurs sought to entertain the pleasure-seeking masses. New York's Coney Island, the nation's premier amusement park at that time, epitomized this trend. In 1903, Luna Park opened to the public and was an immediate success. The amusement park's sparkling lights, fantastic rides, and exotic attractions transported hundreds of thousands of patrons from their ordinary lives. Ambitious realtors and developers opened Dreamland at Coney Island the following year, hoping to outshine the spectacles of Luna Park and capitalize on New Yorkers' thirst for excitement and thrills.

In the following selection, the *New York Times* reviews the opening night at Dreamland and the newly expanded Luna Park. It proclaims that "there were more dazzling, wriggling, spectacular amusements [at Coney Island that night] than had ever before been collected together at any one place at any time."

They took the lid off Coney Island May 15, 1904, and a quarter of a million men and women got a glimpse of a swaying, rocking, glittering magic city by the sea. It was Coney Island's opening day, but Coney Island never before ex-

From "Review of Opening Night at Coney Island," *New York Times*, May 16, 1904.

perienced such a bewildering opening. First of all, there were more people there than had ever been at Coney Island at one time before. Then there were more dazzling, wriggling, spectacular amusements offered than had ever before been collected together at any one place at any time.

Coney Island Is Regenerated

Picturesque Luna Park, with its added acres of new attractions, and the much-talked-about Dreamland presented a bewildering mixture of men, animals, and things that words can scarcely describe. They had been gathered from every corner of the globe, and represented about everything that nature and science have ever produced. Coney Island is regenerated, and almost every trace of Old Coney has been wiped out. Frankfurters, peanuts, and popcorn were among the few things left to represent the place as it was in the old days.

With the new order of things came herds of elephants, genuine Nautch girls, Indian rajahs, snake charmers, Eskimos, Indians, Japs, Russians, Chinamen, acrobats, jugglers, performing camels, pugilistic horses, and bears that could ride a horse as well as some of the jockies of the race track.

Sixteen of the newly acquired acres of land in Luna Park were set aside for the reproduction of the glittering Durbar of Delhi. There was the Vice Royal palace in the city that had been reproduced in miniature, and a pageant of Oriental splendor was presented. There were gilded chariots and prancing horses, and trained elephants and dancing girls, regiments of soldiers, and an astonishing number of real Eastern people and animals in gay and stately trappings. The magnificence of the scene was such as to make those who witnessed it imagine they were in a genuine Oriental city. In fact, there was a charm about the streets of Delhi that kept the people spellbound until the exhibition ended. Five thousand people at a time saw this remarkable show, and then went back to see it a second time.

Clean, Moral, and Magnificent

Outside in Luna Park proper, 20,000 or more men, women, and children gazed in wonderment at the daring feats of the acrobats, tight-rope walkers, and horsemen who appeared in connection with the three-ring circus. They saw two wonderful horses with gloves strapped on their forefeet rear up and box in a manner that would have done credit to old-time pugilists. The pugilistic horses boxed in rounds and clinched now and then with their legs about each other's neck just as prizefighters clinch.

Then came the bears that rode in jockey fashion, much to the amusement of the thousands of children who were there.

The Trip to the Moon, Twenty Thousand Leagues Under the Sea, the chutes, the scenic railway, and the other features of Luna Park were all well patronized. A new feature, known as whirl-the-whirl, proved to be a money coiner. In that boats are arranged to sail through the air in circular fashion at a height of almost a hundred feet. The newly arranged dancing platforms and the new theatres in Luna Park were as well patronized as they possibly could be, for they were crowded from the time the

The Coney Island roller coaster offered a one-minute ride and admission was a nickel.

gates opened until closing time at midnight.

On the way out the crowd found a complete printing plant and newspaper office in operation, turning out a newspaper— *The Evening Star*—which will be published daily in Luna Park. The first issue contained an interview with Police Commissioner McAdoo, in which the Commissioner was quoted as saying that the new Coney Island was clean, moral, and magnificent.

There were many city and country officials among the visitors at Luna Park yesterday. Messrs. Thompson & Dundy, the proprietors of the park, entertained them, together with a thousand other guests, after the banquet in the big dining hall over the dancing pavilion.

A Veritable Fairyland

Dreamland, the site of which extends from Henry's Bathing Pavilion to the Iron Steamboat Company's pier, takes in the old pier and reaches from Surf Avenue far into the ocean. Dreamland opened its gates for the first time yesterday, and scarcely at any time were there less than 20,000 persons visiting its wonderful features. Illuminated at night, it resembled a city in itself. But the visitor who went there yesterday found that after getting in it contained many miniature cities. It proved to be a veritable fairyland, with its mystic palaces and Aladdin-like shows. In addition to these there was a circus in three rings, high divers, jugglers, aerial performances, and other things that are difficult to describe.

Probably one of its most interesting features is the Dwarf City, with its thousand tiny inhabitants. Storekeepers, policemen, firemen, musicians, wagon drivers, and others who live there are all dwarfs. They have a Liliputian Fire Department, with little fire engines, a miniature livery stable, a midget theatre, midget circus, diminutive horses, bantam chickens, and everything else that would go to make up a midget city, even to its midget Chinese laundrymen. Although everything there is on the smallest possible scale, it is perhaps one of the biggest features of the regenerated Coney Island.

The Incubator Building in Dreamland is designed in farmhouse style, the first story being of brick and the upper part in half timber. The tiled roof has a gable with a large stork overlooking a nest of cherubs. It is a scientific demonstration of how the lives of babies can be saved. It cost $36,000, and the building is full of babies.

The Scenic Railway Building in Dreamland has a front that expresses very successfully "l'art nouveau." The Dog and Monkey Building contains Wormwood's Dog and Monkey Show. The front of the structure symbolizes its purpose and is decorated with cocoanut trees, in which monkeys spring from branch to branch.

A GREAT SUCCESS

One of the principal attractions of Dreamland is the famous Bostock animal show.

The attraction called the "Destruction of Pompeii" is lodged in the Pompeiian Building. A painting back of the columns was executed by Charles S. Shean, a gold medalist of the Paris Salon. The subject of the work is the Bay of Naples and the surrounding neighborhood before the destruction of Pompeii.

The ballroom in Dreamland is of generous proportions, and of the style of the French Renaissance. It is reached by passing through the restaurant, the latter being 240 feet long by 100 feet wide. A movable stairway with a capacity of 7,000 persons an hour takes the visitors to the restaurant and grand ballroom, illuminated with 20,000 electric lights. . . .

Chilkoot Pass consists of a huge proscenium arch in classic style. In ascending and descending this arch the visitors are transported by a movable stairway in a reproduction of the game of bagatelle on an enormous scale. After the visitors have ascended to the high platform, they slide down an inclined plane and roll over and strike against various obstructions which take the place of pegs, and finally reach the bottom and land in holes which are numbered, prizes being given according to the numbers entered.

Dreamland was the conception of ex-Senator William H. Reynolds of Brooklyn, and cost more than $3,000,000 to construct. Mr. Reynolds and a number of prominent New Yorkers were present last night when it formally opened with the Fire Show. Four thousand persons were employed in producing this spectacle. Upon the ringing of the fire alarm firemen leaped from their beds in real engine houses, and slid down brass poles as they do in the New York Department. Their machines and horses were hitched in the regular way, and then they attended a real fire, which was certainly startling. A hotel appeared to burn, with scores of guests apparently trying to escape, and altogether this show proved a great success.

1905–1912: Resistance and Reform

CHAPTER 2

THE RISE OF MUCKRAKING JOURNALISM

STEPHEN GOODE

In the early twentieth century, hard-hitting, ambitious investigative journalists provoked the outrage of the American public. Their unflinching, jarring, and often grotesque exposés of corruption in government and industry earned them the name "muckrakers." Among the most influential muckrakers was Upton Sinclair, author of *The Jungle.* In this 1905 novel, Sinclair attacked the American meat packing industry, vividly describing the atrocities that took place within a fictitious Chicago stockyard. These disclosures stunned the nation and led President Theodore Roosevelt to assemble an investigation into Sinclair's allegations.

In the following article, author Stephen Goode claims that the concerted efforts of muckrakers to unmask corruption expanded the federal government's power. He asserts that the first Pure Food and Drug Act, the Meat Inspection Act, and other regulatory laws were direct responses to *The Jungle* and other major muckraking exposés, dramatically increasing the federal government's leverage in state governments and private industry.

Goode is an author and senior editor at *Insight on the News*, a political magazine.

M uckraking journalists uncovered many abuses of power, both in government and private industry, at the turn of the century. They helped save lives and un-

From "Muckrakers Made Mounds of Trouble," by Stephen Goode, *Insight on the News*, July 7, 1997. Copyright © 1997 by News World Communications, Inc. Reprinted with permission.

mask corruption. But they also contributed to the growing power of the federal government and to the mind-set that looks to Washington for the solution for America's problems.

EXPOSÉS OF CORRUPTION AND SUFFERING

The muckrakers gave Americans exposés of corruption in high places and exposed the extreme suffering of some of the nation's poor. In the process, they provided American journalism with what many regard as one of its finest hours. Their name, bestowed by an angry President Roosevelt, doesn't sound pretty and wasn't meant to. Roosevelt was comparing the kind of journalism they did to the raking of dung into a heap.

It was a moniker they nonetheless relished, for it described what it was they believed they did. Journalist Lincoln Steffens, one of their number, began his exposé of large-scale corruption in the St. Louis city government and the government of other major cities, later published in book form as *The Shame of the Cities*, and in *McClure's* magazine in October 1902.

The following month the indefatigable journalist Ida Tarbell published the first installment of her "History of Standard Oil Company" in the same magazine. Behind the innocuous-sounding title was news as Americans rarely had experienced it: a close look at the activities—often questionable and sometimes illegal—of high officials and officers of one of America's biggest corporations.

Tarbell quickly won the name "Terror of the Trusts" and was dubbed, perhaps inevitably, "a modern-day Joan of Arc." In any case, she made her editors and reading public happy. Within a short time, *McClure's* circulation rose from 350,000 to more than 500,000.

BAD FOOD AND BAD DRUGS

Bad food and bad drugs were other issues the muckrakers seized upon and made their own: the mass manufacture and canning of food, for example, which had led to the misuse of preservatives on a large scale and to food tainted—"poisoned" was a favorite word of the muckrakers—in a variety of ways, one of which was by the bodies of meatplant workers who allegedly fell into processing vats and weren't removed until their flesh became part of the food later sold to consumers.

Another target was patent medicines, an industry that often made nearly $100 million a year, selling alleged cures for cancer, "female complaints," tobacco addiction and panaceas of all sorts. The problem was that the medicines usually contained large amounts of alcohol and often cocaine and morphine, described on the containers as "soothing substances," Rodger Streitmatter tells political magazine *Insight on the News*. Streitmatter teaches at American University's communication school in Washington and is author of the recently published *Mightier Than the Sword: How the News Media Have Shaped American History*.

Edward Bok, editor of *Ladies' Home Journal*, launched the first attack on patent medicines in 1904 by calling for a nationwide boycott of such products. In an editorial, the Dutch-born but very Americanized Bok explained: "A mother who would hold up her hands in holy horror at the thought of her child drinking a glass of beer, which contains from 2 to 5 percent alcohol, gives that child with her own hands a patent medicine that contains from 17 to 34 percent alcohol—to say nothing of opium and cocaine!"

What Bok railed against were advertisements he believed misled the public and endangered health, such as this one, which appeared in many magazines and newspapers of the time—even ones carrying the muckrakers' articles:

"Cancer cured with soothing balmy oils. Cancer, Tumor, Catarrh, Piles, Fistula, Ulcers, Eczema and all Skin and Womb diseases, Write for illustrated book, Sent free. Address Dr. Bye, cor. 9th and Broadway, Kansas City, Mo."

The ad is taken from Arthur and Lila Weinberg's *The Muckrakers*, a 1961 compilation of the most important muckraking articles.

JOINING IN THE FRAY

Other magazines joined in the fray. In 1905, *Collier's* found an angle by running an article by Mark Sullivan that included the minutes of a private meeting of members of a trade group organized by patent-medicine manufacturers. The minutes revealed the association chairman claiming that the manufacturers need not fear newspaper and magazine reporters. Because the patent-medicine industry provided a lion's share of newspaper and magazine income through advertising, pressure in the form of refusing advertising dollars could be brought on editors to spike stories by reporters who proved too inquisitive and too rambunctious, the chairman averred.

In response, the editors of *Collier's* announced they would not be bought—and promised readers to drop all advertising from patent-medicine companies. This move cost the magazine $80,000 in income by the end of the year, an enormous sum at the time and one serious at anytime in a field as tenuous and competitive as magazine publishing. But it was a sacrifice that gained *Collier's* new readers and a reputation for hard-knuckled integrity to boot, and it was an example quickly imitated by *McClure's*, *Saturday Evening Post* and *Everybody's*, other leading magazines of the day.

Collier's continued its exposé of the patent-medicine industry with other attacks in a new series launched in October 1905 by former *McClure's* staffer Samuel Hopkins Adams called "The Great American Fraud"; it later appeared as a best-selling book under the same name.

After noting that Americans would spend at least $75 million during the following year on patent medicines, Adams asked what the American public would get. His answer: "In consideration of this sum, it will swallow huge quantities of alcohol, an appalling amount of opiates and narcotics, a wide assortment of varied drugs ranging from powerful and dangerous heart depressants to insidious liver stimulants; and, far in excess of all other ingredients, undiluted fraud."

Along with the Adams article, *Collier's* ran a cartoon that became a major image in the campaign against fraudulent patent medicines, one familiar to an entire generation of Americans, notes American University's Streitmatter. It showed a huge skull on whose forehead was written, "The Patent Medicine Trust: Palatable Poison for the Poor." On papers strewn before the death mask are written, "Slow poison for little children" and "Great lung cure, palatable poison for consumptives."

THE JUNGLE

The year 1905 also witnessed what may be the single most notable muckraking event, when the Socialist weekly *Appeal to Reason* began publishing Upton Sinclair's *The Jungle*. Sinclair had spent seven busy weeks among stockyard workers and meat packers in Chicago. The young journalist, who also was an outspoken Socialist, claimed to have talked with everyone remotely connected with the stockyards in the Windy City— from plant managers to the workers and their families, ministers and priests. But he later admitted he had never entered a packing plant.

It still is easy to see why Sinclair's attack on meat packing raised eyebrows and commanded America's rapt attention. In the installment published on April 29, 1905, he wrote: "For the men who worked in tankrooms full of steam, their peculiar trouble was that they fell into the vats; and when they were fished out, there was never enough of them left to be worth exhibiting. Sometimes they would be overlooked for days, till all but the bones of them had gone out to the world." Americans, in short, and particularly poor Americans who bought the meat canned in Chicago, were told they were eating human flesh. In the words of the late historian Page Smith, *The Jungle*, which became a best-seller when it was sold in book form and made its author a rich man, was nothing short of "hair-raising," one of the few books to alter American history, like Harriet Beecher Stowe's *Uncle Tom's Cabin* had done a half-century earlier.

Sinclair's critics attacked *The Jungle*, which still is in print today, as impressionistic and novel-like. But the author defended it ardently. It would, he wrote, "stand the severest test—it is authoritative as if it were a statistical compilation." One reader who was impressed was Roosevelt, who had denounced Sinclair's kind of journalism, says Streitmatter. By now a "trust buster," the curious Roosevelt sent his own team of investigators to Chicago to look into Sinclair's charges. The team said *The Jungle* was on target.

In the Hands of the People

A powerful activist president's attention was welcome. But the muckrakers had other ways to achieve their goals. In 1906, *Ladies' Home Journal's* indefatigable editor Bok challenged his readers by publishing a bill for federal regulation of the patent-medicine industry, which he and his associates had drawn up. He called it "An Act to Regulate the Manufacture and Sale of Patent Medicines."

Bok urged his readers to clip the sample bill out of the magazine and send it off to their congressmen and senators and to Roosevelt in Washington, along with a clear statement of their own support for the legislation.

Explained Bok: "This and other magazines have done their part" in exposing the wrongs of the patent-medicine and food industries. "The remedy of the fearful evil they have laid bare is in the hands of the people: in your hands. The question is: Will you, now, do your part?" Another editorial repeated the call to arms: "The time has come for YOU to ACT!"

Bok's readers responded quickly "and in great number," notes Streitmatter. Roosevelt responded in turn by asking in his annual message to Congress that the federal government regulate both the food industry and drug manufacturers. In the Senate, legislation complying with the president's wishes immediately was introduced, along with proposals for federal meat inspection. This legislation was in direct response to the articles published by Bok, Sinclair, Adams and others, according to the Weinbergs in their book.

The first Pure Food and Drug Act, passed in 1906, required all medicines to be investigated and approved by the Department of Agriculture. The Meat Inspection Act, passed the following year, said that all meat sold in the United States had to be checked by federal inspectors. The new legislation was based on the constitutional right of Congress to pass laws regulating interstate commerce, the same clause that later was used to expand federal powers so enormously during the New Deal. A precedent had been set.

THE SALOON PROBLEM

JOHN MARSHALL BARKER

By the early twentieth century, Americans' attitudes toward the legal sale and consumption of alcohol had become increasingly conflicted. The movement against the use of alcohol (temperance) was gaining influence, bringing the saloon—where alcohol and beer were freely purchased and consumed—under scrutiny. Temperance advocate John Marshall Barker was one of the most vocal opponents of the saloon. In the following selection, excerpted from his 1905 book, *The Saloon Problem and Social Reform,* Barker argues that the saloon poses a menace to the family and the general public by encouraging the consumption of alcohol. He contends that the saloon lures its once-rational patrons down the path of alcoholism with one small, seemingly harmless "social glass."

The late Barker was a sociology professor in the School of Theology at Boston University.

The influence of the saloon on the social life of the people far exceeds in importance the economic and political aspects. In the first place, the saloon is the enemy of society because of the evil results produced upon the individual. It meets no legitimate demand of human nature, but exists to excite an abnormal appetite for intoxicants. The supply of liquor creates the demand, and not, as in the case of necessities, the demand the supply. In a multitude of ways it fosters and overstimulates a thirst for drink. One of its avowed purposes is to encourage the habit of treating, and by means of free salted lunches

Excerpted from *The Saloon Problem and Social Reform*, by John Marshall Barker (Boston: Everett Press, 1905).

and concocted drinks provoke a wholly unnatural craving for intoxicating liquor. It is this fact that makes the saloon a positive evil, and vicious in the highest degree. It becomes an instrument to make a man intoxicated, and thereby forms the chief contributing cause towards discounting his value in society.

THE PATHOLOGICAL EFFECT OF ALCOHOL

The saloon not only helps to deprave the appetite, but is the important factor from a hygienic point of view in dispensing intoxicants that undermine the health and efficiency of its patrons. Much of the success of man as a productive force in society comes from a sound body and a clear brain. It is an incontrovertible fact that the physical and mental powers cannot be used to the best advantage when under the influence of intoxicating liquors. The insidious and deceptive character of alcohol and beer on the vital functions of the human body is abundantly confirmed by scientists, physiologists, and physicians eminent in their professions. Dr. J.H. Kellog says, "In administering alcohol in small doses to a healthy human being, the result is, first, to diminish nerve activity; second, to reduce cerebral activity; third, to impair the coördinate power of the brain; fourth, to lessen muscular strength to a notable degree; fifth, to diminish digestive activity." Dr. A. Forel, of the University of Zurich, testifies that even a moderate quantity of alcohol contained in a glass of wine or a pint of German beer "is sufficient to paralyze, retard, or disturb the central and centripetal brain functions. The number of mistakes in calculation, setting type, memorizing, is increased. Sensibility is blunted, the reaction is retarded. The subjective consequence of the effect is agreeable: one feels heat, cold, and pain less; one is less afraid, less accurate, less scrupulous. At the same time a very slight illusion spreads over reality, the beginning of the later intoxication by higher doses. Hence, whenever alcohol promotes sociability and loosens the tongue it is the consequence of a cerebral intoxication. Whenever the dose is too weak to produce this result it also fails to have the desired effect. Hence it is evident that the social effect of alcohol is pathological. . . .

THE INSIDIOUS EFFECTS OF BEER

Dr. S.H. Burgen, of Toledo, Ohio, adds the following testimony of a practising physician: "My attention was first called to the insidious effects of beer when I began examining for life insurance. I passed as unusually good risks five Germans—young business men—who seemed in the best of health, and to have superb constitutions. In a few years I was amazed to see the whole five drop off, one after another, with what ought to be mild and easily curable diseases. On comparing my experience with that of other physicians, I found they were all having similar luck with confirmed beer-drinkers, and my practice since has heaped confirmation upon confirmation." The whisky trade paper, *Barrels and Bottles*, adds its testimony to the dangerous use of beer: "Every one bears testimony that no man can drink beer safely, that it is an injury to any one who uses it in any quantity, and that its effect on the general health is far worse than that of whisky, clogging his liver, rotting his kidneys, decaying his heart and arteries, stupefying and starving his brain, choking his lungs and bronchia, loading his body with dropsical fluids and unwholesome fat, fastening upon him rheumatism, erysipelas, and all manner of painful and disgusting diseases, and finally dragging him to his grave when other men are in their prime of mental and bodily vigor."

The deleterious effect of alcohol on the human system is accentuated by expert testimony as to the fearful adulterations. One of the Pure Food Commissioners of Illinois says, "More than 80% of the whisky of the United States is adulterated with harmful deleterious poisons, chemicals, and compounds, 85% of which is sold in barrels and 15% in bottles." Dr. B.H. Warren, the Pure Food Commissioner, of Pennsylvania, found upon examining one thousand samples gathered from over the State, that 95% of them were adulterated. His reports show that more than 85% of all whisky is doctored by wood alcohol and red or India pepper and prussic acid and other drugs. . . .

CAUSE OF INSANITY

Again, the saloon encourages the use of drinks that produce abnormal nerve conditions, and destroy one's dignity as a rational being. Among the many coöperative causes of insanity is the immoderate use of alcohol. It is a potent excitant of the nerves, and stimulates the brain to a feverish activity. The alarming growth of insanity in both Europe and America is traceable to alcoholism. The Massachusetts Bureau of Statistics of 1894 shows that of 1,281 adult insane persons, 659, or 51.44, were addicted to the use of liquors. Dr. Delbruck, of Bremen, Germany, has recently pointed out that of one hundred and forty-nine persons who were treated in a North Germany asylum for drunkenness, forty-one had been alcoholized by drinking spirits, thirty-eight by wine-drinking, and seventy-eight, or more than half, by the excessive consumption of beer. The fifty-sixth annual report of the Pennsylvania Commissioner of Lunacy shows that the ratio of the increase of insanity from intemperance is five to one.

The question has a more dramatic interest when we come to consider that the saloon helps to destroy personal self-respect, and in so far becomes an obstacle to the growth of good society. The saloon lures its patrons to drink, and by means of screens and other devices shields them from public gaze. The harmless social glass with perhaps only a small amount of alcohol is the first step taken to create an uncontrollable desire for more and stronger drink. Gradually the victim reaches a moral plane where conscience is silenced and he is ready to participate in all the accompanying vices of the saloon. Afterwards he wakens to the fact that he has destroyed self-respect and forfeited the good opinion of his fellows. With self-respect gone and all barriers broken down, there is no limit to his moral and social degradation. The passion for drink has caused the expression of the eye to fade and the grace of the human form to depart. He has reached the point where he can practise the art of dissimulation and excuse with the boldest effrontery. Finally, the victim seeks the lowest haunts of vice and becomes submerged in imbecility or a drunkard's grave. What a satire on the life of a human being made a little lower than the angels! Truly, this is no overdrawn picture, but one of the common products of the saloon and its social attractions.

A MENACE TO THE FAMILY

The saloon is likewise a menace to the family. The vice and degradation generated in the saloon do not stop there, but attack the home, and invade the sanctuary of womanhood and childhood. The social and sexual instincts are normally developed in the family. Whatever influence hinders or obstructs these natural relations works an injustice to both individual and social well-being. Many frequenters of the saloon are young men who spend such a large proportion of their money in drink and dissipation that they are thereby debarred from entering into marriage relations and maintaining a family. Those who do assume the responsibility are likely sooner or later to become improvident, squander and waste property, neglect business, and forsake the family. The husband and father who makes the saloon a favorite resort is tempted to waste his money and consume his energy. The economic result of this disablement is to render the man less serviceable to his family, as well as to society. His usefulness is cut short. Instead of being a contributing factor to civilization, he becomes dependent and useless. When the head of a family becomes non-productive because of drink, the wife and children are often compelled to support themselves, and possibly to help pay public fines imposed upon the drunken husband and father. Consequently there is less promise of usefulness in the family when the saloon has occasioned such poverty, squalor, and degradation. . . .

AN UN-AMERICAN SPIRIT

The saloon fosters an un-American spirit among the foreign-born population of our country. The influx of foreigners into our urban centres, many of whom have liquor habits, is a menace to good government. Whole classes of native-born Americans are being redeemed from the saloon, but the foreign-born population is largely under the social and political control of the saloon. If the cities keep up their rapid growth they will soon have the balance of political power in the nation and become the storm centres of political life. The hope of perpetuating our liberties is to help the foreigner correct any demoralizing custom, and, through self-restraint, to assimilate American ideals. At least the children of the heterogeneous foreign population should have a wholesome environment and not be encouraged to cultivate the drink habit because their parents did. However much ethical standards may vary, no citizen has any right to demand that the community support a saloon to satisfy his appetite when it endangers the common welfare of society. . . .

THE DEVASTATION OF HUMAN LIFE

The devastation of human life that is going on silently but effectually all over our land because of drink is fraught with frightful consequences to the nation. Intemperance every year is destroying its victims by the thousands.

THE SAN FRANCISCO EARTHQUAKE OF 1906

DeWitt C. Baldwin

At 5:12 A.M. on April 18, 1906, a 7.8 magnitude earthquake hit the still sleeping city of San Francisco, California. The earthquake spawned devastating fires that ravaged the city for four days, hampering rescue efforts and causing additional losses of property and life. It still stands as America's most deadly earthquake. Although initial reports indicated that 700 people were killed in the earthquake, a reexamination of the 1906 data claimed that more than 3,000 lives were lost.

He was only eight years old at the time, but former San Francisco resident DeWitt C. Baldwin vividly recalls the sights and sounds of the earthquake of 1906. In the following eyewitness account, Baldwin eerily describes the fires, damage, and chaos he encountered the day of the earthquake. The "seriousness of the situation" crept up on him slowly, climaxing when the raging city fires forced the Baldwin family to evacuate their home.

Shortly after five the morning of April 18, 1906, I woke up to dress quickly and have an hour's practice on the piano. (I was eight years old then and Mother insisted that I practice everyday after school. I did not want to give up my hours in the afternoon for that, so we agreed that instead of practicing the piano after school I would practice in the morning before breakfast. That way I could spend the afternoon playing ball with the boys.) At about five fifteen, I had gotten as far as sitting up with my feet over the side of the bed when totally unexpectedly the house began to shake violently. I heard dishes break from different parts of the house; furnitures moved at the violence of the shock.

THE EFFECTS OF THE EARTHQUAKE

I ran across the hall to our parlor from which I had heard crockery and glassware falling off a shelf or a glass cabinet. There I saw the upright piano where I was about to practice on. It shifted about a foot and a half away from the wall. (The shake of the earthquake seemed to be from side to side of our house.)

Then I quickly dashed down the hall to see the effects of the earthquake. I especially wanted to talk to my parents. My elder sister Helen was awakened by the earthquake, but she was still in her room. When I saw her I asked her where our parents and my baby sister were. She hurriedly informed me that "Mother grabbed Virginia and they ran downstairs for safety under the front door.". . .

I was quite excited so I raced to the front windows to look out. There I noticed some people running up and down our street while others were curiously peering out their windows. We all hurried back to our rooms to get dressed. (That must have been a school day or I would not have taken time to wake up early to practice my piano lessons.)

Mother and Father hastily got breakfast ready. Around quarter of eight we were at our table eating and talking over immediate plans when suddenly a second fairly strong earthquake shook the house again. Very soon after the second tremors sirens began to wail at different directions of the city. This indicated to us that local fires had started. After breakfast Father left for work. He realized that he was needed downtown in his office, which was very near the U.S. Mint building. (At that time my father, Clinton D. Baldwin, was the purchasing agent for the United Railroads of San Francisco. There seemed to be a strike in the company and he was then responsible for the food, lodging and other needs of over 100 strike breakers.) Mother and Helen opted to remain at home. They spent the morning listening to the verbal reports of neighbors and other people on the streets sharing their information about on-going fires which were practically [in] every part of the city. (Reportedly there had been fifty-three different fires in progress simultaneously.)

As soon as breakfast was over I requested Mother's permission to go outside our back wooden stairs. (School had already been called off by that time.) I was curious to see the nearest fire at the corner of 22nd and Mission St. Our house was located at 931 Dolores Street in the block between the 22nd and 23rd Streets.

As I ran across Valencia St. going to the Mission St. fire, I noticed on my left down Valencia St. a small old three-story hotel. (Evidently it had been built over a subterranean faultline.) The first story had partly [sunk] in the earth while the second and third had fallen out into the street. That was the first structural destruction I had witnessed.

I had hardly gone on to Mission St. when I came across a large crowd watching a huge department store ablaze. I observed how the firemen desperately attempted to bring the fire under control. After surveilling some time and listening to tales from different folks who were there to see the fire, I turned back home and on the way collected information about other fires from distant places in the city.

(In 1988 I find it difficult to describe my own personal feelings about the earthquake that day. As an eight-year old boy I was not frightened then by the actual earthquake. The tremor and the noise of the breakage did not disturb me. That for me was just a more destructive one than I had known. The rest of the family were quite excited and nervous, but I was not afraid. I guess I felt secure in the knowledge that the house and the family would be all right. Even so, I sensed the seriousness of the situation and I saw the severity of it for many people. My attitude was one of excitement, curiosity and a great desire to see and hear all I could.)

A GRIM EXPERIENCE

Not until mid-afternoon did the first grim experience of the earthquake and the subsequent fires [strike] me. As I went out on our street, Dolores St., the sidewalk began to fill up with people from all parts of the city. They were carrying a load of possessions they considered important to them. There were sights that were a bit laughable to me as a boy. It seemed that some had left their homes quite hurriedly [so] that they had not selected carefully the things to carry with them or that some had not expected to return [so] that they were carrying their whole possessions with them. Folks were carrying bundles, boxes, trunks and even a bird cage. I saw mothers carrying their babies and little children hanging on to their parents hands. Once in a while a boy's playwagon, on which were clothes and food supplies which would help temporarily would pass by.

These lines of people overflowed the sidewalks and were going toward the mountains beyond the Mission area of the city. As the day went on I saw many things that entertained me. . . .

With boys my own age, I wandered as far as I dared to explore some destruction sites and get a view of local fires. In some places there were gaps on the ground. Some were about one foot to five feet wide narrowing toward the inner earth. They seemed anywhere from two feet to over twenty-five feet deep just like a crevice. Sometimes when I dared to peer down the fissure I would see fallen things inside. At times I couldn't see anything because the crack was frightfully deep and dark.

The earthquake of 1906 devastated the city of San Francisco.

EVACUATION TOWARD THE MISSION AREA

All through the night of the first day great numbers of people were constantly passing by our house evacuating toward the Mission Area. On the second day U.S. soldiers were dispatched to every part of the city to keep peace and order, to prevent looting, and to implement emergency regulations set by the Mayor and the City Council [Board of Supervisors]. On our street alone two soldiers were assigned and they had our orders drawn up. Among them were: Stop looting. Fire at robbers or looters. By the second night another order was added. No lighted candles or matches in a building. (If one wanted a light one had to go out on the streets.)

These rules were difficult to follow especially for families with babies or little children. Sometime during that evening Mother felt that she just had to have some warm milk for my baby sister, Virginia, who was just six months old. Cautiously Mother struck a match to light a Sterno. Soon enough an officer knocked at our door and ordered her to "Madam, put out the light and if you do that again I have to shoot you." She protested only to be told that such was the order.

The morning of the third day came and many fires were still in progress. Many structures in our neighborhood were destroyed and leveled to the ground such that one could stand at the foot of Market St. and look as far as the eye could see to the east and to the west. By this time fires were still raging to the east of Market St. and toward the Mission area, likewise in several areas reaching toward the Golden Gate Park.

Later that day as the fires continued, we were ordered to evacuate our homes and find shelter on the hills. At this point the gravity of the situation began to dawn on me. "This is getting serious," I said to myself. The fire had threatened the very place we live. The whole situation set me to thinking of the frailty or the incompleteness of the power of man relative to the power of nature. . . .

SOBERING THOUGHTS

Our family was very fortunate to be provided with a small market wagon. My father, being an officer of the United Railroads of San Francisco, was able to get us what we called a spring wagon to take us and all important possessions on our journey. Hastily Mother packed a small trunk with all the baby's needs that we could bring, a few blankets and some provisions. Soon all of us were on the wagon. Going by Valencia St. looking as far as I could see down the road, I watched the flames bursting on both sides meeting each other on the street.

That sight and the knowledge that soon the flames would reach our home before morning really gave me serious thoughts about the uncertainty of life. My heart developed sober seriousness as to what the situation would mean to us and what it had meant to others. As a boy of eight I had been around the city many times. I was acquainted with the city and I loved it. San Francisco was really a part of me and to say good-bye to it like that surprised me and made me think of what was ahead of us. I doubt if Mother herself slept a wink that night. She held my baby sister close to her and found comfort in prayers.

One of the other sad thoughts I had as we evacuated the city riding on the wagon where Mother had most of the baby's needs and our things was this. I began to feel sorry that others did not have the same transportation. I said to myself how did it happen that others did not have the same resource to carry all that they desperately need to take with them. For me as a boy, the seriousness of the fire and all that it meant was gradually flooding my mind. My mind was then filled with genuine concern for others. I felt so desirous to help in whatever way I [could].

Two lasting impressions were imbedded in my mind the third day. As I looked beyond Mission St. from the back stairs of our three-story building, I saw a powerful blaze consuming everything before it. I began to think of the destructive power of fire and realized that fire was more destructive of man and his environment than any cause I had known then. Later that day when we were ordered to leave our houses to find places of refuge somewhere on the hills so the authorities could better handle the spreading menace, I began to realize as never before the importance of food, shelter and protection. Sobering thoughts! . . .

PROVISIONS AND RECONSTRUCTION

For the thousands of people who had escaped the fire and gone on foot to our part of the city, the military made available provisions, tents, blankets, medicines and food. Father was asked to immediately serve as a member of the city committees and he requisitioned the materials and supplies to provide for the people. Part of his other responsibilities [were] to order and secure materials for the reconstruction of the cable cars, the electric trolleys and other means of transportation for the city. As a member of the First Methodist Church of San Francisco, which was completely burned down, Father became one of the trustees who began to plan for the relocation and rebuilding of the new church.

THEODORE ROOSEVELT AND THE HEPBURN ACT

NATHAN MILLER

By the early twentieth century, railroads had become increasingly important to the economy of the United States. The expanding network of railroads facilitated state-to-state shipping with great efficiency. Capitalizing on the increased reliance on railroads, railroad companies controlled freight charges to their advantage. For instance, railroads offered rebates to large shipping companies to the disadvantage of smaller shipping companies. In addition, particular shippers were arbitrarily charged excessive fees.

President Theodore Roosevelt sought to control the power of the railroad monopolies. In the following excerpt, Nathan Miller asserts that Roosevelt played a major part in the passage of the Hepburn Act of 1906, which allowed the federal government to impose rate limits on railroads. Miller states that in order to win Congress's approval, Roosevelt accepted a less restrictive version of the Hepburn Act, for which he was criticized. However, claims the author, Roosevelt carried out his principles and gave the federal government power over the railroads.

Miller is a critically acclaimed author of numerous books on American history, including *Theodore Roosevelt: A Life*, from which this excerpt is taken.

Excerpted from *Theodore Roosevelt: A Life*, by Nathan Miller (New York: William Morrow, 1992). Copyright © 1992 by Nathan Miller. Reprinted by permission of the publisher.

In his annual message to the new "progressive" Congress on December 5, 1905, President Theodore Roosevelt unleashed a program described by the *New York World* as "the most amazing program of centralization that any President of the United States has ever recommended." This package included a pure food and drug law, governmental supervision of insurance companies, an investigation of child labor by the Department of Commerce and Labor, and an employers' liability law for the District of Columbia that was to become a model for the nation. Most of the programs had little chance of passage, but Roosevelt gave the highest priority to legislation authorizing the Interstate Commerce Commission (ICC) to establish maximum railroad rates after receiving a complaint. These rates would go into effect after a reasonable time, subject to judicial review.[1]

Six days later, this legislative gambit was backed up by the announcement that Attorney General William H. Moody had directed the eighty-five U.S. attorneys to institute proceedings against companies offering or receiving rebates. These cases were to be brought under the conspiracy statutes, so those who were convicted faced the prospect of going to jail. Standard Oil and American Tobacco[2] were already under investigation, and within days, federal grand juries in Chicago and Philadelphia returned indictments against several defendants, including the Armour, Swift, and Cudahy meat-packing companies and the Chicago and Alton railway line.

THE BATTLE OVER RAILWAY REGULATION

The battle over railway regulation was finally joined in January 1906, when Congressman William P. Hepburn of Iowa introduced a bill embodying Roosevelt's program. It gave the ICC general authority to fix limits on railroad rates, a proposal less than that demanded by many progressives such as Wisconsin's Senator Robert La Follette, who wanted the commission to set rate schedules, but it was regarded as a step in the right direction. Railroad reform was popular in the House, and the measure passed with only seven dissenting votes. In the Senate it ran into firm resistance from members opposed to railroad regulation. This might be partially explained by the fact that members of the House were elected by popular vote, while senators

---

1. This was a slight modification of his original position in which the new rate would go into effect immediately.   2. Both corporations had monopolized their markets.

were chosen by state legislatures, which in many cases were dominated by railroad interests.

Senators Nelson Aldrich, Joe Foraker, and Stephen Elkins of West Virginia, all "railroad senators," led the opposition. In an effort to embarrass the president, Elkins, chairman of the Senate Interstate Commerce Committee, refused to sponsor the Senate version of the Hepburn bill, which would have been the normal action in an administration measure, and "Pitchfork Ben" Tillman of South Carolina was designated floor leader for the measure. Tillman was not only a Populist Democrat,[3] but he and the president were anathema to each other; the South Carolinian had even been barred from the White House. The Old Guard [Republican Party] confidently expected that Tillman would turn the bill into a radical measure that would lose the support of moderates, including the president. To everyone's surprise, however, Roosevelt and Tillman put aside their animosities to work together.[4]

For the next sixty days, through March and April 1905, the Senate chamber rang with a debate over railroad regulation. One by one, Republican conservatives—Aldrich, Foraker, Philander Knox, who had been Roosevelt's attorney general, William Allison, even Cabot Lodge—denounced a measure that was a keystone of the legislative program of their own administration. Words like "liar," "unqualified falsehood," and "betrayal" were flung back and forth. Exasperated by opponents within his own party, the president privately called them "a curse" and told Cecil Spring Rice he would be happy to lend the Russian government several eminent statesmen if they would guarantee to place them where a bomb was likely to go off.

NO MERE BYSTANDER

Lacking six of the forty-six votes needed to kill the bill, Aldrich avoided a frontal attack but ate away at its vitals with crippling amendments. While agreeing to grant the ICC power to fix rates after complaints were brought, the Old Guard tried to make it difficult and costly to bring such complaints. "Broad" versus "narrow" court review of rate cases became the issue. Conservatives favored "broad" review, which would allow the courts to establish a lengthy and costly process that would effectively

3. Supporter of the people's power and rights   4. Tillman had been banned from the White House after a brawl on the Senate floor, and he, in turn, had roundly criticized Roosevelt's dinner with Booker Washington as a disgrace.

block rate reform; the moderates wished a swifter, less restrictive review process. La Follette also pushed for a physical evaluation of railroad properties as a basis for rate setting.

The president was no mere bystander during this lengthy debate. He not only worked in bipartisan harmony with a coalition of Republicans and Democrats favoring reform, but tried to influence public opinion with speeches—including a threat to impose stiff inheritance taxes to wipe out family fortunes—and the release of reports, such as one by the Bureau of Corporations on Standard Oil. "The report shows that the Standard Oil Company has benefited enormously up almost to the present moment by secret rates," he declared in transmitting it to Congress. "This benefit amounts to at least three-quarters of a million a year."

But as the deadlock dragged on, it became increasingly apparent that the proregulation coalition did not have the votes to pass the Hepburn bill. Twenty Republicans supported the measure, but it was doubtful if Tillman could produce the twenty-six Democrats needed for a majority. Roosevelt, who wanted a bill, reached out to the conservative bloc for a compromise.

One sign of this was a speech the president gave at a Gridiron dinner on March 17, 1906, in which he denounced crusading journalists as "muckrakers." *Cosmopolitan* magazine had just published "The Treason of the Senate," a series of articles by David Graham Phillips that denounced the general pattern of corruption and conflict of interest that permeated the body. Privately, the president may well have agreed with the articles, but to improve relations with the Old Guard, he attacked Phillips and his fellow muckrakers.

Taking as his text a passage from *The Pilgrim's Progress*, Roosevelt likened these writers to "the Man with the Muckrake, the man who could look no way but downward with the muckrake in his hand; who was offered a celestial crown for his muckrake but who would neither look up nor regard the crown he was offered. . . ." A month later he gave a similar speech at the dedication of the cornerstone of a new House office building in which he warned that this kind of antibusiness journalism could go too far. "The men with the muckrakes are often indispensible to the well being of society," he declared, "but only if they know when to stop raking the muck, and to look upward to the celestial crown above them. . . ."[5]

5. Rather than being offended, investigative journalists accepted the label and in the eyes of most of the public, "muckraker" became a term of approval.

With the approval of Aldrich, Senator Allison drafted an amendment giving the courts authority over cases arising from the law but leaving the exact extent of the review rather vague, which left the bill as it was when it had been approved by the House. Weary of the battle, everyone except the extremists on both sides found merit in Allison's proposal and amid outraged cries of "betrayal" from Tillman, Roosevelt decided to accept it. The Senate approved the Hepburn Act on May 18, 1906, by a margin of 71 to 3, with Foraker casting the only Republican vote against it. The act represented a substantial advance in railway regulation. A stronger ICC now had jurisdiction not only over freight and passenger rates but over pipelines; terminal, refrigeration, and storage facilities, and sleeping car and express service. The railroad interests were also required to disgorge the steamship lines and coal mines they had bought up to stifle competition—a requirement that they managed to evade.

ONGOING PROCESS OF REFORM

Who had won the battle? Critics charged that the president had been too pragmatic and had settled for too little. By obtaining injunctions, the railroads could delay the application of revised rates; moreover, as La Follette emphasized, the ICC lacked knowledge of the true worth of the roads and would be unable to determine what rates should be. Roosevelt obviously conceded the logic of the latter point, for the following year he came out for such a provision.

In the final analysis, however, the president had gotten what he had set out to obtain. He called the new law "a fine piece of constructive legislation, and all that has been done tends toward carrying out the principles I have been preaching." Furthermore, his position was bolstered by the fact that in the first test of the scope of the review provision, the courts rejected the "broad" review favored by the conservatives. Within two years the ICC heard almost twice as many complaints as in the previous nineteen years. Roosevelt recognized the limitations of the law and before the end of his term asked for more stringent procedures. A rebellious Congress refused to enact them, but his actions make it clear that the Hepburn Act was intended to be only one step in an ongoing process of reform and regulation.

THE GREAT AMERICAN VAUDEVILLE INDUSTRY

NEW YORK TIMES

Before radio, motion pictures, and television became popular forms of entertainment, Americans flocked to elaborately staged vaudeville shows in which actors performed comedic skits, magic tricks, monologues, parodies, and short plays. Unlike burlesque, the tawdry variety shows from which it had evolved, vaudeville catered to a wide audience, providing wholesome, light-hearted entertainment at reasonable prices. Popular vaudeville acts toured a circuit, which was a chain of vaudeville houses in different towns and cities that usually went by the same name, hired the same acts, and shared the same booking agents. At each venue, these acts would perform several times a day. The *New York Times* offers a detailed overview of the ins and outs of the vaudeville industry in the following selection. According to the *New York Times*, individuals from all backgrounds auditioned for vaudeville shows; joining a popular show could offer solid, even lucrative, salaries.

T he rumor of a new $30,000,000 vaudeville act—a regular "topline" combination—has been giving Broadway a good deal to talk about. In the slang of the profession, it may make good or it may not.

The theatrical strong family of Klaw & Erlanger, B.F. Keith, Kohl & Castle, and the rest, may succeed in hammering together a big chain of vaudeville houses from Boston to San Francisco; or, as other powerful parties in the field claim, they

From "With the Men and Women of the Twice-a-Day," *New York Times*, May 6, 1906.

may be promising rather more than they can perform. Whatever happens, vaudeville people, far and wide, may be happy in feeling that their doings, their recruits, and their salaries are getting more attention than ever from a devoted public.

AN INTERESTING LOT

They are an interesting lot of people in themselves, these vaudeville folk, quite apart from their value to syndicates and combinations. There are hosts of them. Go up into one of the two big vaudeville booking agencies some morning—either at Keith's or at William Morris's, where the P.G. Williams, Hammerstein, and Frederick F. Proctor circuits have their headquarters. In the outer office you will find a crowd of waiting humanity, in all sizes, ages, complexions, and degrees of prosperity—but all with that indefinable air of being used to being looked at. The place looks like a big railway station. Everybody seems to have just come in from somewhere or to be just starting off for somewhere else. They lounge about, chatting, laughing, or silent, according as they are confident or doubtful of the next bookings. In one group is the smooth-shaven man you could spot anywhere on earth as the fellow who does the rapid-fire-thirteen-to-a-dozen-and-no-periods monologue in front of a row of brownstone houses, with the park in the distance. Over in the corner, with blonde hair and a faded raincoat, is the little girl who plays a cornet, dressed in smart hussar kilts and gold frogs. And so on. The big people don't come much to the office. They have their own private agents, and their booking lists are always as complete as a saint's calendar. When they do come, they "walk right in."

The rank and file of vaudeville people, who book for short periods, are encouraged to keep in touch with the office. They never know when they may be needed for fillers. Inside, with a staff of clerks sits the booking man, like a train dispatcher, with his chart of theatres, acts, and dates, upon which he moves people about like so many freight cars.

For vaudeville has grown, since its humble origin in the old variety show of the Tony Pastor days, when one act had to do service over and over again, into one of the most extensive and complicated branches of the theatrical world. [Pastor was the founder of the first vaudeville theater.] There are now over a hundred first-class vaudeville houses where the higher class acts are sure of continual and profitable booking, besides hundreds of smaller variety houses, with a constant demand for cheaper turns.

The evolution has been in quality as well as in quantity.

BEGINNINGS OF THE CONTINUOUS

When B.F. Keith established his first continuous performance at his little Bijou Theatre, in Boston, in the middle 1880s, and F.F. Proctor introduced the same thing in New York at his Twenty-third Street Theatre, the day of polite vaudeville dawned. Before that, variety acts had been of a rough-and-tumble, strongly flavored sport that went along with beer and sand floors. But to the continuous performance came audiences made up largely of women and children, and parlor vaudeville was soon in full swing. Plenty of people can remember when it came. It marked the first demand for the quieter, cleverer acts that have constantly attracted better and better performers from the legitimate to the variety stage.

The continuous performance proved so profitable, and the public that had been paying 50 cents and finding its own seats, began to come so regularly and in such goodly form, that presently two performances a day, with reserved seats at $1, and a still better class of act, seemed the only way to keep up to the proper level. Since then the constant rise of vaudeville salaries and the frequent beguilement of noted stage people into the vaudeville circuits has been one of the common marvels for the man in the street.

A few nights ago F.F. Proctor, who stands for as much as anybody in the development of vaudeville in America, showed some friends an interesting old bill that he had kept in his archives. It was a variety show bill of the Olympic Theatre, dated in the early 1880s. The top liners—and they were placed in little boxes side by side, so there could be no jealousy—were F.F. Proctor and Nat Goodwin. Mr. Proctor in those days, be it said, was nightly lying on his back and juggling barrels and easy chairs on his feet. Further down the hill, which was a long one, came Flo and Mary Irwin, Weber and Fields, and the Brantz family, the famous troupe of European jugglers. It was regarded at the time as an exceptional bill and highly expensive.

Now, the weekly cost of that "aggregation of talent," as it was probably called in the 1880s, was just $1,100 per week. In 1906 the average weekly programme of from fifteen to eighteen acts costs from $3,000 to $5,000. The "top liner" alone often goes up to $1,500 and even $2,000. Twenty-five years ago $100 a week was big pay for a first-rate variety act, and $150 salaries were rare enough to be underlined.

To-day there is hardly an act in vaudeville, even the one that opens the bill while the audience is straggling in one at a time, that does not get at least $300; $700 and $900 salaries are the rule for families or troupes of three or four members.

A REGULAR TASK

There seems to be a curious bond between vaudeville and circus people in the matter of economy and simplicity. Vaudeville people look upon their daily performance as a kind of regular task. Your actor friends ask, "Where are you playing?" With the vaudeville player it is more likely to be "Where are you working?" He takes a certain quiet pride in thinking of what he does as merely the day's work and he is very likely to tuck away a good share of the proceeds toward future comfort. As a man who has known vaudeville for many years puts it:

"They don't get their money in big chunks, but they hold on to it, and you'll find that later on it's the vaudeville people who are giving the benefits for some busted star."

A surprising number are eager to play seven days in the week for the sake of the extra money. They like to get to New York for just that reason. Of all the hundreds of actors' homes that dot certain parts of Long Island fully two-thirds are said to represent the thrift and domestic instinct of vaudeville folk. They take their profession as a matter of course, and seldom as a pose. They talk about it but little. Go into the greenroom, down at Keith's some afternoon and ten to one you'll find a couple of spangled women, who look on the stage as if they never lifted a finger for housekeeping, sewing away on socks or buttonholes while they wait their turn. Many of the men, and women, too, for that matter are inveterate farmers with a little plot of land somewhere, to which they fly whenever they can. At this time of year their talk is likely to be far less of the Rialto than of "what are you going to raise this year?" and "isn't it time to send work to plant the peas?"

STEAL ONE ANOTHER'S THUNDER

One bad habit these vaudeville people have. They are incorrigible stealers of one another's lines and business. If an act happens to have a clever costume or "gag" in it, ten to one some other team playing at the same theatre will borrow it. When the original proprietor springs his joke in the next town he is lucky if he doesn't find some colleague has been along ahead of him and spoiled his thunder.

There was a case in Indianapolis not long ago of a monologue comedian who originated the line "I've got money to burn, but I don't like the smell of the smoke afterward." For some reason or other he was very proud of it. When he got to St. Louis he found everybody there thoroughly familiar with his pet line. In fact, they accused him of stealing it from an act that had just gone through there. Of course he had copyright protection and all that, but by the time he got the machinery of the law in full action both acts had been taken off and everybody had forgotten all about them. No way has yet been invented to prevent one vaudeville performer from "lifting" the good points from his neighbor's turn.

You rarely hear the word "player" on the stage of a vaudeville house. Whatever you have been, or done elsewhere, in vaudeville you become a plain "performer." Just inside the stage door at the Victoria there hangs a sign. "Performers must be at the theatre one hour before their acts," and elsewhere, "Performers are not to use this exit." These signs have caused some amusement among the big theatrical stars who have recently played in the theatre. As actor Fred Walton remarked when he caught sight of it, "Here I am a vulgar fraction reduced to my lowest terms."

By the same token there are at Hammerstein's two star dressing rooms, side by side, just alike, and both numbered "1"—a fine preventive of faultfinding. While of course vaudeville people have their jealousies and their ambition to stand in good places on the bill, their rating is so definitely understood when they are booked that they just can't fail to realize then and there just where their names are likely to be placed.

TRY OUT FOR NEW ACTS

New acts are constantly being tried out. On certain mornings every week from the big bare stages of empty theatres you will find "funny men" cracking their best jokes and young sopranos singing the "Jewel Song" to a trio of bored managers in the dark orchestra below, who have heard every joke and every song ever sprung in vaudeville.

The past year has seen an unusual number of successful one-act plays translated bodily into vaudeville. In fact, one of the most marked advances in the vaudeville world is its growing tendency to absorb complete productions. In two cases one-act plays have been selected which it will cost from $6,000 to $10,000, merely to put on.

Vaudeville stage managers and agents bear witness to the general promptness and sobriety of vaudeville performers. "Why," said a man connected with Keith, "I only remember one case where we had to turn off a man for drunkenness, and he was a recruit from musical comedy."

There is a certain family of three—father, mother and daughter—who have played for many years in vaudeville circles. For their sketch they receive $250 per week; out of that the father pays 10 per cent. royalty to the author of his sketch and 5 per cent. to the booking agent. Railway fares (which are never paid by the vaudeville manager, except in the case of long jumps) average $3 a week for each person. Out of the remainder this man, of course, defrays the living expenses of his family. He thinks it a very bad week indeed, however, when he doesn't have $100 to put away, and he owns a little farm up in Central New York where he and his wife and daughter spend exactly three weeks every year. But it's there for them later.

Meanwhile, the family go to small hotels and boarding houses, which are not in the least theatrical, and they could probably steer you into a dozen little cafés in New York that you never dreamed could be so good, so clean, and so cheap. This man was once David Belasco's assistant stage manager, but he finds he can make and save money on vaudeville rounds, and he does it as systematically as a man going daily to his desk.

CHANCE FOR FAMILY LIFE

Another good thing about vaudeville from the performer's point of view is the chance it gives for family life, even on the road. In straight drama it is not often that man and wife fit into the same cast. If they do there are almost sure to be complications. If they don't quarrel with each other they quarrel together with the rest of the company. If one leaves, the other is likely to follow, and altogether the manager would infinitely rather have them cast apart in different companies. In vaudeville, on the other hand, if man and wife are in the same act, the whole thing is too small to ever develop serious complications. They are too necessary to each other. If they have separate acts they can easily get the same bookings, and year after year their names will be found together on the same bill.

Nine-tenths of the "families" billed in vaudeville are perfectly genuine. Of course, in certain foreign troupes of jugglers and acrobats there are one or two apprentices; yet acrobatic talent and vaudeville accomplishments in general are very apt to run in families, and vaudeville people are strongly inclined to marry among themselves.

THE FOUNDING OF THE NATIONAL ASSOCIATION FOR THE ADVANCEMENT OF COLORED PEOPLE

CHARLES FLINT KELLOGG

Although the Emancipation Proclamation of 1863 abolished slavery, segregation laws and the threat of racial violence hindered blacks' social mobility in the early twentieth century. Fearful of the arrival of a "new slavery," a group of multiracial activists formed the National Association for the Advancement of Colored People (NAACP) on February 12, 1909. In this excerpt from his book, *A History of the National Association for the Advancement of Colored People*, Charles Flint Kellogg identifies the events and individuals pivotal to the formation of the NAACP. He claims that the race riots of 1908 in Springfield, Illinois, triggered exchanges and meetings that galvanized the powers of prominent civil rights activists, including president of the *New York Evening Post* Oswald Garrison Villard, writer William English Walling, and social worker Mary White Ovington.

O n the fourteenth of August, 1908, race riots broke out in Springfield, Illinois. White mobs raged through the Negro district, burning homes and interfering with the work of firemen. It was two days before 4,200 militiamen brought the riots under control. By that time two persons had been lynched, six had been killed, and over fifty wounded. More than 2,000 Negroes fled the city, and hundreds took shelter in the camps of the militia.

Lynchings and anti-Negro riots in the city where Lincoln had lived and was buried were too much for Oswald Garrison Villard, who, as the grandson of William Lloyd Garrison, had been reared in the abolitionist tradition. In the *New York Evening Post*, of which he was president, Villard spoke out indignantly against the outbreak in Springfield, calling it the climax of a wave of crime and lawlessness that was flooding the country.

The liberal periodical *The Independent* was also shocked that such violence against Negroes could occur in the North. "Springfield," wrote the editor, "will have to carry a heavier burden of shame than does Atlanta, for Illinois was never a slave state." Horrified at the thought that rioting might break out in other cities, *The Independent* urged Negroes, when attacked, first to seek protection from the proper authorities; if that failed, they should defend themselves and resist to the utmost of human power so that invaders of the home would be sorry that they came and be slow to come again. Booker T. Washington, the most prominent Negro of the day, issued a statement which was sharply critical of lynching, although it did not mention the Springfield affair. *The Horizon*, a Negro periodical usually critical of Washington, called his statement the clearest, strongest and most courageous he had uttered. On the whole, Northern newspapers had responded satisfactorily, Villard felt, but he was concerned with the spreading of what he called the Southern attitude in the press.

Neither Villard's indignation at the prevailing lawlessness of the time nor Washington's indictment of lynching resulted in any definite action to combat the rising tide of racism. This stimulus was provided by William English Walling in his article "The Race War in the North," which appeared the following month in *The Independent*.

Walling was a wealthy Southerner from a former slave-owning Kentucky family. He was a writer, settlement house worker, and a socialist. Beginning as a factory inspector in Illinois, he had devoted his life to the labor movement. In 1903, he joined Jane Addams, Lillian Wald, and others in founding the National Women's Trade Union League. He had married Anna

Strunsky, a Jew who, in youth, had been imprisoned in her native Russia for revolutionary activities. The Wallings went to Springfield to investigate the riots. Inquiry convinced them that America's treatment of the Negro was even worse than Russia's treatment of its Jewish minority.

In his article on the Springfield riots, Walling blamed the local press for inflaming public opinion against Negroes prior to the outbreak, and showed how one newspaper subtly linked crime with the race problem, at the same time suggesting to its readers that the South knew how to deal promptly and effectively with such situations. Walling held that the public had shut its eyes to the initiation of a permanent warfare against Negroes, modeled in all respects on that in the South. The small Negro population in Springfield was of no possible threat to white supremacy, and Walling deplored the belief held in the North that there were mitigating circumstances, not for mob violence but for race hatred. No less shocking was Springfield's lack of shame. The common people approved the action of the mob and hoped all Negroes would leave. Prevailing opinion in Springfield, Walling wrote, was expressed by the *Illinois State Journal*, which called the outbreak inevitable and blamed not the white's hatred of the Negro, but the Negro's "misconduct, general inferiority, or unfitness for free institutions."

A FAR MORE SERIOUS ATTACK

Walling reported that after the riot there was a political and business boycott to drive out of Springfield those Negroes who had not already fled, an effort which the local press failed to oppose. He considered this a far more serious attack upon Negroes than the riot. If this kind of attack were allowed to continue, whites would take over the Negroes' property, jobs, and businesses, thus conferring automatic rewards on the rioters. Race baiters would dominate Springfield, and other Northern towns would be tempted to follow the example. Political democracy would die, warned Walling, and American civilization would degenerate if these methods should become general in the North.

"Who realizes the seriousness of the situation?" he asked. "What large and powerful body of citizens is ready to come to [the Negro's] aid?"

One of the readers of Walling's article in *The Independent* was Mary White Ovington, a Unitarian, a socialist, the descendant of an abolitionist, and a social worker of independent means. Her life was already dedicated to the cause of the Negro. She had spent nearly four years gathering material for a study of the Negro in New York, and at the time Walling's article appeared she was living in a Negro tenement. Walling's appeal so moved her that she wrote an answer to his plea within the hour.

Walling had conceived the idea of a national biracial organization of "fair-minded whites and intelligent blacks" to help right the wrongs of the Negro. On returning from Springfield he outlined his plan to his close friend, Charles Edward Russell, and to other sympathetic members of the Liberal Club in New York. There was much enthusiasm at that time in the Liberal Club and in other radical organizations regarding the Negro, but there was little concrete knowledge on which to base a course of action. Then several weeks later Mary White Ovington attended a lecture on Russia given by Walling at Cooper Union, in the course of which Walling stated that the race situation in America was worse, in some respects, than anything in Russia under czarism. After the lecture, Miss Ovington proposed to Walling that they undertake at once to form an organization like the one he had in mind. It was not until she had written him again, however, that he arranged a meeting at his New York apartment for the first week of the year 1909.

THE MEETING

The meeting was to have included Walling's friend Russell, a writer and fellow-socialist, whose father had been an abolitionist editor of a small newspaper in Iowa, but Russell was unable to be present, and Dr. Henry Moskowitz, a social worker among New York immigrants, took his place. These three, Miss Ovington, Moskowitz, and Walling, whose immediate interests were so closely knit, were from widely varied backgrounds—Miss Ovington later reminisced that "one was a descendant of an old-time abolitionist, the second a Jew, and the third a Southerner."

Two steps were taken at this informal gathering at Walling's apartment in January, 1909. It was decided that Lincoln's birthday should mark the opening of a campaign to secure the support of a large and powerful body of citizens, and it was agreed that Oswald Garrison Villard should be invited to become the fifth member of the group. Looking back on this event thirty years later, Villard wrote with feeling: "No greater compliment has ever been paid to me."

Life in a Sweatshop

Rose Cohen

Sweatshops appeared in the American garment industry in the early 1900s. In these factories, workers toiled for long hours in inhumane conditions for substandard wages. Jobs in sweatshops were usually taken by poor, young immigrant women desperate for employment. To many, these factories epitomize the dark side of capitalism, the exploitation of the weakest members of society for profit.

In the following first-person account, Russian immigrant Rose Cohen describes working at the Triangle Shirtwaist Company's sweatshop in New York City. Although Cohen was treated with hostility and exploited at the factory, she did not quit because she and her father were saving money to bring her mother and younger siblings to America. On March 25, 1911, a fire swept through the sweatshop, killing one hundred forty-eight workers. Cohen was among the fortunate and escaped the fire unharmed. In 1918, at the age of twenty-six, she published her autobiography, *Out of the Shadow*, from which this excerpt is taken.

About the same time that the bitter cold came father told me one night that he had found work for me in a shop where he knew the presser. I lay awake long that night. I was eager to begin life on my own responsibility but was also afraid. We arose earlier than usual that morning for father had to take me to the shop and not be over late for his own work. I wrapped my thimble and scissors, with a piece of bread for breakfast, in a bit of newspaper, carefully stuck two needles into the lapel of my coat and we started.

The shop was on Pelem Street, a shop district one block long and just wide enough for two ordinary sized wagons to pass

Excerpted from *Out of Shadow*, by Rose Cohen (New York: George H. Doran, 1918).

each other. We stopped at a door where I noticed at once a brown shining porcelain knob and a half rubbed off number seven. Father looked at his watch and at me.

"Don't look so frightened," he said. "You need not go in until seven. Perhaps if you start in at this hour he will think you have been in the habit of beginning at seven and will not expect you to come in earlier. Remember, be independent. At seven o'clock rise and go home no matter whether the others go or stay."

He began to tell me something else but broke off suddenly, said "good-bye" over his shoulder and went away quickly. I watched him until he turned into Monroe Street.

A Clattering Noise of Machines

Now only I felt frightened, and waiting made me nervous, so I tried the knob. The door yielded heavily and closed slowly. I was half way up when it closed entirely, leaving me in darkness. I groped my way to the top of the stairs and hearing a clattering noise of machines, I felt about, found a door, and pushed it open and went in. A tall, beardless man stood folding coats at a table. I went over and asked him for the name (I don't remember what it was.) "Yes," he said crossly. "What do you want?"

I said, "I am the new feller hand." He looked at me from head to foot. My face felt so burning hot that I could scarcely see.

"It is more likely," he said, "that you can pull bastings than fell sleeve lining." Then turning from me he shouted over the noise of the machine: "Presser, is this the girl?" The presser put down the iron and looked at me. "I suppose so," he said, "I only know the father."

The cross man looked at me again and said, "Let's see what you can do." He kicked a chair, from which the back had been broken off, to the finisher's table, threw a coat upon it and said, raising the corner of his mouth: "Make room for the new feller hand."

One girl tittered, two men glanced at me over their shoulders and pushed their chairs apart a little. By this time I scarcely knew what I was about. I laid my coat down somewhere and pushed my bread into the sleeve. Then I stumbled into the bit of space made for me at the table, drew in the chair and sat down. The men were so close to me at each side I felt the heat of their bodies and could not prevent myself from shrinking away. The men noticed and probably felt hurt. One made a joke, the other laughed and the girls bent their heads low over their work. All at once the thought came: "If I don't do this coat quickly and well he will send me away at once." I picked up the coat, threaded my needle, and began hastily, repeating the lesson father impressed upon me. "Be careful not to twist the sleeve lining, take small false stitches."

Like "the Grown-up Girls"

My hands trembled so that I could not hold the needle properly. It took me a long while to do the coat. But at last it was done. I took it over to the boss and stood at the table waiting while he was examining it. He took long, trying every stitch with his needle. Finally he put it down and without looking at me gave me two other coats. I felt very happy! When I sat down at the table I drew my knees close together and stitched as quickly as I could.

When the pedlar (sic) came into the shop everybody bought rolls. I felt hungry but I was ashamed and would not eat the plain, heavy rye bread while the others ate rolls.

All day I took my finished work and laid it on the boss's table. He would glance at the clock and give me other work. Before the day was over I knew that this was a "piece work shop," that there were four machines and sixteen people were working. I also knew that I had done almost as much work as "the grown-up girls" and that they did not like me. I heard Betsy, the head feller hand, talking about "a snip of a girl coming and taking the very bread out of your mouth." The only one who could have been my friend was the presser who knew my father. But him I did not like. The worst I knew about him just now was that he was a soldier because the men called him so. But a soldier, I had learned, was capable of anything. And so, noticing that he looked at me often, I studiously kept my eyes from his corner of the room.

Seven o'clock came and everyone worked on. I wanted to rise as father had told me to do and go home. But I had not the courage to stand up alone. I kept putting off going from minute to minute. My neck felt stiff and my back ached. I wished there were a back to my chair so that I could rest against it a little. When the people began to go home it seemed to me that it had been night a long time.

A Hard Life Began

The next morning when I came into the shop at seven o'clock, I saw at once that all the people were there and working steadily as if they had been at work a long while. I had just time to put away my coat and go over to the table, when the boss shouted gruffly, "Look here, girl, if you want to work here you better come in early. No office hours in my shop." It seemed very still in the room, even the machines stopped. And his voice sounded dreadfully distinct. I hastened into the bit of space between the two men and sat down. He brought me two coats and snapped, "Hurry with these!"

From this hour a hard life began for me. He refused to employ me except by the week. He paid me three dollars and for this he hurried me from early until late. He gave me only two coats at a time to do. When I took them over and as he handed me the new work he would say quickly and sharply, "Hurry!" And when he did not say it in words he looked at me and I seemed to hear even more plainly, "Hurry!" I hurried but he was never satisfied. By looks and manner he made me feel that I was not doing enough. Late at night when the people would stand up and begin to fold their work away and I too would rise, feeling stiff in every limb and thinking with dread of our cold empty little room and the uncooked rice, he would come over with still another coat.

"I need it the first thing in the morning," he would give as an excuse. I understood that he was taking advantage of me because I was a child. And now that it was dark in the shop except for the low single gas jet over my table and the one over his at the other end of the room, and there was no one to see, more tears fell on the sleeve lining as I bent over it than there were stitches in it.

I did not soon complain to father. I had given him an idea of the people and the work during the first days. But when I had been in the shop a few weeks I told him, "The boss is hurrying the life out of me." I know now that if I had put it less strongly he would have paid more attention to it. Father hated to hear things put strongly. Besides he himself worked very hard. He never came home before eleven and he left at five in the morning.

HALF THE AMOUNT

He said to me now, "Work a little longer until you have more experience; then you can be independent."

"But if I did piece work, father, I would not have to hurry so. And I could go home earlier when the other people go."

Father explained further, "It pays him better to employ you

by the week. Don't you see if you did piece work he would have to pay you as much as he pays a woman piece worker? But this way he gets almost as much work out of you for half the amount a woman is paid."

I myself did not want to leave the shop for fear of losing a day or even more perhaps in finding other work. To lose half a dollar meant that it would take so much longer before mother and the children would come. And now I wanted them more than ever before. I longed for my mother and a home where it would be light and warm and she would be waiting when we came from work.

THE EFFORT TO SAVE YOSEMITE

JOHN MUIR

Hetch Hetchy Valley at Yosemite National Park was the focus of an intense environmental debate in the 1910s. Developers wanted to dam the valley to create a much-needed water supply for the nearby city of San Francisco, California. Environmental preservationists, however, claimed that creating an artificial basin from the Hetch Hetchy Valley floor would rob Yosemite of a unique treasure of nature. Nonetheless, Congress passed a bill authorizing the damming of Hetch Hetchy Valley in 1913 on the basis that it would increase the use of Yosemite's resources. The valley was dammed in the early 1920s.

John Muir was a leading advocate in maintaining the Hetch Hetchy Valley. In the following selection, excerpted from his book *The Yosemite*, Muir claims that the Hetch Hetchy Valley is "one of Nature's rarest and most precious mountain temples" and should be protected against commercial exploitation.

The late Muir was a nationally known preservationist and founder of the Sierra Club, an environmental preservation organization.

Yosemite [Valley] is so wonderful that we are apt to regard it as an exceptional creation, the only valley of its kind in the world; but Nature is not so poor as to have only one of anything. Several other yosemites have been discovered in the Sierra that occupy the same relative positions on the [Sierra Nevada] Range and were formed by the same forces in the same kind of granite. One of these, the Hetch Hetchy Valley, is in the

Excerpted from *The Yosemite*, by John Muir (New York: Century, 1912).

Yosemite National Park about twenty miles from Yosemite and is easily accessible to all sorts of travelers by a road and trail that leaves the Big Oak Flat road at Bronson Meadows a few miles below Crane Flat, and to mountaineers by way of Yosemite Creek basin and the head of the middle fork of the Tuolumne [River].

It is said to have been discovered by Joseph Screech, a hunter, in 1850, a year before the discovery of the great Yosemite. After my first visit to it in the autumn of 1871, I have always called it the "Tuolumne Yosemite," for it is a wonderfully exact counterpart of the [famous] Merced Yosemite, not only in its sublime rocks and waterfalls but in the gardens, groves and meadows of its flowery park-like floor. The floor of Yosemite is about 4000 feet above the sea; the Hetch Hetchy floor about 3700 feet. And as the Merced River flows through Yosemite, so does the Tuolumne through Hetch Hetchy. The walls of both are of gray granite, rise abruptly from the floor, are sculptured in the same style and in both every rock is a glacier monument.

BOLD AND PICTURESQUE

Standing boldly out from the south wall is a strikingly picturesque rock called by the Indians, Kolana, the outermost of a group 2300 feet high, corresponding with the Cathedral Rocks of Yosemite both in relative position and form. On the opposite side of the Valley, facing Kolana, there is a counterpart of the El Capitan that rises sheer and plain to a height of 1800 feet, and over its massive brow flows a stream which makes the most graceful fall I have ever seen. From the edge of the cliff to the top of an earthquake talus it is perfectly free in the air for a thousand feet before it is broken into cascades among talus boulders. . . .

The floor of the Valley is about three and a half miles long, and from a fourth to half a mile wide. The lower portion is mostly a level meadow about a mile long, with the trees restricted to the sides and the river banks, and partially separated from the main, upper, forested portion by a low bar of glacier-polished granite across which the river breaks in rapids.

The principal trees are the yellow and sugar pines, digger pine, incense cedar, Douglas spruce, silver fir, the California and golden-cup oaks, balsam cottonwood, Nuttall's flowering dogwood, alder, maple, laurel, tumion, etc. The most abundant and influential are the great yellow or silver pines like those of Yosemite, the tallest over two hundred feet in height, and the oaks assembled in magnificent groves with massive rugged trunks four to six feet in diameter, and broad, shady, wide-spreading heads. The shrubs forming conspicuous flowery clumps and tangles are manzanita, azalea, spiraea, brier-rose, several species of ceanothus, calycanthus, philadelphus, wild cherry, etc.; with abundance of showy and fragrant herbaceous plants growing about them or out in the open in beds by themselves—lilies, Mariposa tulips, brodiaeas, orchids, iris, spraguea, draperia, collomia, collinsia, castilleja, nemophila, larkspur, columbine, goldenrods, sunflowers, mints of many species, honeysuckle, etc. Many fine ferns dwell here also, especially the beautiful and interesting rockferns—pellaea, and cheilanthes of several species—fringing and rosetting dry rock-piles and ledges; woodwardia and asplenium on damp spots with fronds six or seven feet high; the delicate maidenhair in mossy nooks by the falls, and the sturdy, broad-shouldered pteris covering nearly all the dry ground beneath the oaks and pines.

It appears, therefore, that Hetch Hetchy Valley, far from being a plain, common, rock-bound meadow, as many who have not seen it seem to suppose, is a grand landscape garden, one of Nature's rarest and most precious mountain temples. As in Yosemite, the sublime rocks of its walls seem to glow with life, whether leaning back in repose or standing erect in thoughtful attitudes, giving welcome to storms and calms alike, their brows in the sky, their feet set in the groves and gay flowery meadows, while birds, bees, and butterflies help the river and waterfalls to stir all the air into music—things frail and fleeting and types of permanence meeting here and blending, just as they do in Yosemite, to draw her lovers into close and confiding communion with her.

HETCH HETCHY IN DANGER

Sad to say, this most precious and sublime feature of the Yosemite National Park, one of the greatest of all our natural resources for the uplifting joy and peace and health of the people, is in danger of being dammed and made into a reservoir to help supply San Francisco with water and light, thus flooding it from wall to wall and burying its gardens and groves one or two hundred feet deep. This grossly destructive commercial scheme has long been planned and urged (though water as pure and abundant can be got from sources outside of the people's park, in a dozen different places), because of the comparative cheapness of the dam and of the territory which it is sought to divert from the great uses to which it was dedicated in the Act of 1890 establishing the Yosemite National Park.

The making of gardens and parks goes on with civilization all over the world, and they increase both in size and number as their value is recognized. Everybody needs beauty as well as bread, places to play in and pray in, where Nature may heal and cheer and give strength to body and soul alike. This natural beauty-hunger is made manifest in the little windowsill gardens of the poor, though perhaps only a geranium slip in a broken cup, as well as in the carefully tended rose and lily gardens of the rich, the thousands of spacious city parks and botanical gardens, and in our magnificent National parks—the Yellowstone, Yosemite, Sequoia, etc.—Nature's sublime wonderlands, the admiration and joy of the world. Nevertheless, like anything else worth while, from the very beginning, however well guarded, they have always been subject to attack by despoiling gainseekers and mischief-makers of every degree from Satan to Senators, eagerly trying to make everything immediately and self-ishly commercial, with schemes disguised in smug-smiling philanthropy, industriously, sham-piously crying, "Conservation, conservation, panutilization," that man and beast may be fed and the dear Nation made great. Thus long ago a few enterprising merchants utilized the Jerusalem temple as a place of business instead of a place of prayer, changing money, buying and selling cattle and sheep and doves; and earlier still, the first forest reservation, including only one tree, was likewise despoiled. Ever since the establishment of the Yosemite National Park, strife has been going on around its borders and I suppose this will go on as part of the universal battle between right and wrong, however much its boundaries may be shorn, or its wild beauty destroyed.

A WONDERLAND

The first application to the Government by the San Francisco Supervisors for the commercial use of Lake Eleanor and the Hetch Hetchy Valley was made in 1903, and on December 22nd of that year it was denied by the Secretary of the Interior, Mr. Ethan A. Hitchcock, who truthfully said:

> Presumably the Yosemite National Park was created such by law because of the natural objects of varying degrees of scenic importance located within its boundaries, inclusive alike of its beautiful small lakes, like

Eleanor, and its majestic wonders, like Hetch Hetchy and Yosemite Valley. It is the aggregation of such natural scenic features that makes the Yosemite Park a wonderland which the Congress of the United States sought by law to reserve for all coming time as nearly as practicable in the condition fashioned by the hand of the Creator—a worthy object of National pride and a source of healthful pleasure and rest for the thousands of people who may annually sojourn there during the heated months.

In 1907 when Mr. James R. Garfield became Secretary of the Interior the application was renewed and granted; but under his successor, Mr. Walter L. Fisher, the matter has been referred to a Commission, which as this volume goes to press still has it under consideration. . . .

One of my later visits to the Valley was made in the autumn of 1907 with the late William Keith, the artist. The leaf-colors were then ripe, and the great godlike rocks in repose seemed to glow with life. The artist, under their spell, wandered day after day along the river and through the groves and gardens, studying the wonderful scenery; and, after making about forty sketches, declared with enthusiasm that although its walls were less sublime in height, in picturesque beauty and charm Hetch Hetchy surpassed even Yosemite.

The Dam Scheme

That any one would try to destroy such a place seems incredible; but sad experience shows that there are people good enough and bad enough for anything. The proponents of the dam scheme bring forward a lot of bad arguments to prove that the only righteous thing to do with the people's parks is to destroy them bit by bit as they are able. Their arguments are curiously like those of the devil, devised for the destruction of the first garden—so much of the very best Eden fruit going to waste; so much of the best Tuolumne water and Tuolumne scenery going to waste. Few of their statements are even partly true, and all are misleading.

Thus, Hetch Hetchy, they say, is a "low-lying meadow." On the contrary, it is a high-lying natural landscape garden. . . .

"It is a common minor feature, like thousands of others." On the contrary it is a very uncommon feature; after Yosemite, the rarest and in many ways the most important in the National Park.

"Damming and submerging it 175 feet deep would enhance its beauty by forming a crystal-clear lake." Landscape gardens, places of recreation and worship, are never made beautiful by destroying and burying them. The beautiful sham lake, forsooth, would be only an eyesore, a dismal blot on the landscape, like many others to be seen in the Sierra. For, instead of keeping it at the same level all the year, allowing Nature centuries of time to make new shores, it would, of course, be full only a month or two in the spring, when the snow is melting fast; then it would be gradually drained, exposing the slimy sides of the basin and shallower parts of the bottom, with the gathered drift and waste, death and decay of the upper basins, caught here instead of being swept on to decent natural burial along the banks of the river or in the sea. Thus the Hetch Hetchy dam-lake would be only a rough imitation of a natural lake for a few of the spring months, an open sepulcher for the others.

"Hetch Hetchy water is the purest of all to be found in the Sierra, unpolluted, and forever unpollutable." On the contrary, excepting that of the Merced below Yosemite, it is less pure than that of most of the other Sierra streams, because of the sewerage of camp grounds draining into it, especially of the Big Tuolumne Meadows camp ground, occupied by hundreds of tourists and mountaineers, with their animals, for months every summer, soon to be followed by thousands from all the world.

No Holier Temple

These temple destroyers, devotees of ravaging commercialism, seem to have a perfect contempt for Nature, and, instead of lifting their eyes to the God of the mountains, lift them to the Almighty Dollar.

Dam Hetch Hetchy! As well dam for water-tanks the people's cathedrals and churches, for no holier temple has ever been consecrated by the heart of man.

1913–1917: America Watches the World Go to War

CHAPTER 3

THE WOMAN SUFFRAGE PARADE OF 1913

SHERIDAN HARVEY

By 1913, only six states had granted women the right to vote. Looking for a way to elevate the issue of women's suffrage, suffragists pulled together to organize the Woman Suffrage Parade of 1913, which took place on March 3 in Washington, D.C. In the following article, Sheridan Harvey explains that the women and men marching in the Woman Suffrage Parade were jeered, insulted, and shoved. However, Harvey contends that the parade managed to focus the nation's attention on women's suffrage. The *New York Times* deemed it "one of the most impressively beautiful spectacles ever staged in this country." Harvey is a women's studies specialist in the Humanities and Social Sciences Division at the Library of Congress.

O n Monday, March 3, 1913, lawyer Inez Milholland Boissevain, clad in a white cape and riding a white horse, led the great women's suffrage parade down Pennsylvania Avenue in the nation's capital. Behind her stretched a long procession, including nine bands, four mounted brigades, three heralds, more than 20 floats and more than 5,000 marchers. Women from countries that had enfranchised women held the place of honor in the first section of the procession. Then came the "pioneers" who had struggled for so many decades to secure women's right to vote. The next sections celebrated working women, who were grouped by occupation and wore ap-

Excerpted from "Marching for the Vote: Remembering the Woman Suffrage Parade of 1913," by Sheridan Harvey, *Library of Congress Information Bulletin*, March 1998.

propriate garb—nurses in uniform, woman farmers, home-makers, woman doctors and pharmacists, actresses, librarians—Harriet Hifton of the Library of Congress's Copyright Division led the librarians' contingent—and college women in academic gowns. Next came the state delegations and, finally, the separate section for male supporters of woman suffrage. According to the official program of the suffrage procession, all had come from around the country "to march in a spirit of protest against the present political organization of society, from which women are excluded."

RIBALD JOKES AND LAUGHTER

The procession began late, but all went well for the first few blocks. Soon, however, the crowds—mostly men in town for the inauguration of Woodrow Wilson the following day—surged into the street, making it almost impossible for the marchers to pass. Occasionally only a single file could move forward. Women were jeered, tripped, grabbed, shoved, and many heard "indecent epithets" and "barnyard conversation." Instead of protecting the parade, the police "seemed to enjoy all the ribald jokes and laughter, and part participated in them." One police-man remarked that the women should stay at home where they belonged. The men in the procession heard shouts of "Hen-pecko" and "Where are your skirts?" As one witness explained, "There was a sort of spirit of levity connected with the crowd. They did not regard the affair very seriously."

But to the women, the event was very serious. The *Chicago Tribune* noted that Helen Keller "was so exhausted and un-nerved by the experience in attempting to reach a grandstand . . . that she was unable to speak later at [Constitution Hall]." Two ambulances "came and went constantly for six hours, al-ways impeded and at times actually opposed, so that doctor and driver literally had to fight their way to give succor to the injured." One hundred marchers were taken to the local Emer-gency Hospital. Before the afternoon was over, Secretary of War Henry L. Stimson, responding to a request from the chief of po-lice, authorized the use of a troop of cavalry from nearby Fort Myer to help control the crowd.

AN ALLEGORICAL TABLEAU

Despite enormous difficulties, many of those in the parade com-pleted the route. Upon reaching the Treasury Building, a hundred women and children from the procession presented an allegorical tableau written especially for the occasion to show "those ideals toward which both men and women have been struggling through the ages and toward which, in co-operation and equality, they will continue to strive." The pageant began with "The Star Spangled Banner" and the commanding figure of Columbia dressed in national colors, emerging from the great columns at the top of the Treasury Building steps. Charity entered, her path strewn with rose petals; Liberty followed to the "Triumphal March" from *Aida*, and a dove of peace was released. In the final tableau, Columbia, surrounded by Justice, Charity, Liberty, Peace and Hope, all in flowing robes and colorful scarves, with trumpets sounding, stood to watch the oncoming procession. *The New York Times* described the pageant as "one of the most impressively beautiful spectacles ever staged in this country."

At the railway station a few blocks away, president-elect Woodrow Wilson arrived to little fanfare. One of his staff asked, "Where are all the people?" "Watching the suffrage parade," the police told him. The next day Wilson would be driven down the miraculously clear Pennsylvania Avenue, cheered on by a respectful crowd.

STALLED AT THE NATIONAL LEVEL

The Washington march came at a time when the suffrage movement badly needed an infusion of vigor, a new way to capture public and press interest. Women had been struggling for the right to vote for more than 60 years, and although progress had recently been made at the state level with six western states granting woman suffrage, the movement had stalled at the national level.

Delegates from the National American Woman Suffrage Association (NAWSA, and its predecessor associations) had arrived in the nation's capital every year since 1869 to present petitions asking that women be enfranchised. Despite this annual pilgrimage and the millions of signatures collected, debate on the issue had never even reached the floor of the U.S. House. In 1912 Teddy Roosevelt's Progressive Party became the first major political party to pledge itself "to the task of securing equal suffrage to men and women alike." But the Progressives lost the election.

In November 1912, as suffrage leaders were casting about for new means to ensure their victory, Alice Paul arrived at the NAWSA annual convention in Philadelphia. A 28-year-old Quaker from New Jersey, she had recently returned to the United States fresh from helping the militant branch of the British suffrage movement. She had been arrested repeatedly, been imprisoned, gone on a hunger strike and been forcibly fed. Paul was full of ideas for the American movement. She asked to be allowed to organize a suffrage parade to be held in Washington at the time of the president's inauguration, thus ensuring maximum press attention. She also promised to raise the necessary funds. NAWSA happily accepted her offer and gave her the title Chairman of the Congressional Committee. In December 1912, she moved to Washington, where she discovered that the committee she chaired had no headquarters and most of the members had died or moved away.

Undaunted, Alice Paul convened the first meeting of her new committee on Jan. 2, 1913, in the newly rented basement headquarters at 1420 F Street N.W. She started raising funds. According to one friend, "it was very difficult to refuse Alice Paul." She and the others she recruited worked nonstop for two months. By March 3 this fledgling committee had organized and found the money for a major suffrage parade with floats, banners, speakers and a 20-page official program. The total cost

The women marching in the parade were booed and heckled.

of the event was $14,906.08, a princely sum in 1913, when the average annual wage was $621. The programs and tableau each cost over $1,000.

THE MOST CONSPICUOUS AND IMPORTANT DEMONSTRATION

Suffrage groups across the nation contributed to the success of the procession. From its New York headquarters, NAWSA urged suffrage supporters to gather in Washington:

WHY YOU MUST MARCH

Because this is the most conspicuous and important demonstration that has ever been attempted by suffragists in this country.

Because this parade will be taken to indicate the importance of the suffrage movement by the press of the country and the thousands of spectators from all over the United States gathered in Washington for the Inauguration.

This call was answered. On Feb. 12, with cameras clicking, 16 "suffrage pilgrims" left New York City to walk to Washington for the parade. Many other people joined the original hikers at various stages, and the New York State Woman Suffrage Association's journal crowed that "no propaganda work undertaken by the State Association and Party has ever achieved such publicity." One of the New York group, Elizabeth Freeman, dressed as a gypsy and drove a yellow, horse-drawn wagon decorated with Votes for Women symbols and filled with pro-suffrage literature, a sure way to attract publicity. Two weeks after the procession five New York suffragists, including Elizabeth Freeman, reported to the Bronx motion picture studio of the Thomas A. Edison Co. to make a talking picture known as a Kinetophone, which included a cylinder recording of one-minute speeches by each of the women. This film with synchronized sound was shown in vaudeville houses where it was "hooted, jeered and hissed" by audiences.

SUFFRAGE DELEGATION TO WOODROW WILSON

Officers of NAWSA prepared a strong letter for the New York hikers to deliver to President-elect Woodrow Wilson as they passed through Princeton, N.J. They urged that woman suffrage be achieved during his presidency and warned that the women of the United States "will watch your administration with an intense interest such as has never before been focussed upon the administration of any of your predecessors." When the group reached Princeton, however, they delivered a much more modest proposal. They requested "an audience for not more than two minutes in Washington as soon after your arrival as possible." Less than two weeks after his inauguration, Wilson received a suffrage delegation led by Alice Paul. In response to their impassioned plea, he replied that he had never given the subject any thought but that it would "receive my most careful consideration." Hardly the wholehearted endorsement sought by the women.

The mistreatment of the marchers by the crowd and the police roused great indignation and led to congressional hearings in which more than 150 witnesses recounted their experiences; some complained about the lack of police protection; others defended the police. Before the inquiries were over, the superintendent of police of the District of Columbia had lost his job.

VICTORY DESPITE DISGRACE

The public outcry and its accompanying press coverage proved a windfall for the suffragists. *The Woman's Journal* proclaimed, "Parade Struggles to Victory Despite Disgraceful Scenes; Nation Aroused by Open Insults to Women—Cause Wins Popular Sympathy." The *New York Tribune* announced, "Capital Mobs Made Converts to Suffrage." At its next convention in November 1913, NAWSA praised the "amazing and most creditable year's work" of Alice Paul's Congressional Committee, stating that "their single-mindedness and devotion has been remarkable, and the whole movement in the country has been wonderfully furthered by the series of important events which have taken place in Washington, beginning with the great parade the day before the inauguration of the president."

Not one to mince words, reporter Nellie Bly, who rode as one of the heralds in the parade, bluntly stated in the headline to her article on the march: "Suffragists Are Men's Superiors." With uncanny prescience, she added that it would take at least until 1920 for all states to grant woman suffrage. Despite the pageantry of 1913, Nellie Bly was right. It was to take seven more years before the Nineteenth Amendment to the Constitution, which gave women full rights to vote, finally passed both chambers of Congress and was ratified by the required 36 states.

HENRY FORD INTRODUCES MASS PRODUCTION

ALLAN NEVINS AND FRANK ERNEST HILL

Automobile manufacturer and industrialist Henry Ford brought the Model T, "the universal cheap car," to the masses and made driving possible for the average American. However, Ford's unique approach to assembly line production did much more than place more cars on the road; it transformed the American way of life. In the following selection, historian and Pulitzer Prize winner Allan Nevins and author Frank Ernest Hill contend that Ford's pioneering work in mass production and industry in late 1913 and early 1914 ushered in a new economic era. The authors assert that Ford's theory of mass production brought inexpensive mass-produced goods to the American people. In addition, Nevins and Hill claim that the high wages the Ford Company paid their workers set an industry standard that jump-started consumerism.

O f the many American activities that expressed industrial power, automotive manufacturing was becoming pre-eminent both in size and influence. Nonexistent twenty years earlier, a mere collection of sheds and shops in 1900, it had grown with the rage of Iowa corn in July and the solidity of an oak. Producing only 89,110 vehicles in 1910, it had multiplied that product tenfold (880,489 in 1915)—an output valued at $691,778,000. Another year, and the value would exceed a billion.

Excerpted from *Ford: Expansion and Challenge, 1915–1933*, by Allan Nevins and Frank Ernest Hill (New York: Scribner, 1954). Copyright © 1954 by Meredith Nevins Moyar and Anne Nevins Loftus. Reprinted by permission of the publisher.

But the social and technological impacts of the industry had been even more remarkable than its rapid development. It had created a wholly new type of transportation. Some two and a half million Americans now possessed automobiles, and the life of the nation was changing because of this fact; for the motor vehicle was the first free-ranging form of inland transportation, not tied like locomotives to rails, or steamboats to piers. Remotely situated farmers, miners, or shop owners were no longer isolated economically because they were far from railroad stations or ports. Social isolation was disappearing. The complex of highways that served the nation was being replanned and expanded, with 2340 miles of new concrete-surfaced roads already built, and a vision growing of a future system of 4,000,000 miles.

PROFOUND INDUSTRIAL CONSEQUENCES

The manufacture of motor cars had also made its contribution to the improvement of industrial tools and processes. "The real revolution in American consumption, involving not only radical changes in ways of living but also profound industrial consequences," wrote Ralph C. Epstein some years later, "is in large measure a function of the automobile." From the late eighteen-nineties, starting from the point reached by the successive advances of the arms, sewing machine, and bicycle industries, the automobile makers had taken over the development of machine tools. They had diminished the margin of tolerance for precision elements from a few hundredths of an inch to ten thousandths; they had experimented with alloy and heat-treated steels, immensely extended the possibilities of forgings and stampings, and developed the use of electricity to provide magnetos and batteries, self-starters and lighting systems. Their work in the provision of raw materials and spare parts, of factory layouts, and of mass production methods had been revolutionary.

We shall do well to note at this point the meaning of that term, "mass production." Had an ordinary American been asked in 1915 what was the greatest achievement of the Ford Company, he would erroneously have replied, "The universal cheap car, the Model T." Its most remarkable exploit was actually the creation of the womb in which modern industry was to be reshaped, mass production. If asked to define mass production, the ordinary citizen would again have replied erroneously, "It means large-scale production by the use of uniform interchangeable parts." Indeed, most people still confound mass production with quantity production, which is only one of its elements. Actually, as Henry Ford himself wrote, mass production is the focusing upon a manufacturing operation of seven different principles: power, accuracy, economy, continuity, system, speed, and repetition. When all seven are used to make a car, tractor, refrigerator, airplane, or other complicated commodity,

Henry Ford

then mass production throws open the door to plenty, low prices, and an improved standard of living. Arming a people in peace against want, in war against enemies, it becomes an instrument to alter radically the shape of civilization.

By the end of 1915 the alteration had begun. Mass production had made its first appearance in the world at Highland Park, Michigan, in 1913–14. It was there that the seven principles named were combined in three great creative components. The first was the planned, orderly, and continuous progression of the commodity—the car—through the shop. The second was the systematic delivery of the work to the mechanic, instead of bringing the mechanic to his work. The third was the analysis of all the operations into their constituent parts, with a suitable division of labor and materials.

A KINETIC PLANT

Each one of the components of mass production was in itself more complicated than any amateur student would suppose. We may instance the orderly and continuous progression of the growing commodity through the factory. The assembly line had to move at just the right speed, on just the right level, through just the right sequence of activities. Or, still more complex, we may instance the delivery of the work to the mechanic. This meant that a multitude of subsidiary assembly lines had to feed into the main assembly line at precisely the proper points and pace. A car-spring, for example, did not suddenly appear out of thin air beside the workman charged with fastening it to the chassis. No, the spring (which consisted of seven leaves) had itself passed through a variety of subordinate operations: punch press, bend-ing machine, nitrate bath, bolt insertion, fastening of nuts on bolts, application of two clips, painting and inspection, every operation controlled by automatic gauges. This subsidiary line for providing springs (before long 50,000 a day) had to move without halt. It had to flow into the main assembly line as a small stream flows into a river. But a half-hundred other streams had to flow in, bearing each its vital part, at the same time; and the flow of every one had to be accurately controlled. The whole plant was in motion. Meantime, geared to this motion, every mechanic had his scientifically-ascertained fraction of the labor to perform; for the efficiency expert had found just how much he could best do, and what was the optimum time-allowance for doing it.

A kinetic plant!—moving, moving, moving; every segment— presses, furnaces, welders, stamps, drills, paint-baths, lathes— in use every minute; not an ounce of metal or a degree of heat avoidably wasted; and the economy in time and labor matching the economy in materials. Fascinating in its intricate intermeshing of activities, it meant a new era.

A NEW ERA

It meant a new era not only because mass production turned out far more goods at much lower prices than ever before, but for still larger reasons. It required the constant adoption of new methods and new machines, with the ruthless scrapping of all that was obsolete—even if it had cost a large sum but a few months earlier. It thus stimulated constant advances in the making of better machine-tools, and the installation of an ever-widening variety of single-purpose specialized machines. By lifting more of the load of work off men, and placing more of it on these complex mechanical tools, it reduced the really *hard* labor of the world. Samuel Butler had predicted a civilization in which machines would control men; but mass production implied that men constantly changed, improved, and more fully mastered machines as their servants. Under mass production, if it were properly administered, more skilled artisans and more creative designers would be needed than before; for every large factory would require busy departments devoted to invention, engineering, and art. In a world moulded economically by mass production, the control of industry would be more and more largely withdrawn from the mere financier, and more fully placed in the hands of the engineer, technician, and practical planner.

These were at any rate among the larger results which Henry Ford hoped would flow from this tremendous new force in human affairs. Another result he had already helped give reality. A rich abundance of inexpensive mass-produced goods would require a fast-expanding body of consumers. People must be given the means to buy; and Ford had possessed the insight and the courage to make high wages the concomitant of mass production. The five-dollar day had rung in a new economic era as the moving assembly line had ushered in a new industrial age. All this, could men but have seen it, was bound up in the Ford exhibit at the San Francisco Exposition, and, from that time forward, in most of the assembly lines of other automotive manufacturers.

THE BALKAN CRISIS: ASSASSINATION AT SARAJEVO

EDWARD ROBB ELLIS

Strife within the Balkans, the easternmost peninsula of Southern Europe, created tension in Europe for centuries. That tension erupted into the First World War on June 28, 1914, when Franz Ferdinand, archduke of Austria-Este, and his wife, Sophie were assassinated in Sarajevo. The assassin, Gavrilo Pricip, was part of a team of young Serbian nationalists who sought to overturn Austria-Hungary's rule of Bosnia-Herzegovina. According to early twentieth-century historian Edward Robb Ellis, America's reactions to the Sarajevo assassinations were lukewarm. In the following excerpt from his book *Echoes of Distant Thunder: Life in the United States 1914–1918*, Ellis explains that because the history of the Balkans was rife with religious, cultural, and territorial conflicts, Americans dismissed the tragic event as a remote episode of Balkan violence. Little did they know that the archduke's assassination would start a world war that would eventually draw in the United States.

O n the last day of his life the archduke of Austria arrived by imperial train at Sarajevo in what today is central Yugoslavia.

PAGEANTRY OF ROYALTY

Sunday morning, June 28, 1914. Sunshine glinting from swords and medals of dignitaries waiting at the railway station to greet

Excerpted from *Echoes of Distant Thunder: Life in the United States 1914–1918*, by Edward Robb Ellis (New York: Coward, McCann & Geoghegan, 1975). Copyright © 1975 by Edward Robb Ellis. Reprinted with permission.

Franz Ferdinand von Este and his wife. Sarajevo, the capital of Bosnia, lay in a valley with hills in the foreground and mountains beyond. Most inhabitants were Muslims, and the city had a semi-Oriental look. Mosques pointed slim minarets at the bright sky, hand-woven rugs were displayed in the Turkish bazaar, townspeople clattered down narrow cobblestoned streets to the center of town where a little river called the Miljachka was almost dry, now that summer heat had begun. The archduke, who had been afraid the heat would be oppressive, was pleased to feel his cheeks brushed by a breeze wafting from the dim mountain ranges.

Stepping off the train, he took salutes from officials wearing red fezzes, inspected troops at a nearby parade ground, then got into the second car of a six-car motorcade, maneuvering his sword so the scabbard would not become entangled in his legs. He sank down into a leather seat, and his wife sat down beside him. Peasants, enjoying the pageantry of royalty, gaped at the tall, fleshy man, for he was the nephew of Franz Josef I, the emperor of Austria and king of Hungary, and also heir presumptive to the Dual Monarchy. A vain man, the archduke had insisted upon being sewn into his green uniform, that of an Austrian field marshal. His neck bulged over the collar of his tunic. His decorations clinked. On his head he wore a visored shako, its high crown plumed with white feathers. He was fiercely mustached like Kaiser Wilhelm of Germany, whom he admired. His consort, Sophie, wore a white dress, string of pearls, and a broad-brimmed hat slanting down the right side of her plump and lovely face.

ALONG THE SCHEDULED ROUTE

The mayor and chief of police got into the first car of the royal motorcade. Marshal Oskar Potiorek, the despised military governor of Bosnia, took his place in the second automobile with the visiting couple, riding backward and facing them. The royal car had its top down and flew the gold and black fanion of the House of Hapsburg. The marshal waved his hand, and the procession began rolling along the Appel Quay, a broad avenue rimming the embankment. And along the scheduled route, from the railway station to city hall, there lurked six young terrorists armed with bombs and revolvers. . . .

Franz Ferdinand had come to Sarajevo not from desire but out of a sense of duty. The two Austro-Hungarian army corps regu-

larly stationed in Bosnia were scheduled to stage military maneuvers some thirty kilometers south of the capital, and the
archduke felt he had to make an appearance since he was inspector in chief of the imperial army. But he hesitated. His health
was not the best, he had heard that Sarajevo was a furnace in the
summer, an Austrian flag had been burned only days before his
departure from Vienna, and there even was a rumor that an attempt would be made on his life. Hoping to be urged to stay
home, he had asked Emperor Franz Josef what to do:

"Do as you wish," the emperor grunted. . . .

Now, this summer day in Sarajevo as his limousine purred
along the Appel Quay, he saw houses displaying his picture in
their windows, saw Austrian flags and native rugs unfurled as
decorations. While all this was heartening, every so often he
also saw defiant Serbian flags. Loyal Sarajevo newspapers were
welcoming the archduke to the city, but the town's leading Serbian paper had published only a brief announcement of the
royal visit and then underlined the insult by printing a big picture of King Peter of Serbia. There were no soldiers holding
back the crowds; except for the few at the parade ground, they
were being kept in the field for further military maneuvers. Security, in fact, was dangerously scant; only gaudily dressed gendarmes lined the curbs—too few of them, at that. Some spectators cheered, while others remained ominously silent. The
military governor of Bosnia was pointing out the girls' high
school and the Austro-Hungarian Bank on the left side of the
river. The time was 10 A.M.

THE BLACK HAND

Waiting near the bridge was a teen-ager named Nedjelko
Chabrinovitch. A native of Herzegovina and a communicant of
the Serb Orthodox faith, he had quit school because of poor
grades, quarreled with his father and left home, tried one trade
after another, became a printer, wrangled with his employers,
left Sarajevo for Belgrade, the capital of Serbia. There he got a
job in an anarchist printing shop. A flaming Serb nationalist and
fanatical Pan Slav, he joined a secret Serbian revolutionary society named Union or Death, but more commonly known as the
Black Hand. This society had no ties with the Black Hand so
troublesome to the New York City police of 1914. . . .

Chabrinovitch had left the anarchist printing shop in Belgrade, gone to Trieste to work on a newspaper, then returned to

the Serbian capital, where he got another job in the government printing house. At Eastertime in 1914 a friend in Sarajevo clipped an article about the archduke's impending visit, pasted it on a card with no comment other than "Greetings," mailed it to the Green Garland coffee house in Belgrade where Chabrinovitch picked up his mail. As early as October, 1913, he had told another friend he intended to kill Franz Ferdinand. In February, 1914, Chabrinovitch had been joined in Belgrade by Gavrilo Princip.

Princip was a frail, slim young man of nineteen with burning blue eyes. Born in western Bosnia amid the wild mountains near the Dalmation border, he also belonged to the Serb Orthodox faith. His father was a postman who gave him no financial support, and after many fights, the boy left home. He went to Sarajevo and enrolled in the local high school, finding living quarters in a roominghouse run by the mother of Danilo Ilitch. Ilitch had fallen under the influence of Vladimir Gatchinovitch, who was subsidized by the Black Hand to organize secret cells in Bosnia. . . .

At the urging of Ilitch he left Sarajevo for Belgrade, where he was intitiated into the Black Hand. He met Chabrinovitch, and the two recruited a third conspirator, named Trifko Grabezh. All three were trained in pistol shooting and the use of bombs by agents of the Black Hand. Night after night Princip dreamed he was a political murderer struggling with policemen and soldiers. . . . These teen-agers were dead serious in their intention of assassinating Franz Ferdinand, but they also suffered from adolescent romanticism. They regarded themselves as giant killers, as national heroes. Princip often visited the grave of an earlier political assassin and swore to do his own bloody deed. Chabrinovitch, an hour or so before his attack on the archduke, had his photograph taken.

THE DEADLY PLAN

Three weeks before the archduke was due in Sarajevo the three left Belgrade and slipped out of Serbia carrying six bombs, four Browning revolvers, a map of Bosnia, 150 dinars in cash and phials of potassium cyanide with which to take their lives afterward. They were able to enter Bosnia without being searched and their weapons found because the border guards belonged to the Black Hand. After arriving in Sarajevo, the trio recruited three local youths to help them carry out their deadly plan.

Princip went back to Ilitch's house to live quietly until the moment presented itself.

Ten A.M., Sunday, June 28, with Chabrinovitch lurking near the Cumurja bridge. He was armed with a bomb. When the royal motorcade came abreast of him, he pulled out the bomb, knocked off its cap against a post, stepped forward and hurled it at the archduke's car. The chauffeur saw him and hit the accelerator. The bomb landed on the folded top of the archduke's car, bounced off and exploded beneath the third automobile. The blast injured an aide-de-camp riding in the third car and slightly injured several spectators. Sophie felt something graze her neck and put up her hand to touch her skin. The archduke's face was scratched, probably by the flying cap of the bomb.

Chabrinovitch pulled out his poison and swallowed it. Then he leaped over the embankment and down into the shallow riverbed. Policemen jumped in after him, knocked him down, collared him, jerked him to his feet and beat him with the flats of their swords. Although he was throwing up almond-smelling vomit, Chabrinovitch managed to scream, "I am a Serb! A hero!" In the royal car the military governor of Bosnia cried that a bomb had gone off. The archduke snapped that he had been expecting something of this sort. The governor, Potiorek, then reported that an officer in the third car had been hurt. Courageously but foolishly, the archduke ordered his own car stopped so that they might look after the wounded man. On making sure that everything possible was being done for the aide-de-camp and the bleeding spectators, the archduke shouted, "Come on! The fellow is insane. Gentlemen, let us proceed with our program." Potiorek ordered the chauffeur to drive fast and not stop again until they reached city hall.

THE BRITTLE CEREMONY

After they reached the Rathaus, the mayor began his welcoming speech but had read only a few words when Franz Ferdinand roughly interrupted, "Enough of that! Herr Burgermeister, I come here on a visit and I get bombs thrown at me. It is outrageous!" There was an embarrassed pause. Then the mayor resumed reading his prepared address: "All the citizens of the capital city of Sarajevo find their souls are filled with happiness, and they most enthusiastically greet Your Highness' most illustrious visit with the most cordial of welcomes. . . ." This time the royal visitor let him finish. While this brittle ceremony was proceeding in city hall, Chabrinovitch was being questioned at a police station. The gendarmes, believing the prisoner was involved in a plot and had information that might save the royal couple when they left city hall, were none too gentle. But he refused to talk—just then, at least—buying enough time to let one or another of his five co-conspirators finish the job he had bungled.

At the close of the reception a member of the archduke's retinue asked whether a military guard could be provided. Potiorek barked, "Do you think Sarajevo is filled with assassins?" At last it was decided that when Franz Ferdinand left the Rathaus, he would not follow his scheduled itinerary, calling for him to drive through narrow Franz Josef Street in the crowded part of the city. Instead, he would ride at a fast clip back along the Appel Quay and from there to the hospital; the archduke insisted on going to the hospital to see the injured aide-de-camp. After that he would visit the museum. While no military guard was given him, as requested, an officer did take up a protective position on the running board on the left side of the archduke's car.

But no one thought to tell the archduke's chauffeur of the change in plans. After driving back along the quay, he slowed to make a right turn into the block-long Rudolph Street leading into Franz Josef Street. Potiorek roared at the driver, "Not that way you fool! Keep straight on!" The confused chauffeur stopped the car opposite the Latin bridge so that he might shift into reverse. Princip happened to be standing near the bridge. The time was 10:45 A.M.

Earlier in the day, while the motorcade was en route to city hall, Princip had taken up a position three blocks away from Chabrinovitch, and when he heard the bomb explode and saw the archduke's car leap forward with the archduke unharmed, he realized Chabrinovitch had failed. Princip felt the world collapse. Having run toward the spot, having seen his friend dragged away by angry policemen, Princip thought for a fleeting moment of shooting Chabrinovitch and then taking his own life. Princip carried a loaded Browning revolver. Who knew what tortures would be inflicted on Chabrinovitch? Surely he would talk, name names, reveal everything. But the moment faded before he could act, so Princip wandered away in shock. He did not know that at the sound of the explosion the other four terrorists had panicked and run, one racing to his uncle's house to hide his bomb in a toilet. Princip, his head aswirl and his knees rubbery, stumbled into a coffeehouse to sip shakily from a cup and try to think things through.

PRINCIP'S CHANCE

When he emerged, he stepped into the doorway of a barbershop at the intersection of Appel Quay and Rudolph Street across the quay from the embankment. To his astonishment he saw the archduke in a car with the chauffeur shifting into reverse—less than ten feet from him. Fate, so it seemed, had given Princip his own chance. The officer on the running board stood on the left side of the car opposite Princip. He had a clear shot at the archduke, since Sophie was leaning back against the seat. Princip jerked out his automatic and fired. The bullet pierced the archduke's neck. Princip now aimed at Potiorek and fired a second time, but his hand may have trembled or Sophie may have tried to shield her husband's body with her own, for he accidentally shot her in the abdomen.

Then the assassin turned his gun toward his own head with the intention of killing himself, but passersby grabbed his hand. After firing the two shots into the car, he thought he had missed because for the next couple of seconds the archduke sat as erect as ever. Sophie screamed, fainted, collapsed against her husband. He remained upright, but blood gushed from his mouth and crimsoned his green tunic. Potiorek bellowed at the driver to get the hell to the governor's palace. The car leaped forward and picked up such high speed that the wounded archduke tried to brace himself against his wife's fallen figure. His dulling eyes on his wife's blood-spattered white dress, the archduke murmured, "Sophie! Sophie! . . . Don't die! . . . Live for our children!" Asked if he were in pain, he replied, "It is nothing." Six more times he said, "It is nothing." But each time his voice was weaker. He died about 11:30 A.M. Doctors had lost time cutting him out of his uniform.

THE FIGHTING OF COMIC-OPERA COUNTRIES

The next morning the New York *Times* published a four-column headline:

> HEIR TO AUSTRIA'S THRONE IS SLAIN
> WITH HIS WIFE BY A BOSNIAN YOUTH
> TO AVENGE SEIZURE OF HIS COUNTRY

Summer lay like a pageant across the land, both on the continent and in the United States, each day ripe with a high-hanging sun, and people held faces and hands toward the heavens as they smiled and declared they could not remember a time when the weather was lovelier. Americans were far more concerned with swimming and boating and motoring and such pleasures than with the news from—where? Sarajevo? Never heard of it. Bosnia? What's that? Oh, in the Balkans! Well, that's just a lot of comic-opera countries fighting with one another, so what's it got to do with us? It was not just the average citizen who was unfamiliar with the site of the double assassination. Brand Whitlock, the United States minister to Belgium, was in his summer home outside Brussels writing a new novel of rural life in Ohio, and when he heard the news from Sarajevo, he confessed, "I had not the least idea where it was in this world, if it was in this world." In 1914 few American newspapers maintained European staffs of their own and published very little foreign news. Americans could not be faulted for their ignorance of what was going on in the Balkans. On June 29 the Atlanta *Journal* did not consider the murder of the archduke and his wife sufficiently newsworthy to be published on its front page. That same day the New York *Sun* editorialized, "It is difficult to discuss the tragedy at Sarajevo yesterday without laying oneself open to the reproach of heartlessness. For while it is only natural that one should be stricken with horror at the brutal and shocking assassination of Archduke Francis Ferdinand, it is impossible to deny the fact that his disappearance from the scene is calculated to diminish the tenseness of the situation and to make for peace both within and without the dual empire." . . .

BALKAN LAPSES INTO BARBARISM

Frederic C. Penfield, the American ambassador in Vienna, wired news of the assassinations to the state department in Washington. It was departmental officials, no doubt, who prepared the first draft of a personal telegram to be sent by President Wilson to the old emperor; this left Washington on June 29. The next day State Secretary Bryan had a note of regret hand-delivered to the Austrian ambassador in Washington. David Franklin Houston, the secretary of agriculture, later scribbled a memorandum saying, "I had noted with passing interest the news of the assassinations of the Austrian Archduke and his wife at Sarajevo on June 28th . . . but as . . . there was no clear indication that the developments would be brought very near home

THE PANAMA CANAL OPENS A PATH BETWEEN THE SEAS

David McCullough

The Panama Canal is one of the greatest feats of engineering in the world. It is also an enduring feat of human labor: Efforts to build the canal spanned three decades and cost close to six thousand lives by the time it was completed in 1914. Today, thousands of ships traveling through the Western Hemisphere pass through the Panama Canal annually. However, in the following excerpt from his book, *The Path Between the Seas*, noted historian and lecturer David McCullough contends that the triumph of the Panama Canal was postponed to a later era. World War I, he claims, overshadowed the opening of the canal and was responsible for the slow beginnings of its use as a passage connecting the oceans.

For all practical purposes the canal was finished when the locks [water-filled] were. And so efficiently had construction of the locks been organized that they were finished nearly a year earlier than anticipated. Had it not been for the slides in the Cut [a channel created artificially], adding more than 25,000,000 cubic yards to the total amount of excavation, the canal might have opened in 1913.

The locks on the Pacific side were finished first, the single flight at Pedro Miguel in 1911, Miraflores in May 1913. Morale was at an all-time high. Asked by a journalist what the secret of success had been, [chief engineer Army colonel George Washington]

Goethals answered, "The pride everyone feels in the work."

"Men reported to work early and stayed late, without overtime," Robert Wood remembered. ". . . I really believe that every American employed would have worked that year without pay, if only to see the first ship pass through the completed Canal. That spirit went down to all the laborers."

The last concrete was laid at Gatun on May 31, 1913, eleven days after two steam shovels had met "on the bottom of the canal" in Culebra Cut. Shovel No. 222, driven by Joseph S. Kirk, and shovel No. 230, driven by D.J. MacDonald, had been slowly narrowing the gap all day when they at last stood nose to nose. The Cut was as deep as it would go, forty feet above sea level.

In the second week in June, it would be reported that the newly installed upper guard gates at Gatun had been "swung to a position halfway open; then shut, opened wide, closed and . . . noiselessly, without any jar or vibration, and at all times under perfect control."

On June 27 the last of the spillway gates was closed at Gatun Dam. The lake at Gatun had reached a depth of forty-eight feet; now it would rise to its full height.

Three months later all dry excavation ended. The Cucaracha slide still blocked the path, but Goethals had decided to clear it out with dredges once the Cut was flooded. So on the morning of September 10, photographers carried their gear into the Cut to record the last large rock being lifted by the last steam shovel. Locomotive No. 260 hauled out the last dirt train and the work crews moved in to tear up the last of the track. "The Cut tonight presented an unusual spectacle," cabled a correspondent for *The New York Times*, "hundreds of piles of old ties from the railroad tracks being in flames."

THE FIRST TRIAL LOCKAGE

Then on September 26 at Gatun the first trial lockage was made.

A seagoing tug, *Gatun*, used until now for hauling mud barges in the Atlantic entrance, was cleaned up, "decorated with all the flags it owned," and came plowing up from Colón in the early-morning sunshine. By ten o'clock several thousand people were clustered along the rims of the lock walls to witness the historic ascent. There were men on the tops of the closed lock gates, leaning on the handrails. The sky was cloudless, and in midair above the lower gates, a photographer hung suspended from the cableway. He was standing in a cement bucket, his camera on a tripod, waiting for things to begin.

But it was to be a long, hot day. The water was let into the upper chamber shortly after eleven, but because the lake had still to reach its full height, there was a head of only about eight feet, and so no thunderous rush ensued when the valves were opened. Indeed, the most fascinating aspect of this phase of the operation, so far as the spectators were concerned, was the quantity of frogs that came swirling in with the muddy water.

With the upper lock filled, however, the head between it and the middle lock was fifty-six feet, and so when the next set of culverts was opened, the water came boiling up from the bottom of the empty chamber in spectacular fashion.

The central control board was still not ready. All valves were being worked by local control and with extreme caution to be sure everything was just so. Nor were any of the towing locomotives in service as yet. Just filling the locks took the whole afternoon. It was nearly five by the time the water in the lowest chamber was even with the surface of the sea-level approach outside and the huge gates split apart and wheeled slowly back into their niches in the walls.

The tug steamed into the lower lock, looking, as one man recalled, "like a chip on a pond." [Army engineer William Lother] Sibert, [engineer Edward] Schildhauer, young George Goethals, and their wives were standing on the prow. "The Colonel" and [lock designer Army engineer Harry F.] Hodges were on top of the lock wall from point to point, both men in their shirt sleeves, Goethals carrying a furled umbrella, Hodges wearing glossy puttees and an enormous white hat. The gates had opened in one minute forty-eight seconds, as expected.

The tug proceeded on up through the locks, step by step. The gates to the rear of the first chamber were closed; the water in the chamber was raised until it reached the same height as the water on the other side of the gates ahead. The entire tremendous basin swirled and churned as if being stirred by some powerful, unseen hand and the rise of the water—and of the little boat—was very apparent. Those on board could feel themselves being lifted, as if in a very slow elevator. With the water in the lower chamber equal to that in the middle chamber, the intervening gates were opened and the tug went forward. Again the gates to the stern swung shut; again, with the opening of the huge subterranean culverts, the caramel-colored water came suddenly to life and began its rise to the next level.

IN WORKING ORDER

It was 6:45 when the last gates were opened in the third and last lock and the tug steamed out onto the surface of Gatun Lake. The day had come and gone, it was very nearly dark, and as the boat turned and pointed to shore, her whistle blowing, the crowd burst into a long cheer. The official time given for this first lockage was one hour fifty-one minutes, or not quite twice as long as would be required once everything was in working order.

That an earthquake should strike just four days later seemed somehow a fitting additional touch, as if that too were essential in any thorough testing-and-proving drill. It lasted more than an hour, one violent shudder following another, and the level of magnitude appears to have been greater than that of the San Francisco quake of 1906. The needles of a seismograph at Ancon were jolted off the scale paper. Walls cracked in buildings in Panama City; there were landslides in the interior; a church fell. But the locks and Gatun Dam were untouched. "There has been no damage whatever to any part of the canal," Goethals notified Washington.

Water was let into Culebra Cut that same week, through six big drain pipes in the earth dike at Gamboa. Then on the afternoon of October 10, President Wilson pressed a button in Washington and the center of the dike was blown sky-high. The idea had been dreamed up by a newspaperman. The signal, relayed by telegraph wire from Washington to New York to Galveston to Panama, was almost instantaneous. Wilson walked from the White House to an office in the Executive Building (as the State, War, and Navy Building had been renamed) and pressed the button at one minute past two. At two minutes past two several hundred charges of dynamite opened a hole more than a hundred feet wide and the Cut, already close to full, at once became an extension of Gatun Lake.

THE GREAT, AWKWARD DREDGES

In all the years that the work had been moving ahead in the Cut and on the locks, some twenty dredges of different kinds, assisted by numbers of tugs, barges, and crane boats, had been laboring in the sea-level approaches of the canal and in the two terminal bays, where forty-foot channels had to be dug several miles out to deep water. Much of this was equipment left behind by the French; six dredges in the Atlantic fleet, four in the Pacific fleet, a dozen self-propelled dump barges, two tugs, one drill boat, one crane boat, were all holdovers from that earlier era. Now, to clear the Cut of slides, about half this equipment was brought up through the locks, the first procession from the Pacific side passing through Miraflores and Pedro Miguel on October 25.

The great, awkward dredges took their positions in the Cut; barges shunted in and out, dumping their spoil in designated out-of-the-way corners of Gatun Lake, all in the very fashion that Philippe Bunau-Varilla had for so long championed as the only way to do the job. Floodlights were installed in the Cut and the work went on day and night. On December 10, 1913, an old French ladder dredge, the *Marmot*, made the "pioneer cut" through the Cucaracha slide, thus opening the channel for free passage.

The first complete passage of the canal took place almost incidentally, as part of the new workaday routine, on January 7, when an old crane boat, the *Alexandre La Valley*, which had been brought up from the Atlantic side sometime previously, came down through the Pacific locks without ceremony, without much attention of any kind. That the first boat through the canal was French seemed to everyone altogether appropriate. . . .

In Washington after a drawn-out, often acrimonious debate, Congress determined that the clause in the Hay-Pauncefote Treaty stipulating that the canal would be open to the vessels of all nations "on terms of entire equality" meant that American ships could not use the canal toll free, as many had ardently wanted and as much of the press had argued for. American ships would pay the same as the ships of every other nation, 90 cents per cargo ton.

In Washington also, and in San Francisco, plans were being made for tremendous opening celebrations intended to surpass even those at the opening of the Suez Canal. More than a hundred warships, "the greatest international fleet ever gathered in American waters," were to assemble off Hampton Roads on New Year's Day, 1915, then proceed to San Francisco by way of Panama. At San Francisco they would arrive for the opening of the Panama-Pacific International Exposition, a mammoth world's fair in celebration of the canal. The estimate was that it would take four days for the armada to go through the locks.

Schoolchildren in Oregon wrote to President Wilson to urge that the old battleship *Oregon* lead the flotilla through the canal. The idea was taken up by the press and by the Navy Department. The officer who had commanded the ship on her famous "race around the Horn" in 1898, retired Admiral Charles Clark, hale and fit at age seventy, agreed to command her once again and the President was to be his honored guest.

THE TRIUMPH OF A DIFFERENT ERA

But there was to be no such pageant. The first oceangoing ship to go through the canal was a lowly cement boat, the *Cristobal*, and on August 15 the "grand opening" was performed almost perfunctorily by the *Ancon*. There were no world luminaries on her prow. Goethals again watched from shore, traveling from point to point on the railroad. The only impressive aspect of the event was "the ease and system with which everything worked," as wrote one man on board. "So quietly did she pursue her way that . . . a strange observer coming suddenly upon the scene would have thought that the canal had always been in operation, and that the *Ancon* was only doing what thousands of other vessels must have done before her."

Though the San Francisco exposition went ahead as planned, all but the most modest festivities surrounding the canal itself had been canceled.

For by ironic, tragic coincidence the long effort at Panama and Europe's long reign of peace drew to a close at precisely the same time. It was as if two powerful and related but vastly different impulses, having swung in huge arcs in the forty some years since Sedan, had converged with eerie precision in August 1914. The storm that had been gathering over Europe since June broke on August 3, the same day the *Cristobal* made the first ocean-to-ocean transit. On the evening of the third, the French premier, Viviani, received a telephone call from the American ambassador who, with tears in his voice, warned that the Germans would declare war within the hour. . . .

Across Europe and the United States, world war filled the newspapers and everyone's thoughts. The voyage of the *Cristobal*, the *Ancon's* crossing to the Pacific on August 15, the official declaration that the canal was open to the world, were buried in the back pages.

There were editorials hailing the victory of the canal builders, but the great crescendo of popular interest had passed; a new heroic effort commanded world attention. The triumph at Panama suddenly belonged to another and very different era.

THE ENORMOUS COST

Of the American employees in Panama at the time the canal was opened only about sixty had been there since the beginning in 1904. How many black workers remained from the start of the American effort, or from an earlier time, is not recorded. But one engineer on the staff, a Frenchman named Arthur Raggi, had been first hired by the Compagnie Nouvelle in 1894.

Goethals, Sibert, Hodges, Schildhauer, [engineer Henry] Goldmark, and the others had been on the job for seven years and the work they performed was of a quality seldom ever known.

Its cost had been enormous. No single construction effort in American history had exacted such a price in dollars or in human life. Dollar expenditures since 1904 totaled $352,000,000 (including the $10,000,000 paid to Panama and the $40,000,000 paid to the French company). By present standards this does not seem a great deal, but it was more than four times what the Suez Canal had cost, without even considering the sums spent by the two preceding French companies, and so much more than the cost of anything ever before built by the United States government as to be beyond compare. Taken together, the French and American expenditures came to about $639,000,000.

The other cost since 1904, according to the hospital records, was 5,609 lives from disease and accidents. No fewer than 4,500 of these had been black employees. The number of white Americans who died was about 350.

If the deaths incurred during the French era are included, the total price in human life may have been as high as twenty-five thousand, or five hundred lives for every mile of the canal.

Yet amazingly, unlike any such project on record, unlike almost any major construction of any kind, the canal designed and built by the American engineers had cost less in dollars than it was supposed to. The final price was actually $23,000,000 below what had been estimated in 1907, and this despite the slides, the change in the width of the canal, and an additional $11,000,000 for fortifications, all factors not reckoned in the earlier estimate. The volume of additional excavation resulting from slides (something over 25,000,000 cubic yards) was almost equal to all the useful excavation accomplished by the French. The digging of Culebra Cut ultimately cost $90,000,000 (or $10,000,000 a mile). Had such a figure been anticipated at the start, it is questionable whether Congress would have ever approved the plan.

The total volume of excavation accomplished since 1904 was 232,440,945 cubic yards and this added to the approximately 30,000,000 cubic yards of useful excavation by the French gave a grand total, in round numbers, of 262,000,000 cubic yards, or more than four times the volume originally estimated by Ferdinand de Lesseps for a canal at sea level and nearly three times the excavation at Suez.

The canal had also been opened six months ahead of schedule, and this too in the face of all those difficulties and changes unforeseen seven years before.

Without question, the credit for such a record belongs chiefly to George Goethals, whose ability, whose courage and tenacity, were of the highest order.

That so vast and costly an undertaking could also be done without graft, kickbacks, payroll padding, any of the hundred and one forms of corruption endemic to such works, seemed almost inconceivable at the start, nor does it seem any less remarkable in retrospect. Yet the canal was, among so many other things, a clean project. No excessive profits were made by any of the several thousand different firms dealt with by the I.C.C. There had not been the least hint of scandal from the time Goethals was given command, nor has evidence of corruption of any kind come to light in all the years since.

TRAFFIC THROUGH THE CANAL

Technically the canal itself was a masterpiece in design and construction. From the time they were first put in use the locks performed perfectly.

Because of the First World War, traffic remained comparatively light until 1918, only four or five ships a day, less than two thousand ships a year on the average. And not until July of 1919 was there a transit of an American armada to the Pacific, that spectacle Theodore Roosevelt had envisioned so long before. Thirty-three ships returning from the war zone, including seven destroyers and nine battleships, were locked through the canal, all but three in just two days.

Ten years after it opened, the canal was handling more than five thousand ships a year; traffic was approximately equal to that of Suez. The British battle cruiser *Hood* and the U.S. carriers *Saratoga* and *Lexington* squeezed through the locks with only feet to spare on their way to the Pacific in the 1920's. By 1939 annual traffic exceeded seven thousand ships.

TENSION GROWS IN "NEUTRAL" AMERICA

MARK SULLIVAN

From the outbreak of World War I, President Woodrow Wilson maintained that the United States must assert its neutrality. On August 19, 1914, Wilson issued a declaration of neutrality, stating that "the people of the United States are drawn from many nations, and chiefly from the nations now at war" and that "divisions amongst us . . . might seriously stand in the way of the proper performance of our duty as the one great nation at peace." However, in the following selection, historian Mark Sullivan contends that a pro-Ally sentiment prevailed in the United States prior to America's entry into the war. Sullivan claims that Wilson and other major political figures expressed sympathy for the Allies. In addition, he contends that the cleavage between pro-Ally and pro-German Americans was deepening, creating a climate of race-consciousness in multicultural America. The late Sullivan is author of *Our Times, 1900–1925* and *The Education of an American.*

T he truth is, America was not neutral; American thought, opinion, emotion was strongly pro-Ally. President Woodrow Wilson in his heart sympathized with the Allies (though he was conscientiously careful to keep his personal feelings separate from his public duty and his official attitude, which was one of strict neutrality). Vice-President Thomas R. Marshall was pro-Ally—when Wilson said that Americans "must put a curb upon our sentiments" Marshall obeyed the injunction of his superior, but said "I am the only American possessed of a voice

Excerpted from *Our Times, 1900–1925*, by Mark Sullivan (New York: Charles Scribner's Sons, 1936). Copyright © 1933 by Charles Scribner's Sons. Reprinted with permission.

who followed that request." Chief Justice of the Supreme Court Edward D. White, officially neutral and mute, was in heart strongly pro-Ally; once he said to a member of Wilson's cabinet: "I wish I were thirty years younger, I would go to Canada and enlist." The leading Republican, ex-President Theodore Roosevelt, was pro-Ally (though at the beginning he did not feel we should take part). One of the most distinguished leaders of thought in America, President Emeritus Charles W. Eliot of Harvard University, was pro-Ally; he spoke of "ultimate defeat of Germany and Austria-Hungary" as "the only tolerable result of this outrageous war." Most of our men of letters were pro-Ally; a representative one, William Roscoe Thayer, biographer of Roosevelt, Hay, and Cavour, proclaimed: "I make no spurious claim to neutrality; only a moral eunuch could be neutral in the sense implied by the malefic dictum of the President."

THE PRO-GERMANS

So general was pro-Ally sentiment in America, that many of us came to feel that to be not pro-Ally was to be not patriotically American. In our overwhelmingly pro-Ally emotion, our conviction that Germany was in the wrong and should be defeated, our latent impulse to help, if only vicariously, in the pro-Ally cause—in that condition the pleas of the German-born professors gave us something concrete to complain against, something occurring on our own soil.

Complain many of us did, and presently we extended our complaint to include our German-American citizens generally. They, in natural resentment against being treated so, and partly on account of the spokesmanship given them by the German professors, partly on account of the sum of all the conditions, became self-consciously pro-German, vocal, and organized. Some of them acted through the "National German-American Alliance," which urged German-Americans to "organize press bureaus and combat the attitude of the English language press." A conspicuous American of German parentage, George Sylvester Viereck, conducted a weekly paper, "*The Fatherland*, devoted to Fair Play to Germany." The quite considerable German language press in America, hitherto a rather innocuous medium of news from the homeland and of neighborhood items for German immigrants and their descendants, became aggressively pro-German. Many, though not all, ministers of Lutheran churches called meetings, adopted resolutions: "We German-Americans" protest "against the common calumnies against the head of a nation friendly to us . . . [brand as false the charge] that Germany and its Emperor have sought and forced this war."

Between German-Americans and pro-Germans and, on the other hand, anti-Germans, academic war, kept within oral and polemic limits, went on constantly. Friends of Germany, thinking mainly in terms of the German people, pointed to their kindliness, quoted their poets, cited German achievement in science. Anti-Germans, thinking mainly in terms of the German ruling caste, the Hohenzollerns,[1] the militarists, and the Kultur [culture] they had fastened on the people, pointed to the Kaiser's[2] bombast, cited some of the German philosophers and about all the German authors of treatises on military science, the schrecklichkeit [horror] they preached or condoned. Philosopher Friedrich Nietzsche, through quotations from his "Will to Power" and other works, became almost as familiar a name as that of the contemporary holder of the highest batting average in professional baseball. Source for the most bloodthirsty quotations was Austrian Commander Friedrich von Bernhardi—that name, too, became as familiar to readers of editorials as the name of any of the generals at the front. Some of Bernhardi's sentiments were, to the American point-of-view, pretty shocking. An often quoted one—"Weak nations do not deserve to exist and should be absorbed by powerful ones"—ran counter to a deep American sentiment, and seemed to explain Germany's invasion of Belgium, which, to America, was the outstanding wrong of the war.

INCONSISTENT NEUTRALITY

As the tension grew, activities of some pro-Germans went to a point inconsistent with our neutrality, inconsistent indeed with loyalty to the United States. They established connections with the German government, received money which they spent on propaganda, in some cases on criminal conspiracy, even criminal violence. This, as it became known, excited strong feeling. The cleavage between pro-Germans and the rest of the people became tense.

The Germans were joined by some Irish, comparatively few but very much moved, and with a racial capacity for making their emotion vocal; the beginning of the Great War had

1. Family who occupied the German Imperial House until German Emperor Wilhelm II abdicated in 1918.   2. German Emperor Wilhelm II.

happened to coincide with an acute outbreak of the seven-centuries-long struggle of the Irish against England. An organization of Irish-Nationalists, meeting in Philadelphia, "pledge ourselves to do all in our power . . . to bring Irishmen and Germans together to fight for a common cause, the national welfare of Germany. . . ." One Irish organization that became active and resourceful in pro-German propaganda was called "The American Truth Society." At many an exalted meeting "The Wearing of the Green" mingled, rather incongruously, with "Die Wacht am Rhein."[3]

As feeling grew, race-consciousness became infectious. In the bedevilling cleavages by which America was thus beset, an intricate line of division separated various foreign groups each from each: Italian-Americans, Irish-Americans, Polish-Americans, Russian-Americans, Hungarian-Americans, and other groups from the peculiarly polyglot Austro-Hungarian Empire. All began to organize, take sides, and express their emotions in foreign-language newspapers, including demands that their adopted country should take one side or the other. Thus arose another war-created term, "hyphenated American." The phenomenon disturbed us, caused many to wonder if our policy of unrestricted immigration had been wise, whether America was really a nation, or just an international boarding-house. It was not a happy time for average Americans—occasions arose when they were obliged to wonder whether they existed, whether there was such a thing as "the average American." Some, conspicuously Theodore Roosevelt, then ex-President, took the situation very seriously, started movements for "Americanization"—Roosevelt popularized a phrase, "hundred per cent American." One more tolerant, or more timorous, expressed himself in poetry, at least in words that rhymed, in the New York *Sun*:

> The barber to the right of me was hoching for the Kaiser.
> The barber to the left of me was hacking for the Czar.
> A gentleman from Greece was shearing off my fleece,
> While very near a swart Italian stropped his scimitar.
> And when presently discussion, polyglot and fervid,
> On political conditions burst about my chair,
> I left the place unshaven—I hope I'm not a craven,
> But I sort of like to wear a head beneath my hair!

3. "The Watch on the Rhein," the German national anthem until 1922.

AMERICANS REACT TO THE SINKING OF THE *LUSITANIA*

THOMAS A. BAILEY AND PAUL B. RYAN

When British naval forces blockaded the Germans during World War I, preventing them from receiving supplies and raw materials from overseas, Germany declared that any enemy vessel entering the waters surrounding Great Britain and Ireland would be destroyed without warning. On the afternoon of May 7, 1915, the British luxury liner *Lusitania*, sailing off the coast of Ireland, was torpedoed by a German submarine. The *Lusitania* sank, taking with it the lives of 1,198 passengers and crew members, including 128 Americans.

The sinking of *Lusitania* compelled the United States to sympathize with the Allied forces. In this excerpt from their book *The Lusitania Disaster*, history professor Thomas A. Bailey and retired U.S. Navy captain Paul B. Ryan examine the reaction of the American public to this tragedy. According to Bailey and Ryan, Americans condemned the attack on the *Lusitania* but did not unanimously demand retribution against Germany. In addition, the authors contend that much of the American press felt that the nation could not contribute much more to the Allied cause than it was already contributing materially.

T he reaction of American citizens to the [*Lusitania*] tragedy was compounded of shock, revulsion, indignation, and anger. Extreme bitterness evidently was most strident along the eastern seaboard, especially in New York City. From here the liner had departed, and from here many of the most prominent victims had come, including the theatrical genius Charles Frohman and the wealthy sportsman Alfred G. Vanderbilt. President Woodrow Wilson had announced with much publicity that Germany would be held to "a strict accountability," and Berlin had not only defied him but had published an insulting counterwarning in the American newspapers. National pride had suffered a humiliating blow.

A MONUMENTAL FOLLY

Many newspaper editors and other prominent Americans condemned the "premeditated" "massacre" or "slaughter" as "deliberate murder" or a "deed of wholesale murder." If the loss of the *Titanic* was an act of God, the torpedoing of the *Lusitania* was an act of the Devil (the Kaiser[1]), "the most momentous moral crisis since the crucifixion of Christ." The "foul deed" or "outrage" was an act of "war" or "piracy," or even worse than piracy. "Mad dog" Germany, led by "the Beast of Berlin," was running amuck like "savages drunk with blood." Even a rattlesnake had the decency to warn before striking. The torpedoing was "piracy organized, systematized, and nationalized." The New York *Nation* branded the attack as "a deed for which a Hun would blush, a Turk be ashamed, and a Barbary pirate apologize. . . . The law of nations and the law of God have been alike trampled upon. . . . The torpedo that sank the *Lusitania* also sank Germany in the opinion of mankind. . . . It is at once a crime and a monumental folly. . . . She has affronted the moral sense of the world and sacrificed her standing among the nations." The Reverend Billy Sunday, the sensational evangelist, cried, "Damnable! Damnable! Absolutely Hellish!" Some extremists wondered why Wilson did not hurry up and "declare war," which of course he could not do under the Constitution. The New York *Tribune* wrote darkly, "The nation which remembered the *Maine* will not forget the civilians of the *Lusitania*."

The myth persists that America with almost one voice demanded a war of retribution against Germany, and that Wilson was able, only with the greatest difficulty, to sidetrack such a declaration by Congress. (That body was not to be in session until December, seven months later.) In this pre-Gallup Poll era

1. German Emperor Kaiser Wilhelm II.

the best rough index of public opinion was thought to be the newspaper editors. Author David Lawrence reported that about 1,000 editorial reactions were compiled by telegraph within three days after the "massacre," and that fewer than a half-dozen of these indicated a belief that Congress should declare war. Many favored going no further than to demand from Germany disavowal, apology, and the payment of an indemnity. This editorial survey was not a scientific poll, but for what it was worth it indicated that only about one half of one percent of the entire voting population favored war as the most desirable response. The American people discussed the dread possibility of an armed clash; they did not demand it. General Leonard Wood wrote in his diary, "Rotten spirit in the *Lusitania* matter. Yellow spirit everywhere in spots."

No Clamor for War

A few outspoken men prominent in public life, conspicuously former President Theodore Roosevelt, demanded two-fisted action to protect the "right" of American passengers to sail freely on blockade-runners carrying ammunition. He found some support among other influential pro-Ally partisans, such as Colonel Edward M. House, Senator Henry Cabot Lodge, and Elihu Root, the former Secretary of State. One noteworthy effect of the sinking was to cause leaders of this stripe to move even more strongly in the direction of intervention.

Yet the overwhelming majority of the American people clearly wanted the President to voice their moral indignation through diplomacy, without risking hostilities with an embattled Germany. They condemned "murder" but they did not clamor for war. The views of dozens of Congressmen and Senators were widely publicized, but apparently only two Senators and one Representative publicly voiced warlike sentiments. Most Congressmen evidently believed that the issue was safe in Wilson's diplomatic hands, that Americans should not be permitted to travel on contraband-carrying belligerent ships, and that one wholesale tragedy should not be allowed to precipitate a far more horrible shooting war.

Much of the American press concluded that there was no point in fighting. The republic, with no army to boast of and no conscription in prospect, could not contribute much more to the common cause than it was already sending in military supplies and in money. In significant respects a blockaded United States would actually be a handicap to the Allies as a war partner. Fear was also expressed that the millions of German aliens in the United States might rise in a civil war and paralyze the nation; in fact, there were thought to be considerably more German and Austrian reservists in the country (about 500,000) than there were soldiers in the United States Army (about 100,000).

On September 13, 1907, the **Lusitania** *made its first appearance in New York Harbor.*

MISREADING THE NATIONAL CHARACTER

The so-called "right" of American passengers to sail on British ships was sharply questioned by certain men prominent in public affairs. Vice President Thomas Marshall [of Wilson's administration] told the press that when a person boarded an English vessel he was virtually on English soil and must expect to stand the consequences. This was a view since then ably argued by various international lawyers. Among other prominent personages who opposed permitting American passengers to embark on belligerent ships were Senator Jones of Washington; Senator Stone of Missouri, who had a large German-American constituency; and Judge A. Mitchell Palmer of Pennsylvania, whom Wilson later appointed Attorney General. Two days after the sinking, Secretary of State William Jennings Bryan wrote privately to Wilson to argue that Germany had a "right to prevent contraband going to the Allies, and a ship carrying contraband should not rely upon passengers to protect her from attack—it would be like putting women and children in front of an army." Arbitration was the solution proposed by the Governor of Connecticut for any deadlock growing out of the issue. The Governor of Nebraska reported that 90% of his people favored settling such differences of opinion by methods of arbitration and conciliation, as Secretary Bryan had been quietly urging behind the scenes. Ex-President William Taft privately favored arbitration of questions involving international law.

From Washington the British Ambassador, Sir Cecil Spring Rice, wrote home that the American people wanted above all else to keep out of the overseas bloodbath. He did not believe that America would even contemplate intervention unless its own material interests were directly affected. As for himself, he did not blame the United States for acting as the British had done in 1870, when they sat on the sidelines while Germany invaded and crushed France. All this suggests that if British Prime Minister Winston Churchill had expected the Americans to enter the war over the torpedoing of a British ship, he was gravely misreading the national character, some knowledge of which he could claim from his American mother.

GERMAN SYMPATHIZERS

Not many American citizens were foolhardy enough to applaud in public the sinking of the *Lusitania*, but many of them expressed considerable sympathy for the German point of view. This was especially true among German-Americans and their journals, as well as among Irish-Americans and their press. In the casinos and restaurants of New York many partisans of Germany drank to the "great victory" of the Fatherland. One German-American spokesman insisted that "Germany is not bluffing; she means business." Another declared that "nothing is to be gained by Americans shooting off their mouths; war is war."

[According to author Charles Callan Tansill,] even some "one hundred percent Americans" were critical of the British for permitting their munitions ships to carry passengers or were convinced that the "living shield" argument had much force. Rear Admiral F.E. Chadwick, U.S.N., whose Americanism needed no defense, felt that the real "outrage" was for the British to be carrying ammunition on a mail ship, along with women and children. He quoted General Leonard Wood as saying, "You can't cover 10,000 tons [?] of ammunition with a petticoat."

A MILITARY ACTION

The Chicago *Tribune,* with its many German-American sub-
scribers, was more anti-British than pro-German. It argued that
if the United States accorded Britain the right to buy munitions,
then the State Department should not deny the Germans the
right to sink them with their most effective sea weapon. The
movement of military supplies was clearly a military action. A
transport that was carrying a regiment could be legally sunk on
sight; then why demand immunity for a transport that was carrying enough ammunition to wipe out a regiment? If such vessels could not be sunk legally by U-boats, international law
should be modified to accommodate the new weapon.

Such pro-German justifications, as soon became apparent,
were only those of a decided minority. Viewed in terms of the
propaganda warfare then being conducted in America by the
Germans, the sinking of the Cunarder was about as disastrous
to them as the loss of the Battle of the Marne in France in 1914.
The torpedo that destroyed the *Lusitania* also sank the German
campaign in America for people's minds, and thus ended all
hope of persuading the United States to embargo shipments of
arms to the Allies. German ambassador to the United States Jo-
hann von Bernstorff wrote candidly to his superiors in Berlin
that "our propaganda here has *collapsed completely* under the im-
pact of the *Lusitania* incident." The ineptitude of German agents
in America also contributed to this end. Captain Franz von Papen, the German Military Attaché, remarked to the press that it
was "absolutely criminal" for Cunard [British liners] to be carrying passengers on a munitions transport. Doctor Bernhard
Dernburg, the leading German propaganda agent in America,
told reporters that Germany had an undoubted right to sink
without warning all ships carrying contraband, especially aux-
iliary cruisers like the *Lusitania.* This kind of talk merely compounded the so-called felony, and von Bernstorff had no choice
but to bundle Dernburg off home before the State Department
requested his expulsion.

THE BIRTH OF A NATION: A LANDMARK IN FILM HISTORY

WARD GREENE

D.W. Griffith's 1915 film *The Birth of a Nation* took motion pictures to a new artistic level. This film epic on the Civil War and Reconstruction period introduced innovative filming and editing techniques and topped three hours in running time, the longest film at that time. *The Birth of a Nation* was also a box-office smash, grossing $18 million by the time "talking" motion pictures gained popularity. However, many critics called *The Birth of a Nation* (which was based on Thomas Dixon's novel of racial conflict, *The Clansman*) a work of racist propaganda. Griffith rebuked this claim and insisted that "in filming *The Birth of a Nation,* I gave to my best knowledge the proven facts . . . about the Reconstruction period in the American south."

Ward Greene, a Southerner and prominent newspaper executive at the time, endorsed *The Birth of a Nation.* In the following review, Greene praises the film for its glorification of the South and contends that "the picture does every credit to the negro race." In addition, he asserts that *The Birth of a Nation* is a magnificent cinematic event, stirring passion, dismay, and fascination in a way no other motion picture ever has before.

T he story of the Creation was told in eight words, but should the pen of another Moses be raised today he would need ten times that number of pages to do credit to *The Birth of a Nation.*

Excerpted from Ward Greene's review of *The Birth of a Nation, Atlanta Journal,* 1915.

There has been nothing to equal it—nothing. Not as a motion picture, nor a play, nor a book does it come to you; but as the soul and spirit and flesh of the heart of your country's history, ripped from the past and brought quivering with all human emotions before your eyes.

It swept the audience at the Atlanta Theater Monday night like a tidal wave. A youth in the gallery leaped to his feet and yelled and yelled. A little boy downstairs pounded the man's back in front of him and shrieked. The man did not know it. He was a middle-aged, hard-lipped citizen; but his face twitched and his throat gulped up and down. Here a young girl kept dabbing and dabbing at her eyes and there an old lady just sat and let the tears stream down her face unchecked.

THE AWAKENER OF EVERY FEELING

For *The Birth of a Nation* is the awakener of every feeling. Your heart pulses with patriotism when those boys in grey march to battle with banners whipping and the band playing "Dixie"; you are wrung with compassion for the mother and her girls desolate at home; you are shocked by the clamor of mighty armies flung hell-bent into conflict; your throat chokes for a boy who dies with a smile on his face beside the body of his chum, the enemy. Then "the South's best friend" crumples under the assassin's bullet and the land of the lost cause lies like a ragged wound under a black poison that pours out upon it. Loathing, disgust, hate envelop you, hot blood cries for vengeance. Until out of the night blazes the fiery cross that once burned high above old Scotland's hills and the legions of the Invisible Empire roar down to rescue, and that's when you are lifted by the hair and go crazy.

Race prejudice? Injustice? Suppression? You would not think of those things had you seen *The Birth of a Nation*. For none but a man with a spirit too picayunish and warped for words would pick such flaws in a spectacle so great and whole-hearted as this. In the first place, the picture does every credit to the negro race, lauds those faithful old black people whose fealty to their masters led them to dare the anger of mistaken fanatics, shows the true progress they have since made in industry and education. This picture is too big a thing to be bothered by such a gnat's sting of criticism.

Technically, *The Birth of a Nation* is perfect. Its stage settings, the acting of the principals, its faithfulness to historic fact, its every intimate detail, its photography, and its skillful blending of scenes laughable and pathetic—all are so well done that you don't even think about them during the picture.

Yet in retrospect they loom big. There is the scene which gives you the flash of a desolate family huddled on a hilltop and far below Sherman's invaders putting the city to the torch and raiding onward to where the sea laps the sand at Savannah.

There is the old Southern home in the very first part of the picture, when the orchestra plays "Sewanee Ribber." An old man sits there and by his side a cat and a puppy mawl each other. The cat claws viciously, you can almost hear the puppy whimper. And you laugh out loud at the joy of it.

When they go to war, your breast swells at the sight of the flower of the Confederacy tripping away to the strains of "The Bonnie Blue Flag." But you smile sympathetically, too, at the darky buck-dancing on the corner and the little pickaninnies rolling funnily in the dust.

You marvel again at the rolling smoke and flash of shell and canister across a far-flung battle line, but you feel as much the pathos when the boy of the North pauses with uplifted bayonet above the body of his chum of the South, until he jerks back from the bullet and wavers down across that body and before he dies smiles that roguish lad's smile and steals his arm across the other's face before he, too, lets his curly head fall in the shadows of the other's shoulder blades.

There is the scene where the "Little Colonel" comes home after the war, wasted, wan, hopeless, pausing, uncertain outside the old mansion where the shattered gate hangs broken on the hinges. And his little sister comes to greet him. She flies out of the house and stops at the threshold and smiles at him. They do not fall into each other's arms, but stand there and try to joke a little to hide the pity in each other's eyes. He fingers the "Southern ermine" on her dress and it ravels away, just like the raw cotton she had bravely donned in honor of his homecoming. And then she cleaves to him with both arms around his neck. And when the picture fades away as he is drawn inside the door, the last thing you feel is the spasm of pain in his face, the last thing you see are twin hands clutched convulsively across his shoulders.

THRILLING TO THE CORE

That little sister—she is wonderful. Mae Marsh is the girl who plays the role, plays it with an abandon and sincerity that is not acting but living. There, at the last, when she goes to the dark spring for water, you see her smile gayly at a squirrel on a limb; you see the bright-eyed little animal swallow a nut. You follow her mad race through the woods from the black crazed by power. You are with her when she pauses on the precipice and when she plunges downward and rolls over and over at the bottom to writhe for a moment, crushed and broken, before her head snaps back.

She is but one of the stars. That gives you an idea of the lavishness of the picture. Wallace Reid, who is featured in other films as the whole show, is in this picture in but one scene. Yet he is worth it, for his battle with ten negroes in the ginshop of "White-armed Joe" thrills you to the core. He uppercuts one and hurls another across the room, brains a third with a chair, pitches a fourth out of the window, beats them back until a shot spurts grey smoke and he totters into the street and drops forward in a heap.

Then the Ku Klux Klan gathers. The scenes which follow defy description. In the little town of Piedmont the blacks are celebrating, far away across the hills the Klan assembles. Back and forth the scene changes—one moment a street in Piedmont swirling with mad negroes, the next a bugle blast from the orchestra and out of the distance the riders of the Klan sweeping on and on. Back to the street and a house where a white girl trembles in fear before the black horde without, back with the bugle blast to the onrush of the Klan. They are coming, they are coming!

A NATION REBORN

You know it and your spine prickles and in the gallery the yells cut loose with every bugle note. The negro mob grows wilder and wilder, the white-shrouded riders are tearing nearer and nearer. Then, with a last mighty blast from the bugle, they sweep into the town and with a shattering volley hammer into the crowd. They fire back, they break, they flee. The Klan beats on them and over them, here a rider knocked off his horse and there another whizzing clean out of the window to the back of his steed—on them and over them to rescue and retribution and final triumph.

And after it's all over, you are not raging nor shot with hatred, but mellowed into a deeper and purer understanding of the fires through which your forefathers battled to make this South of yours a nation reborn!

That's why they sold standing room only Monday night and why every matinee at 2:30 and every night performance at 8:30 this week will be packed.

"I wouldn't pay $2 to see any movie in the world," scoffed one man Monday.

A friend took him Monday night. Tuesday he spent $10 to take himself again, his wife, his two children, and his maiden aunt.

And if you haven't seen it, spend the money, borrow it, beg it, get it any old way. But see *The Birth of a Nation*.

Margaret Sanger and the Birth Control Movement

Ellen Chesler

As a firsthand witness to atrocities of self-induced abortions, an American nurse named Margaret Sanger became the champion of female birth control in the early twentieth century. On October 16, 1916, with the help of her younger sister Ethel Byrne, Sanger opened America's first birth control clinic in Brooklyn, New York. According to Ellen Chesler, author of the book *Woman of Valor: Margaret Sanger and the Birth Control Movement of America,* the opening of the clinic was a milestone in the birth control movement. In the following excerpt, Chesler recounts how the police shut down the clinic and imprisoned Byrne and Sanger for dispensing contraceptives and promoting contraception. She explains that Sanger was able to use the controversy of the birth control clinic, her arrest, and her trial to gain publicity and support for the birth control movement. Chesler is a senior fellow and the director of the Program on Reproductive Health and Rights at the Open Society Institute.

O n October 16, 1916, Margaret Sanger opened the first birth control clinic in America, behind the curtained windows of a storefront tenement on Amboy Street near the corner of Pitkin Avenue in the Brownsville district of Brooklyn. Handbills, advertising the location in English, Yiddish, and Italian, promoted the benefits of contraception over abortion:

MOTHERS! Can you afford to have a large family? Do you want any more children? If not, why do you have them? DO NOT KILL, DO NOT TAKE LIFE, BUT PREVENT.

The women of Brownsville patiently stood in line for service—there were 464 recorded clients during the several weeks the facility remained open. Surviving photographs show them handsomely attired in shirtwaists and billowing skirts. Draped in a shawl to protect against the autumn chill, one young mother hovers over a graceful wicker baby carriage in a romantic tableau that conceals the full dimension of the neighborhood's dispiriting poverty.

PROCEEDING SLOWLY AND CAREFULLY

Margaret had been advised "to proceed slowly and carefully in the matter of the clinic" and "avoid all unnecessary antagonisms." She may have intended to . . . staff the clinic with a doctor, but failing to find a willing recruit, gave authority to her sister, Ethel Byrne, who was still working as a registered nurse at Mt. Sinai Hospital. Assisting with client intake and record keeping were Fania Mindell, a volunteer from Chicago who spoke three languages, and Elizabeth Stuyvesant, a social worker with Associated Charities of New York, who was apparently acting without institutional endorsement. That the presence of a doctor would have saved the clinic from attack was not clear, but in the interests of caution, Margaret and Ethel ostensibly agreed to provide only contraceptive information and sex education, rather than themselves dispense condoms and suppositories or fit the cervical appliances they advocated as a preferred birth control method. They charged 10 cents for each consultation. A device called the Mizpah Pessary was available at local pharmacies as a womb support for multiparous women who suffered from the then commonly diagnosed condition of prolapsed or distended uterus, which results when multiple or strenuous pregnancies weaken the vaginal muscles that hold the uterus in place. This pessary could also be effective as a contraceptive, and boxes of them were part of the clinic's inventory.

On day nine of the clinic's operation, a modishly attired woman, identifying herself as a "Mrs. Whitehurst," arrived and immediately aroused suspicion. When she left, according to Margaret, the $2 bill she had paid for a 10-cent sex education pamphlet was pinned to the wall with a note that read "received from Mrs. Whitehurst of the Police Department as her contribution." The following day she returned with three plain-clothesmen from the department's vice squad and arrested Margaret and Fania Mindell. The police impounded pamphlets, furnishings, and supplies, along with the case histories that had been compiled as a record of the clinic's activities.

THROWING CAUTION TO THE WIND

Provoked by this confrontation, Margaret threw all caution to the winds, betraying her radical roots. The afternoon edition of the *Brooklyn Daily Eagle* on October 26, 1916, described the scene:

> Mrs. Whitehurst placed Mrs. Sanger under arrest. The little woman was at first taken aback but in an instant she was in a towering rage. "You dirty thing," she shrieked. "You are not a woman. You are a dog." "Tell that to the judge in the morning," calmly responded Mrs. Whitehurst. "No. I'll tell it to you, now. You dog, and you have two ears to hear me too!"

According to the story, Sanger and Mindell were then "half-dragged, half carried" to a patrol wagon. With a gaggle of Brownsville mothers defiantly following behind them, they were taken to the local station house, where they were arraigned and released on $500 bail. But they chose to reap the publicity value of remaining overnight in a cold, vermin-infested jail. Several weeks later Margaret reopened the clinic, pending action by the courts, but it was closed down once again, and she was charged this time with maintaining a public nuisance.

Though Margaret managed the publicity surrounding her arrest much like an old-fashioned Wobbly,[1] her choice of counsel reflected a new and determined political savvy. Jonah J. Goldstein was a young liberal Democrat. . . . Though he failed to win her the jury trial she desired, he did manage—after impassioned testimony from Margaret herself during the pre-trial hearings—to remove from the three-man panel that heard the case in Brooklyn's Court of Special Sessions the judge who had convicted her husband and was known for his extreme bias on the birth control issue.

Goldstein's actual courtroom strategy, however, was not so successful. Ethel Byrne had not been there when the clinic was raided, but she was arrested shortly thereafter, and the charges

---

1. Member of the Industrial Workers of the World, an organization aimed at overthrowing capitalism.

brought against her came up first, on the court calendar of January 4, 1917. In pretrial arguments he had argued for dismissal on the grounds that the Comstock statutes[2] were unconstitutional because they interfered with the free exercise of conscience and the pursuit of happiness; that they were arbitrary and unduly oppressive, because they allowed for no exceptions; that they failed to promote the health, welfare, and morals of the community; that they were so unreasonable as to place the life of women in jeopardy, thereby violating the equal protection provisions of the Fourteenth Amendment. His various entreaties failed, however, and during the trial itself, he took still a different approach, telling the judges that Section 1145 of New York's Comstock law, which provided a medical exception, infringed the constitutional rights of the poor, denying them the right to choose how many children they would have, a right enjoyed by middle-class citzens who could afford the services of private physicians. . . .

In the kind of racist accusation that would continue to haunt her sister, Ethel Byrne was accused by the prosecution of intending "to do away with the Jews" by dispensing contraception in an immigrant ghetto, and of hoping to make money in the process, because she had charged a small fee. She was found guilty of violating the statutory prohibition on giving birth control information and was sentenced to one month's imprisonment in the workhouse on Blackwell's Island. Goldstein applied to the State Supreme Court and to the Federal District Court to void her sentence pending an appeal, but he was denied by both.

BYRNE'S HUNGER STRIKE

Disappointed by the failure of their legal strategy but emboldened by the sudden spate of publicity they were receiving, Sanger and Byrne embarked on an audacious course. They announced that Mrs. Byrne would undertake a hunger strike in jail in the manner of the British suffragists. Newspapers throughout the country bannered her vow to "die, if need be, for my sex." A farewell dinner of turkey and "plenty of ice cream" sustained the theatrics on the eve of her incarceration, and for the entire week that followed, news from prison of her deteriorating physical and emotional status vied for front-page

---

2. These laws prohibited the distribution of obscene materials, which included birth control devices and information.

headlines with stories of German belligerence against American ships in the seas of Europe. Ethel kept her fast for four days, giving rise to allegations, which were later denied, that she was drinking water when not observed. When the New York City corrections commissioner announced that forcible feeding of the prisoner through a tube inserted into the esophagus would begin, for the first time in United States penal history, the national wire services literally went wild. Even the normally sensation-shy *New York Times* carried the story on its front page for four days in a row, alternating reports from prison officials that Mrs. Byrne's response was " passive" to her thrice-daily feedings of a mixture of milk, brandy, and eggs, with overstated claims from Sanger that her sister could not resist because she was extremely weak and near death.

SUPPORT FROM THE COMMITTEE OF 100

Throughout this ordeal, Ethel and Margaret enjoyed the support of a group of women from the National Birth Control League, who called themselves the Committee of 100 and included Mary Ware Dennett, Rose Stokes, Jessie Ashley, Crystal Eastman, and Elsie Clews Parsons, along with others willing to associate themselves with Sanger's direct action. Their chairwoman was Gertrude Pinchot, who had earlier given the Sangers the money to keep their children in school, and their official credo was drafted by the prepossessing Juliet Barrett Rublee, an heiress from Chicago who would become Margaret's intimate friend and whose husband, George, served on the Federal Trade Commission as a Wilson appointee. The document, though not elegantly phrased, emphatically announced their purpose:

> We maintain that it is no more indecent to discuss sexual anatomy, physiology and hygiene in a scientific spirit than it is to discuss the functions of the stomach, the heart and the liver. We believe that the question as to whether or not, and when, a woman should have a child, is not a question for the doctors to decide, except in cases where the woman's life is endangered, or for the state legislators to decide, but a question for the woman herself to decide.

Margaret had impressed these women when she first appeared at one of what they called their "parlor meetings," and by dominating the media after the clinic raid, she persuaded them to support her activities along with their preferred legislative solution to the birth control problem. As a measure of their effectiveness and power, moreover, they raised $700 for birth control work by just informally passing around a hat, and pledged part of it for her legal expenses.

When Ethel was sentenced, the Committee of 100 called a protest rally at Carnegie Hall. Falling right in the middle of her sensationalized hunger strike, the event attracted 3,000 supporters, most of them women, and raised another $1,000. Admission to the upper galleries was only 25 cents, and according to the newspapers, the seats were filled with poor working women, offering a sharp contrast to the "richly dressed" society types who adorned the boxes below. Margaret was, of course, the featured speaker of the evening, and her impassioned oratory elicited sustained cheers. She began:

> I come to you from a crowded courtroom, from a vortex of persecution. I come not from the stake of Salem where women were tried for blasphemy, but from the shadow of Blackwell's Island where women are tortured for obscenity.

At her suggestion, a group of Brownsville mothers were given "places of honor" on the platform behind her "to let everybody see what kind of women we are fighting for," and by all accounts this dramatic touch was extremely effective. One observer likened the spirit of the evening to that of the abolition days.

THE PARDON

Several days after the event, a well-connected delegation of the Committee of 100, upset that Ethel's militancy was getting out of hand and truly endangering her life, took Margaret to meet with New York Gov. Charles Whitman. Their intent was to win commutation of Ethel's sentence and to secure a pledge from the governor to appoint a commission to investigate birth control. Whitman was willing to pardon Byrne only if she pledged never to break the law again, a condition Margaret declared unacceptable, and no investigation ever took place. Through his intervention, however, Margaret was granted a pass to visit her sister in jail, which she had previously been denied. On discovering what appeared to be a genuinely alarming physical deterioration, she decided to accept the terms of the pardon on her sister's behalf. Given the extraordinary public interest in the situation, prison officials were only too happy to be rid of their charge, and Ethel was carried prostrate from the workhouse, wrapped in the fur coat of one of her rich new benefactors.

Once recovered, Ethel told Margaret that "I couldn't have lived or fought through anything if I hadn't known and loved you," and Margaret assured her in response that she had fought "the finest fight ever made by any woman in the U.S.A." Later, Margaret would gallantly identify the hunger strike as the most significant act of "self-sacrifice in the history of the birth control movement." Yet it effectively ended Ethel's participation in birth control activities and regrettably cast a permanent pall on relations between the two sisters. An undercurrent of rivalry had long festered beneath their deep and abiding affection, and these extraordinary events brought it to the surface. Ethel greatly resented Margaret's ambitious pursuit of the new social and political connections their sudden celebrity had wrought. . . .

MARGARET'S TRIAL

The trials of Margaret Sanger and Fania Mindell got underway on January 29, 1917, while Ethel was still imprisoned and making headlines. Thirty Brownsville mothers who had been clients of the clinic were subpoenaed by the prosecution, and they filled the courtroom laden with bags of bread and fruit to eat, and with pacifiers and extra diapers to service the infants they held at their breasts. Newspaper reporters described a courtroom configuration of those who could barely afford the carfare to bring them to downtown Brooklyn seated beside the fashionable, formidable representatives of the Committee of 100, whose chauffeurs waited outside to drive them back to Manhattan. These accounts created an indelible impression of the birth control movement as a respectable alliance of wealthy and powerful women helping their less fortunate sisters, distinctions of class giving way to the common bond of gender.

The prosecution called Mindell first, and she was summarily charged with selling Margaret's pamphlet, *What Every Girl Should Know.* Her case was adjourned until the judges had time to read the disputed copy, at which time she was found guilty on obscenity charges and given a $50 fine, which Gertrude Pinchot graciously agreed to pay. (This decision was subsequently reversed on appeal, essentially disposing of the definition of birth control literature as "obscene" under New York State law and providing the basis for Goldstein's later defenses of Sanger and others on charges brought against them in 1919 for distributing birth control propaganda.)

Margaret's own trial began after additional technical objections by Jonah Goldstein were overruled. The policewoman, Mrs. Whitehurst, took the stand first as a witness for the prosecution. She testified that she had found Mrs. Sanger in the clinic's back room holding a box of suppositories and a rubber birth control appliance. A second witness also claimed to have heard her make abusive comments about the Jewish people, a canard that a third witness disputed, but the tactic, alas, had already done its damage.

LITTLE TO DO WITH GUILT OR INNOCENCE

Since Margaret openly admitted that she had given out birth control information, the question of her guilt under the state Comstock law was never in question. Most of the trial testimony, however, centered on the narrower issue of whether she had gone beyond verbal instruction to actually fit her clients with cervical devices. To the prosecutor this seemed an even more heinous crime. Boxes of confiscated pessaries, condoms and douching solutions were introduced as evidence, and one Brownsville mother did testify that Margaret had not only explained the contraceptive utility of the pessary when properly fitted but also offered to "adjust it myself," yet it was never clear that she, in fact, had done so. Margaret only admitted that she had "lectured" women on sexual physiology and hygiene, because they often did not themselves understand the reproductive functions and could not, therefore, comprehend how contraception worked. "Their gratitude was touching," she had earlier told one newspaper reporter. "Some of them sought to kiss our hands because we had taken an interest in them."

The discrepancy between the prosecutor's allegations and the testimony of witnesses evidently troubled the three presiding judges. Indeed the most sympathetic among them, Judge Freschi, then specifically raised the basic question Margaret set out to test—whether the statute's Section 1145 medical exemption did countenance contraception when prescribed for the prevention of disease. This was an important breakthrough in the legal proceedings, because Margaret as a nurse did not have technical standing in court to demand clarification of physician's rights under the existing statutes. Goldstein seized on the opening, and recognizing that the court had not been willing to hear expert medical witnesses, he had the Brownsville mothers tell their own tragic stories about multiparity, miscarriage, infant death, poverty, hunger, and disease.

Their testimony may have been compelling, but it had little to do with the question of Margaret's guilt or innocence under the law. Goldstein therefore tried to strike a deal in the judge's chambers, requesting a suspended sentence for his client in exchange for her promise not to violate the law again, while he appealed to higher courts on the larger issue of the clear intent of the state's Comstock laws with respect to physicians' rights to prescribe contraception on medical grounds. The court, however, would only comply if she promised to obey the law without limit of time, an agreement she refused to make. "I cannot promise to obey a law I do not respect," she calmly responded to clapping and shouting in the courtroom. When order was restored, Goldstein asked for leniency on his client's behalf, but she was found guilty and given the choice of paying a $5,000 fine or being sentenced. She chose prison and was given thirty days in the workhouse. By the newspaper accounts of the trial, a single word was then uttered loudly from a far corner of the room. The word was "Shame!"

MARGARET'S PRISON SENTENCE

Margaret vowed publicly to repeat her sister's hunger strike in jail, and with that threat the women's facility on Blackwell's Island refused to have anything to do with her. She was instead sent to a quieter, more commodious penitentiary for women in Queens. Sobered by having seen Ethel's condition, and recognizing the diminished news value of a repeat performance, especially during a week when the Germans were sinking more American battleships and diplomatic relations between the two countries had been broken, she spent her incarceration compliantly in a private cell. She actually welcomed the rare opportunity to rest and be alone, and told her supporters in a published letter that their "loving thoughts pouring into her" protected her from sadness. She found that what she most resented was the poor quality of the prison food and, desperately hungry, wrote lightheartedly to Ethel questioning which fate was worse, slow starvation over thirty days or "getting the job done quick." In subsequent years, she would support movements for penal reform and prisoners' rights. . . .

The only drama in Margaret's prison sentence came as she

was about to be released on the bright but cold morning of March 6, 1917. For a month she had flatly refused on civil libertarian principles to submit to the indignity of the routine fingerprinting of prisoners. As the hour of her departure approached, several prison guards attempted to force her hands down on an ink pad, but she resisted and finally emerged the victor to a welcoming party of friends and supporters.

Ethel was there, along with Jonah Goldstein, Anna Lifschiz, Margaret's secretary, and Kitty Marion, a veteran of British suffrage militancy. The civic-minded Women's City Club of New York, which had recently appointed a birth control committee, was also represented, and the Committee of 100 sent the social worker, Helen Todd, chairwoman of the successful Carnegie Hall rally, as its standard bearer. A Russian Jewish immigrant by the name of Rose Halpern carried a bouquet of flowers from the mothers of Brownsville, and just before she died at the age of ninety-three, nearly sixty years later, she spoke to her daughter of her delight in having been present on this historic occasion.

1918–1919: The War Changes America

CHAPTER 4

America Enters World War I

Woodrow Wilson

President Woodrow Wilson struggled to maintain the United States' neutrality during the early years of World War I, resorting to diplomatic actions to keep Germany's naval belligerence at bay following the sinking of the British liner *Lusitania*. However, in 1917, Germany resumed unrestricted warfare around the waters of Great Britain and sank three U.S. ships in order to stop supplies from entering France and Great Britain. These events compelled Wilson to persuade Congress to declare war on Germany. In the following excerpt from his April 2, 1917, congressional speech, Wilson explains why the United States should enter the war. He asserts that the German submarine attacks on neutral U.S. vessels are nothing less than cunning acts of war against the United States. In addition, Wilson claims that Germany is taking further actions against the peace of the United States in neighboring Mexico. Won over by his speech, Congress passed the War Resolution four days later, bringing the nation into World War I.

I have called the Congress into extraordinary session because there are serious, very serious, choices of policy to be made, and made immediately, which it was neither right nor constitutionally permissible that I should assume the responsibility of making.

Cruel and Unmanly Business

On the 3d of February last I officially laid before you the extraordinary announcement of the Imperial German Government

Excerpted from "President Woodrow Wilson's War Message," by Woodrow Wilson, *War Messages* (Washington, DC: Government Printing Office, 1917).

that on and after the 1st day of February it was its purpose to put aside all restraints of law or of humanity and use its submarines to sink every vessel that sought to approach either the ports of Great Britain and Ireland or the western coasts of Europe or any of the ports controlled by the enemies of Germany within the Mediterranean. That had seemed to be the object of the German submarine warfare earlier in the war, but since April of last year the Imperial Government had somewhat restrained the commanders of its undersea craft in conformity with its promise then given to us that passenger boats should not be sunk and that due warning would be given to all other vessels which its submarines might seek to destroy, when no resistance was offered or escape attempted, and care taken that their crews were given at least a fair chance to save their lives in their open boats. The precautions taken were meagre and haphazard enough, as was proved in distressing instance after instance in the progress of the cruel and unmanly business, but a certain degree of restraint was observed. The new policy has swept every restriction aside. Vessels of every kind, whatever their flag, their character, their cargo, their destination, their errand, have been ruthlessly sent to the bottom without warning and without thought of help or mercy for those on board, the vessels of friendly neutrals along with those of belligerents. Even hospital ships and ships carrying relief to the sorely bereaved and stricken people of Belgium, though the latter were provided with safe-conduct through the proscribed areas by the German Government itself and were distinguished by unmistakable marks of identity, have been sunk with the same reckless lack of compassion or of principle.

I was for a little while unable to believe that such things would in fact be done by any government that had hitherto subscribed to the humane practices of civilized nations. International law had its origin in the attempt to set up some law which would be respected and observed upon the seas, where no nation had right of dominion and where lay the free highways of the world. By painful stage after stage has that law been built up, with meagre enough results, indeed, after all was accomplished that could be accomplished, but always with a clear view, at least, of what the heart and conscience of mankind demanded. This minimum of right the German Government has swept aside under the plea of retaliation and necessity and because it had no weapons which it could use at sea except these which it is impossible to employ as it is employing them without throwing to the winds all scruples of humanity or of respect for the understandings that were supposed to underlie the intercourse of the world. I am not now thinking of the loss of property involved, immense and serious as that is, but only of the wanton and wholesale destruction of the lives of noncombatants, men, women, and children, engaged in pursuits which have always, even in the darkest periods of modern history, been deemed innocent and le-

Woodrow Wilson

gitimate. Property can be paid for; the lives of peaceful and innocent people can not be. The present German submarine warfare against commerce is a warfare against mankind.

A WAR AGAINST ALL NATIONS

It is a war against all nations. American ships have been sunk, American lives taken, in ways which it has stirred us very deeply to learn of, but the ships and people of other neutral and friendly nations have been sunk and overwhelmed in the waters in the same way. There has been no discrimination. The challenge is to all mankind. Each nation must decide for itself how it will meet it. The choice we make for ourselves must be made with a moderation of counsel and a temperateness of judgment befitting our character and our motives as a nation. We must put excited feeling away. Our motive will not be revenge or the victorious assertion of the physical might of the nation, but only the vindication of right, of human right, of which we are only a single champion.

When I addressed the Congress on the 26th of February last, I thought that it would suffice to assert our neutral rights with arms, our right to use the seas against unlawful interference, our right to keep our people safe against unlawful violence. But armed neutrality, it now appears, is impracticable. Because submarines are in effect outlaws when used as the German submarines have been used against merchant shipping, it is impossible to defend ships against their attacks as the law of nations has assumed that merchantmen would defend themselves against privateers or cruisers, visible craft giving chase upon the open sea. It is common prudence in such circumstances, grim necessity indeed, to endeavour to destroy them before they have shown their own intention. They must be dealt with upon sight, if dealt with at all. The German Government denies the right of neutrals to use arms at all within the areas of the sea which it has proscribed, even in the defense of rights which no modern publicist has ever before questioned their right to defend. The intimation is conveyed that the armed guards which we have placed on our merchant ships will be treated as beyond the pale of law and subject to be dealt with as pirates would be. Armed neutrality is ineffectual enough at best; in such circumstances and in the face of such pretensions it is worse than ineffectual; it is likely only to produce what it was meant to prevent; it is practically certain to draw us into the war without either the rights or the effectiveness of belligerents. There is one choice we can not make, we are incapable of making: we will not choose the path of submission and suffer the most sacred rights of our nation and our people to be ignored or violated. The wrongs against which we now array ourselves are no common wrongs; they cut to the very roots of human life.

A MORE THOROUGH STATE OF DEFENSE

With a profound sense of the solemn and even tragical character of the step I am taking and of the grave responsibilities which it involves, but in unhesitating obedience to what I deem my constitutional duty, I advise that the Congress declare the recent course of the Imperial German Government to be in fact nothing less than war against the Government and people of the United States; that it formally accept the status of belligerent which has thus been thrust upon it, and that it take immediate steps not only to put the country in a more thorough state of defense but also to exert all its power and employ all its resources to bring the Government of the German Empire to terms and end the war.

What this will involve is clear. It will involve the utmost practicable cooperation in counsel and action with the governments now at war with Germany, and, as incident to that, the extension to those governments of the most liberal financial credits, in order that our resources may so far as possible be added to theirs. It will involve the organization and mobilization of all the material resources of the country to supply the materials of war and serve the incidental needs of the nation in the most abundant and yet the most economical and efficient way possible. It will involve the immediate full equipment of the Navy in all respects but particularly in supplying it with the best means of dealing with the enemy's submarines. It will involve the immediate addition to the armed forces of the United States already provided for by law in case of war at least 500,000 men, who should, in my opinion, be chosen upon the principle of universal liability to service, and also the authorization of subsequent additional increments of equal force so soon as they may be needed and can be handled in training. It will involve also, of course, the granting of adequate credits to the Government, sustained, I hope, so far as they can equitably be sustained by the present generation, by well conceived taxation. . . .

NEUTRALITY NO LONGER FEASIBLE

While we do these things, these deeply momentous things, let us be very clear, and make very clear to all the world what our motives and our objects are. My own thought has not been driven from its habitual and normal course by the unhappy events of the last two months, and I do not believe that the thought of the nation has been altered or clouded by them. I have exactly the same things in mind now that I had in mind when I addressed the Senate on the 22d of January last; the same that I had in mind when I addressed the Congress on the 3d of February and on the 26th of February. Our object now, as then, is to vindicate the principles of peace and justice in the life of the world as against selfish and autocratic power and to set up amongst the really free and self-governed peoples of the world such a concert of purpose and of action as will henceforth ensure the observance of those principles. Neutrality is no longer feasible or desirable where the peace of the world is involved and the freedom of its peoples, and the menace to that peace and freedom lies in the existence of autocratic governments backed by organized force which is controlled wholly by their will, not by the will of their people. We have seen the last of neutrality in such circumstances. We are at the beginning of an age in which it will be insisted that the same standards of conduct and of responsibility for wrong done shall be observed among nations and their governments that are observed among the individual citizens of civilized states.

We have no quarrel with the German people. We have no

feeling towards them but one of sympathy and friendship. It was not upon their impulse that their Government acted in entering this war. It was not with their previous knowledge or approval. It was a war determined upon as wars used to be determined upon in the old, unhappy days when peoples were nowhere consulted by their rulers and wars were provoked and waged in the interest of dynasties or of little groups of ambitious men who were accustomed to use their fellow men as pawns and tools. Self-governed nations do not fill their neighbour states with spies or set the course of intrigue to bring about some critical posture of affairs which will give them an opportunity to strike and make conquest. Such designs can be successfully worked out only under cover and where no one has the right to ask questions. Cunningly contrived plans of deception or aggression, carried, it may be, from generation to generation, can be worked out and kept from the light only within the privacy of courts or behind the carefully guarded confidences of a narrow and privileged class. They are happily impossible where public opinion commands and insists upon full information concerning all the nation's affairs.

No Real Friendship

A steadfast concert for peace can never be maintained except by a partnership of democratic nations. No autocratic government could be trusted to keep faith within it or observe its covenants. It must be a league of honour, a partnership of opinion. Intrigue would eat its vitals away; the plottings of inner circles who could plan what they would and render account to no one would be a corruption seated at its very heart. Only free peoples can hold their purpose and their honour steady to a common end and prefer the interests of mankind to any narrow interest of their own. . . .

One of the things that has served to convince us that the Prussian autocracy was not and could never be our friend is that from the very outset of the present war it has filled our unsuspecting communities and even our offices of government with spies and set criminal intrigues everywhere afoot against our national unity of counsel, our peace within and without our industries and our commerce. Indeed it is now evident that its spies were here even before the war began; and it is unhappily not a matter of conjecture but a fact proved in our courts of justice that the intrigues which have more than once come perilously near to disturbing the peace and dislocating the industries of the country have been carried on at the instigation, with the support, and even under the personal direction of official agents of the Imperial Government accredited to the Government of the United States. Even in checking these things and trying to extirpate them we have sought to put the most generous interpretation possible upon them because we knew that their source lay, not in any hostile feeling or purpose of the German people towards us (who were, no doubt, as ignorant of them as we ourselves were), but only in the selfish designs of a Government that did what it pleased and told its people nothing. But they have played their part in serving to convince us at last that that Government entertains no real friendship for us and means to act against our peace and security at its convenience. That it means to stir up enemies against us at our very doors the intercepted [Zimmermann] note to the German Minister at Mexico City is eloquent evidence.[1]

FOR THE ULTIMATE PEACE

We are accepting this challenge of hostile purpose because we know that in such a government, following such methods, we can never have a friend; and that in the presence of its organized power, always lying in wait to accomplish we know not what purpose, there can be no assured security for the democratic governments of the world. We are now about to accept gage of battle with this natural foe to liberty and shall, if necessary, spend the whole force of the nation to check and nullify its pretensions and its power. We are glad, now that we see the facts with no veil of false pretense about them, to fight thus for the ultimate peace of the world and for the liberation of its peoples, the German peoples included: for the rights of nations great and small and the privilege of men everywhere to choose their way of life and of obedience. The world must be made safe for democracy. Its peace must be planted upon the tested foundations of political liberty. We have no selfish ends to serve. We desire no conquest, no dominion. We seek no indemnities for ourselves, no material compensation for the sacrifices we shall freely make. We are but one of the champions of the rights of mankind. We shall be satisfied when those rights have been made as se-

---

1. The Zimmerman note revealed that the German Minister in Mexico proposed to form a German-Mexican alliance against the United States.

cure as the faith and the freedom of nations can make them.

Just because we fight without rancour and without selfish object, seeking nothing for ourselves but what we shall wish to share with all free peoples, we shall, I feel confident, conduct our operations as belligerents without passion and ourselves observe with proud punctilio the principles of right and of fair play we profess to be fighting for.

I have said nothing of the governments allied with the Imperial Government of Germany because they have not made war upon us or challenged us to defend our right and our honour. The Austro-Hungarian Government has, indeed, avowed its unqualified endorsement and acceptance of the reckless and lawless submarine warfare adopted now without disguise by the Imperial German Government, and the Ambassador recently accredited to this Government by the Imperial and Royal Government of Austria-Hungary; but that Government has not actually engaged in warfare against citizens of the United States on the seas, and I take the liberty, for the present at least, of postponing a discussion of our relations with the authorities at Vienna. We enter this war only where we are clearly forced into it because there are no other means of defending our rights.

It will be all the easier for us to conduct ourselves as belligerents in a high spirit of right and fairness because we act without animus, not in enmity towards a people or with the desire to bring any injury or disadvantage upon them, but only in armed opposition to an irresponsible government which has thrown aside all considerations of humanity and of right and is running amuck. We are, let me say again, the sincere friends of the German people, and shall desire nothing so much as the early reestablishment of intimate relations of mutual advantage between us—however hard it may be for them, for the time being, to believe that this is spoken from our hearts. We have borne with their present government through all these bitter months because of that friendship—exercising a patience and forbearance which would otherwise have been impossible. We shall, happily, still have an opportunity to prove that friendship in our daily attitude and actions towards the millions of men and women of German birth and native sympathy, who live amongst us and share our life, and we shall be proud to prove it towards all who are in fact loyal to their neighbours and to the Government in the hour of test. They are, most of them, as true and loyal Americans as if they had never known any other fealty or allegiance. They will be prompt to stand with us in rebuking and restraining the few who may be of a different mind and purpose. If there should be disloyalty, it will be dealt with with a firm hand of stern repression; but, if it lifts its head at all, it will lift it only here and there and without countenance except from a lawless and malignant few.

SACRIFICE AHEAD

It is a distressing and oppressive duty, gentlemen of the Congress, which I have performed in thus addressing you. There are, it may be, many months of fiery trial and sacrifice ahead of us. It is a fearful thing to lead this great peaceful people into war, into the most terrible and disastrous of all wars, civilization itself seeming to be in the balance. But the right is more precious than peace, and we shall fight for the things which we have always carried nearest our hearts—for democracy, for the right of those who submit to authority to have a voice in their own governments, for the rights and liberties of small nations, for a universal dominion of right by such a concert of free peoples as shall bring peace and safety to all nations and make the world itself at last free. To such a task we can dedicate our lives and our fortunes, everything that we are and everything that we have, with the pride of those who know that the day has come when America is privileged to spend her blood and her might for the principles that gave her birth and happiness and the peace which she has treasured. God helping her, she can do no other.

AMERICA ASSERTS ITS MILITARY POWER

ARTHUR S. LINK, WILLIAM A. LINK, AND WILLIAM B. CATTON

When the United States entered the First World War in 1917, it played a role greater than it had anticipated, beyond providing the British and French with material and monetary contributions and naval support. In the following selection, Arthur S. Link, William A. Link, and William B. Catton contend that the United States asserted its military and naval powers, tipping the war in favor of the Allies. For example, the authors claim that American reinforcements played a decisive role in ending the stalemate on the Western front by giving the Allied forces an advantage of manpower over Germany when the French and British had come close to diminishing their reserves. In addition, the U.S. Navy effectively countered German submarine warfare, greatly cutting the Allies' shipping losses, according to the authors. The late Arthur S. Link was an American history professor at Princeton University and a leading authority on President Woodrow Wilson. William A. Link is professor and head of the Department of History in the College of Arts and Sciences at the University of North Carolina at Greensboro. William B. Catton is professor emeritus at Middlebury College in Middlebury, Vermont.

N either President Woodrow Wilson nor his military advisers understood the weakness of the Allied military situation in the spring of 1917. Since 1914, Americans had assumed as a matter of course that the Allies would win. Even after it was evident that the United States would enter the

Excerpted from *American Epoch: A History of the United States Since 1900*, vol. I, by Arthur S. Link, William A. Link, and William B. Catton (New York: Alfred A. Knopf, 1987). Copyright © 1987 by Alfred A. Knopf. Reprinted with permission.

war, most Americans visualized their contribution only in terms of shipping, naval support, credit, and materials. Allied war missions to Washington soon counseled differently.

SELECTIVE SERVICE

Wilson and his advisers were shocked when British and French generals revealed that their governments were reaching their last reserves of manpower. Drawing on an Army War College plan for raising a large army, administration and army officials agreed that "Selective Service," or conscription, offered the only rational and democratic method. Even so, the selective service bill, presented to Congress soon after adoption of the war resolution, ignited a bitter contest in the House of Representatives. Wilson insisted that selective service was essential to victory. In the end he had his way, although there was a hard struggle over age limits and the sale of alcoholic beverages at or near army camps. In the measure that Wilson signed in May 1917, the House won its fight to set the minimum age at twenty-one instead of nineteen, as the army demanded. . . .

Secretary of War Newton D. Baker enlisted state and local officials in making the first registration on June 5, 1917, a nationwide demonstration of patriotism. On that date 9,586,508 men between the ages of twenty-one and thirty-one registered with local civilian boards without commotion, riot, or organized resistance. In August 1918, Congress expanded the age limits to include all men between eighteen and forty-five. All told, draft boards registered 24,234,021 men, of whom 6,300,000 were found to be fit for service and 2,810,296 were inducted into the army. In addition, volunteer enlistments in the army, navy, and marine corps brought the total number of men and women under arms by November 1918 to 4,800,000.

For commander of the projected American Expeditionary Force (AEF) the president and secretary of war turned to Major General John J. Pershing. . . . He arrived in June 1917 in Paris and established AEF headquarters at Chaumont, southeast of the French capital. While Allied military leaders argued that available American troops should be integrated into the existing structure and subordinated to Allied field commanders, Pershing insisted on preserving the identity and integrity of his command and even demanded a share of the front. The French command gave him the small and quiet Toul sector east of Verdun to defend with his initial force of 14,500 men.

THE GERMANS' HEAVY BLOWS

The Germans began a series of heavy blows in October 1917 that pointed up the urgent need of large American reinforcements and forced the Allied governments to unite effectively for the first time. Following a near rout of the Italian armies by the Germans and Austrians at Caporetto, Italy, in October 1917, came the triumph of the Bolsheviks in Russia. This raised the possibility that Russia would soon withdraw from the war. The Allied prime ministers assembled in extraordinary conference at Rapallo, Italy, in November 1917 and created a Supreme War Council to sit at Versailles and coordinate and direct military operations. During the next few months, Pershing and President Wilson were subjected to heavy pressure by British and French leaders to permit American troops, even troops inadequately trained, to be amalgamated into their armies. Pershing refused, promising that he would have an army of a million men in France by the end of 1918. Yet it seemed that the Germans might win the war before the arrival of Pershing's reinforcements. The imperial German army hit hard at the British Fifth Army in the Somme Valley in March 1918 and rolled it back. The Allied leaders and President Wilson elevated Marshal Ferdinand Foch to the post of supreme commander five days later, and Pershing offered his four divisions for use anywhere on the front. The Germans renewed their offensive against the British in early April, captured enormous quantities of booty and 60,000 prisoners—but failed to break the British lines. The German forces then turned hard against the French in May and pushed to Château-Thierry on the Marne, only fifty miles from Paris. Foch sent the American Second Division and several regiments of marines to bolster French colonial troops in this sector, and American troops for the first time participated in an important way. For most of June, they pushed the Germans back across the Marne at Château-Thierry and cleared the enemy out of Belleau Wood.

THE LAST GREAT DRIVE

The German General Staff began its last great drive—to break through the Marne pocket between Rheims and Soissons and reach Paris—in mid-July 1918. Some 85,000 Americans were engaged in this battle. The German thrust was quickly parried, and the force of the German drive was spent. Foch then began a counter-offensive against the weak western flank of the German line from the Aisne to the Marne, between Rheims and Soissons. In this engagement, which lasted until August 6, eight American divisions and French troops wiped out the German salient. British and French armies, reinforced by new American divisions, shortly afterward began offensives that did not end until they neared the Belgian frontier in November.

American soldiers began to pour into France in large numbers while Foch was mounting his offensive mainly with British and French troops. The American First Army, 550,000 strong, and under Pershing's personal command, was placed in front of the St. Mihiel salient at the southern end of the front in August. The Americans pressed forward in the morning of September 12; within three days they had wiped out the German salient and captured 16,000 prisoners and 443 guns. It was the first independent American operation of the war.

The tide was turning rapidly. Pershing had 1.2 million men, 2,417 guns, and 324 tanks by September 26 and was eager, as he afterward said, "to draw the best German divisions to our front and to consume them." He now hurled his force against the German defenses between Verdun and Sedan. His goal was the Sedan-Mézières railroad, the main supply line for the German forces in this sector. Both sides threw every available man into the battle that raged all during October. The German lines began to crumble on November 1; Americans reached the outskirts of Sedan and cut the Sedan-Mézières railroad on November 7. The American victory in this so-called Meuse-Argonne offensive destroyed a major portion of the German defenses and, coupled with British and French successes in the central and northern sectors, brought the war to an end.

A Decisive Contribution

Americans tempted to exaggerate their country's contribution to the victory will be less inclined to boast when they recall that only 112,432 Americans died while in service, as compared with 1.7 million Russians, 1.4 million Frenchmen, and 900,000 Britons. Belated though it was, the American contribution came in the nick of time to enable the Allies to withstand the last great German assault. On April 1, 1918, at the beginning of the German drive and before the American buildup in France, the Germans had a superiority of 324,000 infantrymen on the western front. By June American reinforcements gave the Allies a majority in manpower. By November the Allied preponderance was more than 600,000 men, enough to overwhelm the German defenses. Americans could rightly say, therefore, that their contribution had at least been decisive.

ON THE SEAS

As U-boats set out in February 1917 to destroy all seaborne commerce, the most dangerous threat to the Allied cause came first not on land but on the seas. The German Admiralty had calculated that sinkings at the rate of 600,000 tons a month would bring England to her knees within six months, and it seemed for a time that the promise of the U-boat champions would be fulfilled. All told, submarines destroyed more than 6.5 million tons of shipping during 1917, while all American, Allied, and neutral shipyards combined built only 2.7 million tons. "They will win, unless we can stop these losses—and stop them soon," Admiral Jellicoe, first sea lord of the admiralty, told the American liaison admiral in London, William S. Sims, in mid-April 1917.

The adoption of the war resolution found the American navy ready and eager to join the battle. Secretary Josephus Daniels and his staff conferred with British and French admirals in April 1917 and mapped out a preliminary division of duty. The American navy would defend and patrol the western hemisphere, while the British fleet would carry the brunt of the antisubmarine campaign in waters around the British Isles with what help the American navy could spare. American assistance was not long in coming. The first six destroyers reached Queenstown, Ireland, in early May; there were thirty-five American destroyers stationed at that base by July; and 383 American craft were overseas by the end of the war.

BRINGING THE U-BOATS UNDER CONTROL

The British system of defense against submarines in April 1917 consisted of dispersing sea traffic widely and then channeling merchant ships through heavily patrolled waters around the British Isles. The system created a positive deathtrap for merchantmen, as there simply were not enough ships to patrol the area. To the obvious alternative—the convoy system—British naval planners and masters of merchant ships objected, arguing that convoys were slow and merchant ships could not stay in formation. But, as the submarine toll mounted, a minority in the British Admiralty joined Secretary Daniels and Admiral

Sims in virtually demanding the use of convoys. Even after the feasibility of the plan had been demonstrated in the latter part of May 1917, the British Admiralty contended that it did not have enough warships to use the system generally. The American reinforcement of destroyers turned the tide in July, however, and convoys for merchant ships were begun. The intensified antisubmarine campaign and inauguration of the convoy system were the two decisive factors that brought the U-boats under control. Shipping losses fell from 881,027 tons in April to half that figure in December 1917; and losses never ran above 200,000 tons a month after April 1918.

TRANSPORTING AND SUPPLYING THE TROOPS

The American navy's next task was to transport and supply the AEF. The Navy Department had seven troop and six cargo ships, totaling 94,000 tons, on hand in July 1917. By November 1918, it had created a Cruiser and Transport Force of 143 vessels, aggregating 3.3 million tons, which carried 911,047 soldiers to France. In addition, every available British transport was pressed into service in the Atlantic Ferry when the need for American manpower grew acute in 1918. Slightly more than 1 million soldiers were carried by British vessels. The troop carriers were so fast and so closely guarded by naval escorts that only two of them, both British vessels, were sunk on the eastbound voyage.

The American navy, with more than 2,000 vessels and 533,000 officers and men in service at the end of the war, had attained unparalleled size and fighting effectiveness. By November 1918, American ships were patrolling the far reaches of the western hemisphere and cooperating with Japanese and British forces in the Far East, while 834 vessels and 200,000 men were either serving in European waters or else transporting troops and supplies to France. By insisting on the adoption of the convoy system, American naval strategists had made a significant contribution to operations that assured an Allied-American victory at sea. By throwing its destroyers into the campaign against the submarines, the American navy perhaps turned the tide against the U-boats. And by transporting nearly half the AEF and almost all the army's cargo to France, the navy made possible the defeat of Germany in 1918 instead of 1920, as the Allied leaders had originally anticipated.

Eugene Debs's Antiwar Speech

EUGENE DEBS

As an outspoken socialist and an exceptional orator, labor leader Eugene Debs had both dedicated followers and vigorous opponents. He boldly dissented America's involvement in World War I, producing some his most eloquent and controversial statements of his political career during the war. In the following selection, excerpted from his famous June 16, 1918, speech before the Ohio Socialist Party in Canton, Ohio, Debs calls for the socialist opposition to the war. He claims that politicians use the guise of patriotism to win support for the war, which he argues is being fought to advance the interests of capitalism and oppress the socialist movement. His antiwar speech provoked a swift reaction from the government: Debs was tried and convicted for violating the Espionage Act by supposedly obstructing American participation in World War I. As a result, he lost his citizenship and served two years of a ten-year prison sentence.

A re we opposed to Prussian militarism? Why, we have been fighting it since the day the Socialist movement was born; and we are going to continue to fight it, day and night, until it is wiped from the face of the earth. Between us there is no truce—no compromise.

A LITTLE HISTORY

But, before I proceed along this line, let me recall a little history, in which I think we are all interested. . . .

Excerpted from Eugene Debs's speech to the Ohio Socialist Party, Canton, Ohio, June 16, 1918.

You remember that, at the close of Theodore Roosevelt's second term as President, he went over to Africa to make war on some of his ancestors. You remember that, at the close of his expedition, he visited the capitals of Europe; and that he was wined and dined, dignified and glorified by all the Kaisers and Czars and Emperors of the Old World. He visited Potsdam while the Kaiser [German Emperor Wilhelm II] was there; and, according to the accounts published in the American newspapers, he and the Kaiser were soon on the most familiar terms. They were hilariously intimate with each other, and slapped each other on the back. After Roosevelt had reviewed the Kaiser's troops, according to the same accounts, he became enthusiastic over the Kaiser's legions and said: "If I had that kind of an army, I could conquer the world." He knew the Kaiser then just as well as he knows him now. He knew that he was the Kaiser, the Beast of Berlin. And yet, he permitted himself to be entertained by that Beast of Berlin; had his feet under the mahogany of the Beast of Berlin; was cheek by jowl with the Beast of Berlin. And, while Roosevelt was being entertained royally by the German Kaiser, that same Kaiser was putting the leaders of the Socialist Party in jail for fighting the Kaiser and the Junkers of Germany. Roosevelt was the guest of honor in the white house of the Kaiser, while the Socialists were in the jails of the Kaiser for fighting the Kaiser. Who then was fighting for democracy? Roosevelt? Roosevelt, who was honored by the Kaiser, or the Socialists who were in jail by order of the Kaiser?

BIRDS OF A FEATHER
"Birds of a feather flock together."

When the newspapers reported that Kaiser Wilhelm and ex-President Theodore recognized each other at sight, were perfectly intimate with each other at the first touch, they made the admission that is fatal to the claim of Theodore Roosevelt, that he is the friend of the common people and the champion of democracy; they admitted that they were kith and kin; that they were very much alike; that their ideas and ideals were about the same. If Theodore Roosevelt is the great champion of democracy—the arch foe of autocracy, what business had he as the guest of honor of the Prussian Kaiser? And when he met the Kaiser, and did honor to the Kaiser, under the terms imputed to him, wasn't it pretty strong proof that he himself was a Kaiser at heart? Now, after being the guest of Emperor Wilhelm, the

Beast of Berlin, he comes back to this country, and wants you to send ten million men over there to kill the Kaiser; to murder his former friend and pal. Rather queer, isn't it? And yet, he is the patriot, and we are the traitors. I challenge you to find a Socialist anywhere on the face of the earth who was ever the guest of the Beast of Berlin except as an inmate of his prison—the elder Wilhelm Liebknecht and the younger Karl Liebknecht, the heroic son of his immortal sire.[1]

JUNKERS OF THE UNITED STATES

A little more history along the same line. In 1902 Prince Henry paid a visit to this country. Do you remember him? I do, exceedingly well. Prince Henry is the brother of Emperor Wilhelm. Prince Henry is another Beast of Berlin, an autocrat, an aristocrat, a Junker [a Prussian militarist] of Junkers—very much despised by our American patriots. He came over here in 1902 as the representative of Kaiser Wilhelm; he was received by Congress and by several state legislatures—among others, by the state legislature of Massachusetts, then in session. He was invited there by the capitalist captains of that so-called commonwealth. And when Prince Henry arrived, there was one member of that body who kept his self-respect, put on his hat, and as Henry, the Prince, walked in, that member of the body walked out. And that was James F. Carey, the Socialist member of that body. All the rest—all the rest of the representatives in the Massachusetts legislature—all, all of them—joined in doing honor, in the most servile spirit, to the high representative of the autocracy of Europe. And the only man who left that body, was a Socialist. And yet, and yet they have the hardihood to claim that they are fighting autocracy and that we are in the service of the German government.

A little more history along the same line. I have a distinct recollection of it. It occurred fifteen years ago when Prince Henry came here. All of our plutocracy, all of the wealthy representatives living along Fifth Avenue—all, all of them—threw their palace doors wide open and received Prince Henry with open arms. But they were not satisfied with this; they got down and grovelled in the dust at his feet. Our plutocracy—women and men alike—vied with each other to lick the boots of Prince

---

1. Wilhelm Liebknecht was the leader of a German working class movement during the nineteenth century.

Henry, the brother and representative of the "Beast of Berlin." And still our plutocracy, our Junkers, would have us believe that all the Junkers are confined to Germany. It is precisely because we refuse to believe this that they brand us as disloyalists. They want our eyes focused on the Junkers in Berlin so that we will not see those within our own borders.

I hate, I loathe, I despise Junkers and junkerdom. I have no earthly use for the Junkers of Germany, and not one particle more use for the Junkers in the United States.

THE LAST REFUGE OF THE SCOUNDREL

They tell us that we live in a great free republic; that our institutions are democratic; that we are a free and self-governing people. This is too much, even for a joke. But it is not a subject for levity; it is an exceedingly serious matter.

To whom do the Wall Street Junkers in our country marry their daughters? After they have wrung their countless millions from your sweat, your agony and your life's blood, in a time of war as in a time of peace, they invest these untold millions in the purchase of titles of broken-down aristocrats, such as princes, dukes, counts and other parasites and no-accounts. Would they be satisfied to wed their daughters to honest workingmen? To real democrats? Oh, no! They scour the markets of Europe for vampires who are titled and nothing else. And they swap their millions for the titles, so that matrimony with them becomes literally a matter of money.

These are the gentry who are today wrapped up in the American flag, who shout their claim from the housetops that they are the only patriots, and who have their magnifying glasses in hand, scanning the country for evidence of disloyalty, eager to apply the brand of treason to the men who dare to even whisper their opposition to Junker rule in the United States. No wonder [eighteenth century English wit] Sam Johnson declared that "patriotism is the last refuge of the scoundrel." He must have had this Wall Street gentry in mind, or at least their prototypes, for in every age it has been the tyrant, the oppressor and the exploiter who has wrapped himself in the cloak of patriotism, or religion, or both to deceive and overawe the people. . . .

AN EXPANDING PHILOSOPHY

Socialism is a growing idea; an expanding philosophy. It is spreading over the entire face of the earth: It is as vain to resist it as it would be to arrest the sunrise on the morrow. It is coming, coming, coming all along the line. Can you not see it? If not, I advise you to consult an oculist. There is certainly something the matter with your vision. It is the mightiest movement in the history of mankind. What a privilege to serve it! I have regretted a thousand times that I can do so little for the movement that has done so much for me. The little that I am, the little that I am hoping to be, I owe to the Socialist movement. It has given me my ideas and ideals; my principles and convictions, and I would not exchange one of them for all of [Standard Oil Company Founder and tycoon] John D. Rockefeller's bloodstained dollars. It has taught me how to serve—a lesson to me of priceless value. It has taught me the ecstasy in the handclasp of a comrade. It has enabled me to hold high communion with you, and made it possible for me to take my place side by side with you in the great struggle for the better day; to multiply myself over and over again, to thrill with a freshborn manhood; to feel life truly worthwhile; to open new avenues of vision; to spread out glorious vistas; to know that I am kin to all that throbs; to be class-conscious, and to realize that, regardless of nationality, race, creed, color or sex, every man, every woman who toils, who renders useful service, every member of the working class without an exception, is my comrade, my brother and sister—and that to serve them and their cause is the highest duty of my life.

And in their service I can feel myself expand; I can rise to the stature of a man and claim the right to a place on earth—a place where I can stand and strive to speed the day of industrial freedom and social justice.

THE BOLSHEVIKI OF RUSSIA

Yes, my comrades, my heart is attuned to yours. Aye, all our hearts now throb as one great heart responsive to the battle cry of the social revolution. Here, in this alert and inspiring assemblage our hearts are with the Bolsheviki of Russia. Those heroic men and women, those unconquerable comrades have by their incomparable valor and sacrifice added fresh luster to the fame of the international movement. Those Russian comrades of ours have made greater sacrifices, have suffered more, and have shed more heroic blood than any like number of men and women anywhere on earth; they have laid the foundation of the first real democracy that ever drew the breath of life in this world. And the very first act of the triumphant Russian revolution was to proclaim a state of peace with all mankind, coupled with a fervent moral appeal, not to kings, not to emperors, rulers or diplomats but to the people of all nations. Here we have the very breath of democracy, the quintessence of the dawning freedom. The Russian revolution proclaimed its glorious triumph in its ringing and inspiring appeal to the peoples of all the earth. In a humane and fraternal spirit new Russia, emancipated at last from the curse of the centuries, called upon all nations engaged in the frightful war, the Central Powers as well as the Allies, to send representatives to a conference to lay down terms of peace that should be just and lasting. Here was the supreme opportunity to strike the blow to make the world safe for democracy. Was there any response to that noble appeal that in some day to come will be written in letters of gold in the history of the world? Was there any response whatever to that appeal for universal peace? No, not the slightest attention was paid to it by the Christian nations engaged in the terrible slaughter.

THE CZAR AND HIS ROTTEN BUREAUCRACY

It has been charged that [Bolsheviks] Lenin and Leon Trotsky and the leaders of the revolution were treacherous, that they made a traitorous peace with Germany. Let us consider that proposition briefly. At the time of the revolution Russia had been three years in the war. Under the Czar she had lost more than four million of her ill-clad, poorly-equipped, half-starved soldiers, slain outright or disabled on the field of battle. She was absolutely bankrupt. Her soldiers were mainly without arms. This was what was bequeathed to the revolution by the Czar and his regime; and for this condition Lenin and Trotsky were not responsible, nor the Bolsheviki. For this appalling state of affairs the Czar and his rotten bureaucracy were solely responsible. When the Bolsheviki came into power and went through the archives they found and exposed the secret treaties—the treaties that were made between the Czar and the French government, the British government and the Italian government, proposing, after the victory was achieved, to dismember the German Empire and destroy the Central Powers. These treaties have never been denied nor repudiated. Very little has been said about them in the American press. I have a copy of these treaties, showing that the purpose of the Allies is exactly the purpose of the Central Powers, and that is the conquest and spoilation of the weaker nations that has always been the purpose of war.

FOR CONQUEST AND PLUNDER

Wars throughout history have been waged for conquest and plunder. In the Middle Ages when the feudal lords who inhabited the castles whose towers may still be seen along the Rhine concluded to enlarge their domains, to increase their power, their prestige and their wealth they declared war upon one another. But they themselves did not go to war any more than the modern feudal lords, the barons of Wall Street go to war. The feudal barons of the Middle Ages, the economic predecessors of the capitalists of our day, declared all wars. And their miserable serfs fought all the battles. The poor, ignorant serfs had been taught to revere their masters; to believe that when their masters declared war upon one another, it was their patriotic duty to fall upon one another and to cut one another's throats for the profit and glory of the lords and barons who held them in contempt. And that is war in a nutshell. The master class has always declared the wars; the subject class has always fought the battles. The master class has had all to gain and nothing to lose, while the subject class has had nothing to gain and all to lose—especially their lives.

They have always taught and trained you to believe it to be your patriotic duty to go to war and to have yourselves slaughtered at their command. But in all the history of the world you, the people, have never had a voice in declaring war, and strange as it certainly appears, no war by any nation in any age has ever been declared by the people.

And here let me emphasize the fact—and it cannot be repeated too often—that the working class who fight all the battles, the working class who make the supreme sacrifices, the working class who freely shed their blood and furnish the corpses, have never yet had a voice in either declaring war or making peace. It is the ruling class that invariably does both. They alone declare war and they alone make peace.

> Yours not to reason why;
> Yours but to do and die.

That is their motto and we object on the part of the awakening workers of this nation.

If war is right let it be declared by the people. You who have your lives to lose, you certainly above all others have the right to decide the momentous issue of war or peace. . . .

You need at this time especially to know that you are fit for something better than slavery and cannon fodder. You need to know that you were not created to work and produce and impoverish yourself to enrich an idle exploiter. You need to know that you have a mind to improve, a soul to develop, and a manhood to sustain.

You need to know that it is your duty to rise above the animal plane of existence. You need to know that it is for you to know something about literature and science and art. You need to know that you are verging on the edge of a great new world. You need to get in touch with your comrades and fellow workers and to become conscious of your interests, your powers and your possibilities as a class. You need to know that you belong to the great majority of mankind. You need to know that as long as you are ignorant, as long as you are indifferent, as long as you are apathetic, unorganized and content, you will remain exactly where you are. You will be exploited; you will be degraded, and you will have to beg for a job. You will get just enough for your slavish toil to keep you in working order, and you will be looked down upon with scorn and contempt by the very parasites that live and luxuriate out of your sweat and unpaid labor. . . .

THE MOST IMPORTANT CHANGE

To turn your back on the corrupt Republican Party and the still more corrupt Democratic Party—the gold-dust lackeys of the ruling class counts for still more after you have stepped out of those popular and corrupt capitalist parties to join a minority party that has an ideal, that stands for a principle, and fights for a cause. This will be the most important change you have ever made and the time will come when you will thank me for having made the suggestion. It was the day of days for me. I remember it well. It was like passing from midnight darkness to the noontide light of day. It came almost like a flash and found me ready. It must have been in such a flash that great, seething, throbbing Russia, prepared by centuries of slavery and tears and martyrdom, was transformed from a dark continent to a land of living light. . . .

The government is now operating its railroads for the more effective prosecution of the war. Private ownership has broken down utterly and the government has had to come to the rescue. We have always said that the people ought to own the railroads and operate them for the benefit of the people. We advocated that twenty years ago. But the capitalists and their hench-men emphatically objected. "You have got to have brains to run the railroads," they tauntingly retorted. Well, the other day [William Gibbs] McAdoo, the governor-general of the railroads under government operation; discharged all the high-salaried presidents and other supernumeraries. In other words, he fired the "brains" bodily and yet all the trains have been coming and going on schedule time. Have you noticed any change for the worse since the "brains" are gone? It is a brainless system now, being operated by "hands." But a good deal more efficiently than it had been operated by so-called "brains" before. And this determines infallibly the quality of their vaunted, high-priced capitalist "brains." It is the kind you can get at a reasonable fig-ure at the market place. They have always given themselves credit for having superior brains and given this as the reason for the supremacy of their class. It is true that they have the brains that indicates the cunning of the fox, the wolf, but as for brains denoting real intelligence and the measure of intellectual capacity they are the most woefully ignorant people on earth. Give me a hundred capitalists just as you find them here in Ohio and let me ask them a dozen simple questions about the history of their own country and I will prove to you that they are as ignorant and unlettered as any you may find in the so-called lower class. They know little of history; they are strangers to science; they are ignorant of sociology and blind to art but they know how to exploit, how to gouge, how to rob, and do it with legal sanction. They always proceed legally for the reason that the class which has the power to rob upon a large scale has also the power to control the government and legalize their rob-bery. I regret that lack of time prevents me from discussing this phase of the question more at length.

PATRIOTIC DUTY

They are continually talking about your patriotic duty. It is not *their* but *your* patriotic duty that they are concerned about. There is a decided difference. Their patriotic duty never takes them to the firing line or chucks them into the trenches.

And now among other things they are urging you to "culti-vate" war gardens, while at the same time a government war report just issued shows that practically 52 percent of the arable, tillable soil is held out of use by the landlords, speculators and profiteers. They themselves do not cultivate the soil. They could not if they would. Nor do they allow others to cultivate it. They keep it idle to enrich themselves, to pocket the millions of dollars of unearned increment. Who is it that makes this land valuable while it is fenced in and kept out of use? It is the people. Who pockets this tremendous accumulation of value? The landlords. And these landlords who toil not and spin not are supreme among American "patriots."

In passing I suggest that we stop a moment to think about the term "landlord." "LANDLORD!" Lord of the Land! The lord of the land is indeed a superpatriot. This lord who practically owns the earth tells you that we are fighting this war to make the world safe for democracy—he who shuts out all humanity from his private domain; he who profiteers at the expense of the people who have been slain and mutilated by multiplied thousands, under pretense of being the great American patriot. It is he, this identical patriot who is in fact the archenemy of the people; it is he that you need to wipe from power. It is he who is a far greater menace to your liberty and your well-being than the Prussian Junkers on the other side of the Atlantic ocean. . . .

POLITICAL AND INDUSTRIAL ACTION

Now what you workers need is to organize, not along craft lines but along revolutionary industrial lines. All of you workers in a given industry, regardless of your trade or occupation, should belong to one and the same union.

Political action and industrial action must supplement and sustain each other. You will never vote the Socialist republic into existence. You will have to lay its foundations in industrial organization. The industrial union is the forerunner of industrial democracy. In the shop where the workers are associated is where industrial democracy has its beginning. Organize according to your industries! Get together in every department of industrial service! United and acting together for the common good your power is invincible. . . .

When we unite and act together on the industrial field and when we vote together on election day we shall develop the supreme power of the one class that can and will bring permanent peace to the world. We shall then have the intelligence, the courage and the power for our great task. In due time industry will be organized on a cooperative basis. We shall conquer the public power. We shall then transfer the title deeds of the railroads, the telegraph lines, the mines, mills and great industries to the people in their collective capacity; we shall take possession of all these social utilities in the name of the people. We shall then have industrial democracy. We shall be a free nation whose government is of and by and for the people.

And now for all of us to do our duty! The clarion call is ringing in our ears and we cannot falter without being convicted of treason to ourselves and to our great cause.

Do not worry over the charge of treason to your masters, but be concerned about the treason that involves yourselves. Be true to yourself and you cannot be a traitor to any good cause on earth.

The Sun of Socialism Is Rising

Yes, in good time we are going to sweep into power in this nation and throughout the world. We are going to destroy all enslaving and degrading capitalist institutions and re-create them as free and humanizing institutions. The world is daily changing before our eyes. The sun of capitalism is setting; the sun of socialism is rising. It is our duty to build the new nation and the free republic. We need industrial and social builders. We Socialists are the builders of the beautiful world that is to be. We are all pledged to do our part. We are inviting—aye challenging you this afternoon in the name of your own manhood and womanhood to join us and do your part.

In due time the hour will strike and this great cause triumphant —the greatest in history—will proclaim the emancipation of the working class and the brotherhood of all mankind.

THE INFLUENZA EPIDEMIC HITS AMERICA

A.A. HOEHLING

Although it vanished as quickly as it appeared, the influenza epidemic of 1918 claimed the lives of half a million Americans and twenty-one million lives worldwide—twice the overall death toll of the First World War. In the United States, the first outbreak of the virus occurred in the spring of 1918 at Fort Riley, Kansas, infecting one hundred men in less than a day. By the fall, the epidemic had the nation it its deadly grip, and thousands of its victims died on a weekly basis. In the following excerpt, A.A. Hoehling recounts how the infection hit Massachusetts, Michigan, Oregon, and other states. He contends that the epidemic did not leave small towns and remote areas untouched, killing young and old, patient and caretaker, alike. A.A. Hoehling is the author of *Lonely Command*, *The Fierce Lambs*, and *The Great Epidemic*, from which this excerpt is taken.

While Spanish influenza shared the blind wantonness of a forest fire, it also had a seemingly directed venom and often hit where it could be the least substantially withstood.

The infection sought out for its own an increasingly great number of pregnant women, suffocating them as they struggled with their uncustomary, heavy burden. It felled young mothers —thirty-six in one New Hampshire town alone. Fathers under forty years of age were stricken. The stronger the man, seemingly the more rapid was his total physical collapse.

"The husky male," observed Dr. Victor C. Vaughan, now acting Surgeon General of the Army since Dr. William Crawford Gorgas had sailed for France, "either made a speedy and rather abrupt recovery or was likely to die. Nature overdoes the resistance, kills the invading organisms too rapidly and sets free such an amount of poison that death occurs . . . Infection, like war, kills the young, vigorous, robust adults."

A CHEERLESS SUNDAY

Boston had spent a cheerless Sunday, this last one in September. Church doors were closed. Their bells were silent, though they might appropriately have tolled in mourning. Motorists, to conserve gasoline and discourage fraternizing, had been ordered to keep their automobiles garaged. Boylston Street was strangely deserted, and no one walked along the banks of the Charles River or watched the lonely swans in the Public Garden. The wind whined across Bunker Hill past a familiar monument around which few children would play or adults pause this Sabbath. Boston could have been the community Defoe referred to when he observed, "What a desolate place the city was at that time."

In Winthrop, Massachusetts, police fought to subdue a man crazed with fever. Finally trussed in a straitjacket, he was taken to a hospital. His wife and three children were left abed, too ill to be moved.

ONE FIFTH OF THE CITY

In Brockton, Massachusetts, the flu raged implacably. Its eight thousand cases, nearly one fifth of the city's population, made a total nearly unparalleled throughout the country. More and more schoolrooms were converted into emergency kitchens. More and more volunteers were sought to feed and care for those who suffered through the illness in their own bedrooms. Age barriers were discarded. Old women and old men appeared behind the soup lines, ladles in hand.

Nurses were arriving from distant states and from Canada to help the almost prostrate city. Among their number were Georgena and Winnifred Flemming, sisters from Londonderry, Nova Scotia. At the Brockton Hospital, where the Flemmings went immediately on duty, there was only one intern, Dr. Helen

Haynes. Her male colleagues had gone to war, leaving her with almost around-the-clock responsibilities. There were not only the flu cases, but surgery and the routine assortment of medical ailments, as well as accident patients.

In its cruelty, the disease did not spare doctor or nurse. Two nurses died this Sunday evening at the Brockton Hospital: Gladys Clark, a twenty-five-year-old student within three weeks of graduation, and Julia Murley, night supervisor. By Monday noon, seventeen patients had succumbed at the same hospital. In alarm, Mayor Gleason called Boston to request the services of state guardsmen.

Harvard opened for its fall term among emergency tents spread on the city's banks. Most of the students kept to the Yard.

CHECKMATED BY THE EPIDEMIC

Into Gloucester, Massachusetts, harbor limped the fishing schooner *Athlete*, appearing as though it had sailed from out of the ghostly pages of *The Ancient Mariner*.[1] She was almost a derelict, with her entire crew suddenly, desperately stricken. One member, Frank Poole, was dead. The picturesque fishing port was more effectively checkmated by the epidemic than it had been by winter ice storms and blizzards. Admissions overflowed the modest new Addison Gilbert Hospital, and tents were spread across its broad lawns.

"The whole city is stricken," wrote Lydia Griffin of Gloucester's District Nursing Association. "No help is available from the other cities, and as one of our nurses is also ill with it, it leaves Miss Thomas and Miss Riley to do it all. I called for volunteers who had taken the nursing course and only one was willing to report for duty this afternoon.

"The situation is critical, the hospitals are filled, the doctors are ill . . . We were taken quite unawares."

Half the population of Watkins, New York, was prostrate. The town's largest fraternal organization, the Red Men, offered its hall as a hospital. The high school principal put on an apron and became the emergency institution's chief cook.

The much larger community, San Antonio, Texas, was similarly hit; its military neighbor, Fort Sam Houston, had difficulty finding a bugler well enough to sound Reveille—or, for that matter, Retreat, with all its connotations.

1. *The Rime of the Ancient Mariner,* Samuel Taylor Coleridge.

Far to the north, in Michigan's wooded Upper Peninsula, a slight, wiry woman in Luce County was combating the Spanish influenza in a unique way, dictated by the geography of the area. Annie L. Colon, a public health nurse, accompanied by a doctor, used a handcar to reach her patients. With a red oil lantern on the back of the car and a white one as an imperfect headlight, the two, doctor and nurse, pumped the little vehicle's handbar up and down, up and down. Since Annie was a fraction the weight of the doctor, her problem was one of balance: not to be lifted off her feet every time he pumped down.

PENETRATING THE FORESTS

It was the only way to penetrate the dense forests into remote lumber camps. With them, over these logging tracks, went as odd a cargo as was ever carried by a handcar: bottles of aspirin, quinine, cough syrup, whiskey, gin and rum, milk cans sloshing with soup, baskets of bread, blankets, bedsheets and even baby toys. If the pair set out at 4 A.M., they could reach the first patients shortly after dawn. It was frosty at that hour, but doctor and nurse worked so unremittingly that they were soon forced to remove overcoats. Nurse Colon wrote to the State Health Department in Lansing, Michigan:

> We have had a terrible time in this county, losing 100 people or one person out of every 50. . . . I worked with Dr. Perry, our health officer, going to the logging camps, in the hospital, in the homes, wherever the need was greatest at the time. We all worked day and night, hardly taking time to eat.

> Some of our patients lived miles back in the woods; not even a road could reach them, but the train could, so we had to go after them in handcars, and so saved many a life.

> We hitched a flat-car to a handcar with wire, put a board floor on, mattresses over that, plenty of covers and a canvas to cover the top and break the wind, and we carried the patients 15 or more miles to a decent bed and a chance to live.

> We rode 20 and 30 miles at night through the deepest woods and over the roughest roads to camps, and many times we would find 30 or 40 cases, sometimes

10 people all huddled together fully drest in a tiny log cabin, probably all in two beds and all with fevers over 104°.

On long trips we had one doctor, a driver, one helper and myself, and we just worked and instructed and showed those among them who could help what to do, when we had to leave . . . Everybody worked hard and long with unselfish spirit.

Whiskey proved effective medicine for the lumberjacks. Bottle in hand, they curled up under their blankets, confident of being cured.

DISPROPORTIONATE SEVERITY

Newberry, the county seat [of Luce], was a ghost town. Even the hotel had been turned into a hospital. The lack, as elsewhere, was of doctors and nurses. One social worker who had been dispatched from Lansing aroused the ire of citizens who charged that he had done "little except give the local people hell for not making out daily reports when they were already dead on their feet." Across Lake Michigan, taps had been sounded for 489 sailors at the Great Lakes Naval Training Station, though the doctors believed the rate was downward. Nonetheless, one fourth of the 45,000 men stationed there were ill.

In Chicago, an Influenza Commission had just been created. The city's West Side Hospital was attacked with disproportionate severity. At least twenty-five of its nurses were now bedded with the fever. Dr. C. St. Clair Drake, Director of the State Department of Public Health, ordered all hospital attendants to wear masks. He hoped this expedient would insure against repetition of the West Side Hospital's crippling experience.

In suburban Glencoe and Winnetka, Illinois, soldiers of the Home Guard patrolled closed schoolyards, as well as the padlocked saloons and movie theaters. Bulletins apprising the citizenry of the rapidly changing situation were printed each morning and distributed by the Boy Scouts.

THE BACTERIAL TIDE

How to stem this bacterial tide? Advice poured into the Surgeon General's office, to the White House, to the Public Health Service, to Congressmen and to every daily or weekly newspaper in America.

Take two pieces of flannel each 12 × 14 inches [wrote J.J.C. Elliott, Former Superintendent of the Methodist Hospital in Los Angeles], sprinkle over one or two of the small packages of wormwood purchased from drug stores usually for ten cents. Lay the other over the sprinkled wormwood and stitch around the edges and quilt them across each way so the wormwood may be held evenly over the entire bag. Place one of these bags in vinegar as hot as it can possibly be wrung from the vinegar and place the bag over the chest of the patient, covering the flannel with bed clothing.

SOUGHT OUT IN ISOLATION

In Seattle, policemen were ordered to wear masks at all times. Citizens must don them in order to ride the public transit. Oregon was confronted with medical challenges for which there was little precedent: sick sheepherders. It was bewildering to rationalize how the flu had sought them out in their isolation, and it was yet more vexing to treat them. A public health nurse at Denio, Oregon, wrote headquarters of her special problems:

Our patients are mostly families of sheepherders; they live in miserable cabins scattered in most inaccessible places, a house to a hill and each hill from 12 to 15 miles apart. There is no food, no bedding and absolutely no conception of the first principles of hygiene, sanitation or nursing care.

I have taken over the hotel as a hospital and the Big Boss, who employs the sheepherders, is having all who are not too ill to be moved brought in here.

The men are willing, some are intelligent, but most are sick, and if it were not for the grit and brains of the nurses who have been working here before and for the women of the community, God help us!

I am working by fits and starts, as I can snatch a minute off to jot down our needs, hoping that the situation may be clear to you and that you will be able to get us some supplies before we get snowed in for the winter. Our greatest need (next to fruit and malted milk) is feeding cups and drinking tubes, also need lots of gauze and cheesecloth and cotton for pneumonia jackets; also rubber sheeting and quantities of old rags, to be used and burned, also gallons of formaldehyde, if we are to stamp out the disease; everything is thrown on the ground and will thaw out next spring and release all these germs again if we do not take precautions against it.

AMERICA WAS SHAKEN

At Norfolk, Virginia, five thousand sailors were ill. In West Virginia, uncounted thousands of coal miners were absent from the shafts. Coal shortages, at a time when warmth was needed, were coupled with rocketing prices, and there was no ceiling in sight.

Three thousand residents of Wilmington, Delaware, were sick. Delaware College, at nearby Newark, Delaware, sent its few well students home and sealed the campus.

America was shaken. Many who could scarcely remember the last time they went to church now belatedly and passionately beseeched the Lord to spare them. For some there was a lurking suspicion that Judgment Day was near, man having been called to account for his sin and wickedness. "Epidemics," opined the *New York Evening Post*, "are the punishment which nature inflicts for the violation of her laws and ordinances." Others, perhaps mindful of September's last hours, turned to poetry. They would have found these doleful lines of Edgar Allan Poe peculiarly appropriate:

The skies they were ashen and sober;
The leaves they were crispèd and sere—
The leaves they were withering and sere;
It was night in the lonesome October . . .

THE TREATY OF VERSAILLES AND THE LEAGUE OF NATIONS

THOMAS C. REEVES

Woodrow Wilson's last acts as president mirrored his relentless, if not lofty, idealism. When a crippled Germany sought an end to World War I through an armistice in 1918, Wilson viewed the peace deliberations in Paris, France—which included delegates from Germany and the majority of the Allied nations—as an opportunity to achieve an end to all wars. Despite opposition at home, Wilson attended the conference, which was an unparalleled act of American involvement in foreign policy.

In the following excerpt from his book *Twentieth-Century America: A Brief History*, author Thomas C. Reeves contends that the outcome of the peace conference reflected the influence of Wilson's idealist goal for peace: The terms of the Treaty of Versailles were less vengeful against Germany than anticipated and included Wilson's proposal for a League of Nations Covenant, an international organization designed to prevent future wars by establishing open, just, and cooperative relations between the nations of the world. However, Reeves claims Wilson's unwillingness to compromise the conditions of the Treaty with his opponents in Congress prevented the United States from joining the League of Nations. According to the author, Wilson's opponents rejected Article X of the League of Nations because it called for unprecedented American engagement in foreign relations, which Wilson strongly desired. The absence of the United States in the League, asserts Reeves, weakened its effectiveness.

Many put their trust in Woodrow Wilson and the United States to heal their wounds, create a just peace, and put an end to all war. Wilson had brought America into the conflict declaring the highest principles, and throughout 1918 he had won the hearts of millions in a series of speeches laden with lofty idealism about the peace that was to follow. Indeed, this oratory was instrumental in persuading the German people to seek an armistice.

WILSONIAN IDEALISM

If Wilson had consulted with the Allies before writing his war message he would have discovered that they did not accept much of his idealistic rhetoric. This important truth became apparent in late 1917 when the Bolshevik government of Russia began disclosing secret treaties among the Allies for dividing the colonies of their enemies after the war. Wilson was determined to prevent such traditional statecraft and to create a peace in line with his own goals.

After attempting unsuccessfully to work out a joint statement with the Allies, he took the initiative and became the self-appointed spokesman of the war aims. With the British and French relatively silent on the issue, people assumed that the president was speaking for them as well as the United States. Wilson assumed his new role confident that he could control the British and French after the war and with a certainty that he represented the aspirations of most men and women everywhere.

On January 8, 1918, in a speech before Congress, Wilson outlined what he said were America's war aims. These Fourteen Points contained several guidelines for the future handling of international affairs, including open covenants instead of secret treaties, freedom of the seas in peace and war, the removal of economic barriers between nations, a reduction of national armaments, and an impartial adjustment of colonial claims. The most important point of all, to Wilson, was the fourteenth: the call for a "general association of nations" to guarantee world peace.

The British and French were delighted that Wilson's pronouncements helped bring an end to the war. Even before the combat stopped, however, they were quietly preparing to resist the peace plans of their American "associate." Having suffered mightily for four years, they were eager to wring as much out of their enemies as possible. At no time were the Allied leaders genuinely committed to Wilsonian idealism.

REPUBLICAN OPPOSITION

In the spring of 1918 the GOP launched an intensive campaign to win the fall congressional elections. Despite a general reluctance to attack the chief executive during wartime, several leading Republicans, including Theodore Roosevelt, former President Taft, and Senator Henry Cabot Lodge, made angry speeches against the president. In late October Wilson fired back with a personal appeal to the American people to vote for Democrats as an expression of confidence in his leadership "at home and abroad." Republicans, who had loyally supported the administration's wartime programs, were infuriated by this partisan tactic and stepped up their attacks. The Fourteen Points and the League of Nations were favorite targets.

On election day Republicans captured the Senate by a two-seat margin, making Senator Lodge chairman of the Foreign Relations Committee. They gained twenty-five seats in the House and now outnumbered Democrats 237 to 190. The returns largely reflected unhappiness about big government, high taxes, low wheat prices, the Eighteenth Amendment, and violations of civil liberties. The election was widely interpreted throughout the country and overseas, however, as a public repudiation of the president.

When Wilson made the stunning announcement on November 18 that he would personally attend the Peace Conference at Paris, many observers thought he would be an ineffective spokesman in light of his rebuke by the electorate. Theodore Roosevelt roared, "Our allies and Mr. Wilson himself should all understand that Mr. Wilson has no authority whatever to speak for the American people at this time." Republican leaders in general agreed, declaring their firm opposition to Wilson's postwar aims and activities.

No president had ever traveled to Europe while in office, and even some Democrats were opposed to this innovation in American foreign policy. Allied leaders, moreover, subtly objected to Wilson's presence at the peace table because they feared he would demand a "soft peace" and block their efforts to grab the spoils of war. But Wilson dismissed all objections. Always a rather rigid and self-righteous man, he now saw himself as an apostle of a new world order, a prophet with a burning moral mission to create a just peace and end war forever. This supremely important task, he believed, required his personal presence at Paris.

Republican hostility toward the president intensified when he selected four men to join him on the Peace Commission. Only one, career diplomat Henry White, was a Republican, and he was a minor figure in the party. It was undoubtedly a mistake not to appoint at least one distinguished Republican to the commission in order to create bipartisan support for the momentous decisions that lay ahead. But Wilson had long disliked and distrusted the opposition party and had deeply resented the recent campaign attacks. The logical choice would have been Senator Lodge, but he and the president were personal as well as political enemies. On December 4, 1918, Wilson sailed for Europe convinced that he alone represented the millions in the world crying for peace and justice.

THE PARIS PEACE CONFERENCE

After spending two weeks in France, Wilson made brief visits to England and Italy. Wherever he appeared crowds cheered and wept. In Rome people cried "Viva Wilson, god of peace," and in Milan wounded soldiers attempted to kiss his clothes. The tumultuous ovations further convinced Wilson that the common people of Europe backed his high-minded principles. In fact, the very people who cheered the president were as eager as their leaders to punish Germany severely and to gain as much as possible from the peace talks.

The Peace Conference began its deliberations in mid-January. Hundreds of delegates and experts from twenty-seven nations were on hand (the American contingent alone numbered about 1,300), and some sixty different commissions were created to handle a mountain of largely technical issues. At first, a Council of Ten, including the United States and the major Allied powers, handled the important decisions. Before long this task was assumed by the Council of Four: Wilson, Georges Clemenceau of France, David Lloyd George of Great Britain, and Vitorrio Orlando of Italy. Orlando represented the weakest of the four powers and had little influence. In April he left the conference in a huff. This meant that three men, often meeting in private, bore the responsibility of restructuring much of the world. It was an ironic ending to a war fought in the name of democracy, and was inconsistent with the goal of the Fourteen Points to put an end to secret diplomacy.

Wilson worked extremely hard at Paris to master every detail of the complex issues brought to the peace table and was the best prepared of the Big Four. Although he did not dominate the talks as he had hoped, he was able within the first five weeks to score two important victories: adoption of the mandate principle and the incorporation of the League of Nations Covenant in the peace treaty.

THE MANDATE PLAN

The mandate plan was a compromise. Germany was stripped of all its colonies in Africa and the Far East. Rather than being parceled out among the victors, however, these territories were to be held as mandates by certain nations under the supervision of the League of Nations. This arrangement was more in harmony with the Fourteen Points than naked annexation, it offered eventual self-rule to the people of the colonies, and it provided the league with some immediate duties. Still, critics later noted that the major powers wound up possessing most of what they had sought to own and that the mandates bore a close relation to the terms of the dozen or so secret treaties the Allied powers had made among themselves during the war.

During April the Council of Four hammered out the specifics of the treaty. Wilson fought bitterly with Clemenceau, who was determined to defend French security and was committed to the return of balance-of-power politics. Compromises were soon reached, however, forced in large part by deteriorating economic and political conditions throughout the world. Germans were starving, for example, central Europe was in chaos, and Bolsheviks were winning the civil war in Russia and communism was spreading into the West.

Article 231 of the Treaty of Versailles, the "war guilt clause," declared that Germany and its allies were responsible for the war and all the losses suffered by the Allied and associated nations. Germany was required to sign a "blank check" by agreeing to pay whatever reparation figure an expert commission would later arrive at, a sum that would include all civilian damages and future Allied war pensions. (The final tally, established in 1921, was $33 billion, far beyond anything Germany could pay.) Among other penalties, Germany also lost its colonies, was stripped of Alsace-Lorraine in the west and Polish territories in the east, and was virtually disarmed.

The treaty fell far short of guaranteeing the "self-determination" of peoples. Italy, for example, was given a section of the Austrian South Tyrol containing more than 200,000

Austrian-Germans. The four new states of central Europe—
Poland, Czechoslovakia, Rumania, and Yugoslavia—incorporated an assortment of nationalities. Mandates ignored the
wishes of those inhabiting the former German colonies. The
treaty also saddened Wilsonians by omitting references to free
trade, freedom of the seas, "open covenants openly arrived at,"
and disarmament. . . .

An Extraordinarily Moderate Document

Considering the passions of those first months after armistice,
the Treaty of Versailles was an extraordinarily moderate document. Wilson's presence among the peacemakers undoubtedly
kept the terms of the agreement from being far more vengeful
than they were.

Wilson was keenly aware of the discrepancies between the
Fourteen Points and the treaty but was confident that the document's inadequacies would be ironed out by the new League
of Nations. He returned home certain that the American people
would back his efforts at the peace table and embrace their new
international responsibilities.

The president was physically and mentally exhausted, and
often moody and irritable. He had been forced to compromise
on numerous issues during the past several months in order to
create the League and was unwilling to give further ground.
"Anyone who opposes me . . . I'll crush!," he told a Democratic
Senator. "I shall consent to nothing. *The Senate must take its medicine.*" Wilson biographer Arthur Link later revealed that Wilson suffered from serious arterial disease at the time. "In his
normal, healthy state, Wilson would have found compromise
with the large group of moderate Republicans."

The Ratification Struggle

Among other things, Article X of the League of Nations
Covenant was certain to face stiff opposition. By it each member nation promised to protect "the territorial integrity and existing political independence" of all other members. Collective
security was to replace balance of power, and the United States
would be committed to a fully active participation in international affairs for the first time.

There were many other reasons for opposing the treaty and
the Covenant. At the core of much of the opposition, however,
was political partisanship. Republicans, looking ahead to the

1920 elections, were determined to discredit the President.

At the same time, Lodge realized that Wilson had a great deal of support across the country. Thirty-three governors and thirty-two state legislatures had endorsed the League. A poll of newspaper editors revealed an overwhelming majority in favor of American membership in the international body. To give the antiratification forces more time to mobilize public opinion against the treaty, Lodge used the Foreign Relations Committee to stall consideration of the document. After nearly two months had passed, and efforts to win over GOP senators had failed, Wilson announced that he would take his case directly to the American people.

On September 3, 1919, the President embarked on a speaking tour through the Midwest and Far West. In twenty-two days he traveled more than 8,000 miles and delivered thirty-seven addresses to cheering crowds that grew larger and more enthusiastic the farther west he went. Now 63, Wilson had begun this exhausting journey against the advice of his physician. The strains of the presidency and a severe case of influenza suffered while he was in France had severely taxed his strength.

What drove him on was the belief that he could rally the public and force senators to accept the treaty as he had handed it to them. On September 25, in Pueblo, Colorado, his health gave out and the remainder of the tour was canceled. Back in Washington, on October 2, he suffered a near fatal stroke that paralyzed his left side.

Wilson was totally disabled for almost two months, and he would never again be able to fulfill all of his presidential duties. His mind was undamaged, but the illness permanently upset his emotional balance. Cabinet members ran the government. The First Lady, Edith Galt Wilson, covered up the extent of her husband's illness and thwarted suggestions that he resign. As he slowly regained his strength, Wilson grew increasingly certain that he was locked in combat with the forces of evil.

LODGE'S RESERVATIONS

In early November Senator Lodge presented for his committee a series of fourteen reservations to the treaty—a number designed to match Wilson's Fourteen Points. The second reservation was the most significant, declaring that the United States would not assume obligations under Article X of the Covenant without a joint resolution of Congress. From his sickbed, Wilson rejected numerous appeals to compromise and demanded that Democrats oppose all reservations. On November 19, following a bitterly partisan struggle, the Senate defeated the treaty with and without reservations. Still, the votes revealed that nearly four-fifths of the senators favored the league in some form.

Pleas for compromise poured into the White House, and the British government said publicly that the Allies would be willing to accept the reservations if that was the price for bringing the United States into the league. But Wilson, like the haughty Senator Lodge, refused to budge. On July 21, 1921, a joint resolution of Congress simply declared the war at an end.

The failure by the president, Senator Lodge, and a number of senators from both parties to place the welfare of the nation and the world ahead of their political goals and personality conflicts blocked what was undoubtedly a desire by the majority of Americans to join the league. The tragic course of events that followed might have been altered had America assumed the international leadership Wilson envisioned. We can never be certain. Without the United States, however, the league proved ineffective, and the ghastly specter of the Second World War was not far away.

THE MAKING OF A RED

ROBERT BENCHLEY

World War I created a climate of mass paranoia in America. Dissenters of the war, capitalism, and democracy were perceived as threats to America's political and social order. Fear of these individuals, called the Red Scare, gripped the country in 1919, spurring anti-radical legislation and the persecution of socialists, Communists, and other "subversives." In the following essay, Robert Benchley satirizes the Red Scare, fictitiously narrating how a man descended from the status of an "eminently safe citizen" to a TNT-toting radical because of overreactions to his innocuous comments on war. His satire reflects the view that the Red Scare was a deleterious, counterproductive phenomenon. Benchley was a noted humorist and drama critic.

Y ou couldn't have asked for anyone more regular than Peters. He was an eminently safe citizen. Although not rich himself, he never chafed under the realization that there were others who possessed great wealth. In fact, the thought gave him rather a comfortable feeling. Furthermore, he was one of the charter members of the war. Long before President Wilson saw the light, Peters was advocating the abolition of German from the public-school curriculum. There was, therefore, absolutely nothing in his record which would in the slightest degree alter the true blue of a patriotic litmus. And he considered himself a liberal when he admitted that there might be something in this man [labor leader Samuel] Gompers, after all. That is how safe he was.

From "The Making of a Red," by Robert Benchley, *Nation*, March 15, 1919.

A TINY SLIP

But one night he made a slip. It was ever tiny a slip, but in comparison with it author Guy de Maupassant's famous piece of string was barren of consequences.[1] Shortly before the United States entered the war, Peters made a speech at a meeting of the Civic League in his home town. His subject was "Interurban Highways: Their Development in the Past and Their Possibilities for the Future." So far, 100 percent American. But, in the course of his talk, he happened to mention the fact that war, as an institution, has almost always had an injurious effect on public improvements of all kinds. In fact (and note this well—the government's sleuth in the audience did) he said that, all other things being equal, if he were given his choice of war or peace in the abstract, he would choose peace as a condition under which to live. Then he went on to discuss the comparative values of macadam and wood blocks for paving.

In the audience was a civilian representative of the Military Intelligence Service. He had a premonition that some sort of attempt was going to be made at this meeting of the Civic League to discredit the war and America's imminent participation therein. And he was not disappointed (no Military Intelligence sleuth ever is), for in the remark of Peters, derogatory to war as an institution, his sharp ear detected the accent of the Wilhelmstrasse [German Emperor Wilhelm II].

THE CHILLING HEADLINE

Time went by. The United States entered the war, and Peters bought Liberty Bonds. He didn't join the Army, it is true, but, then, neither did James M. Beck, and it is an open secret that Mr. Beck was for the war. Peters did what a few slangy persons called "his bit," and not without a certain amount of pride. But he did not hear the slow, grinding noise from that district in which are located the mills of the gods. He did not even know that there was an investigation going on in Washington to determine the uses to which German propaganda money had been put. That is, he didn't know it until he opened his newspaper one morning and, with that uncanny precipitation with which a man's eye lights on his own name, discovered that he had been mentioned in the dispatches. At first he thought that it might be an honor list of Liberty Bond holders, but a glance

1. Reference to de Maupassant's short story, "A Piece of String."

at the headline chilled that young hope in his breast. It read as follows:

PRO-GERMAN LIST BARED BY ARMY SLEUTH
Prominent Obstructionists Named at Senate Probe

And then came the list. Peters' eye ran instinctively down to the place where, in what seemed to him to be 24-point Gothic caps, was blazoned the name "Horace W. Peters, Pacifist Lecturer, Matriculated at Germantown (Pa.) Military School." Above his name was that of Emma Goldman, "Anarchist." Below came that of Fritz von Papen, "agent of the Imperial German Government in America," and Jeremiah O'Leary, "Irish and Pro-German Agitator."

Peters was stunned. He telegraphed to his senator at Washington and demanded that the outrageous libel be retracted. He telegraphed to the Military Intelligence office and demanded to know who was the slanderer who had traduced him, and who in h—l this Captain Whatsisname was who had submitted the report. He telegraphed to Secretary Baker and he cabled to the President. And he was informed, by return stagecoach, that his telegrams had been received and would be brought to the attention of the addressees at the earliest possible moment.

Then he went out to look up some of his friends, to explain that there had been a terrible mistake somewhere. But he was coolly received. No one could afford to be seen talking with him after what had happened. His partner merely said "Bad business, Horace. Bad business!" The elevator starter pointed him out to a subordinate, and Peters heard him explain "That's Peters, Horace W. Peters. Did'je see his name in the papers this morning with them other German spies?" At the club, little groups of his friends dissolved awkwardly when they saw him approaching, and, after distant nods, disappeared in an aimless manner. After all, you could hardly blame them.

THE DOUBLE-LEADED EDITORIAL

The next morning the *Tribune* had a double-leaded editorial entitled "Oatmeal," in which it was stated that the disclosures in Washington were revealing the most insidious of all kinds of German propaganda—that disseminated by supposedly respectable American citizens. "It is not a tangible propaganda. It is an emotional propaganda. To the unwary it may resemble real-estate news, or perhaps a patriotic song, but it is the pap of

Prussianism. As an example, we need go no further than Horace W. Peters. Mr. Peters' hobby was interurban highways. A very pretty hobby, Mr. Peters, but it won't do. It won't do." The *Times* ran an editorial saying, somewhere in the midst of a solid slab of type, that no doubt it would soon be found that Mr. Peters nourished Bolshevist sentiments, along with his teammate Emma Goldman. Emma Goldman! How Peters hated that woman! He had once written a letter to this very paper about her, advocating her electrocution.

He dashed out again in a search of someone to whom he could explain. But the editorials had done their work. The doorman at the club presented him with a letter from the House Committee saying that, at a special meeting, it had been decided that he had placed himself in a position offensive to the loyal members of the club and that it was with deep regret that they informed him, etc. As he stumbled out into the street, he heard someone whisper to an out-of-town friend, "There goes Emma Goldman's husband."

As the days went by, things grew unbelievably worse. He was referred to in public meetings whenever an example of civic treachery was in order. A signed advertisement in the newspapers protesting, on behalf of the lineal descendants of the Grand Duke Sergius, against the spread of Bolshevism in northern New Jersey, mentioned a few prominent snakes in the grass, such as Trotzky, Victor Berger, Horace W. Peters, and Emma Goldman.

THE EASY DESCENT

Then something snapped. Peters began to let his hair grow long and neglected his linen. Each time he was snubbed on the street he uttered a queer guttural sound and made a mark in a little book he carried about with him. He bought a copy of "Colloquial Russian at a Glance," and began picking out inflammatory sentences from the *Novy Mir*. His wife packed up and went to stay with her sister when he advocated, one night at dinner, the communization of women. The last prop of respectability having been removed, the descent was easy. Emma Goldman, was it? Very well, then, Emma Goldman it should be! Bolshevist, was he? They had said it! "After all, who is to blame for this?" he mumbled to himself "Capitalism! Militarism! Those Prussians in the Intelligence Department and the Department of Justice! The damnable bourgeoisie who sit back and read their *Times* and their *Tribune* and believe what they read there!" He had tried explanations. He had tried argument. There was only one thing left. He found it on page 112 of a little book of Emma Goldman's that he always carried around with him.

You may have read about Peters the other day. He was arrested, wearing a red shirt over his business cutaway and carrying enough TNT to shift the Palisades back into the Hackensack marshes. He was identified by an old letter in his pocket from Henry Cabot Lodge thanking him for a telegram of congratulation Peters had once sent him on the occasion of a certain speech in the Senate.

The next morning the *Times* said, editorially, that it hoped the authorities now saw that the only way to crush Bolshevism was by the unrelenting use of force.

AN AMERICAN TOWN GREETS PROHIBITION

The Historical Society of Quincy and Adams County, Illinois.

Although alcohol was not officially prohibited until the Eighteenth Amendment was ratified on January 16, 1920, the Volstead Act of November 21, 1918, proclaimed that after June 29, 1919, until the conclusion of America's demobilization in World War I, it would be illegal to manufacture, transport, and sell alcoholic beverages. In the following selection, the Historical Society for Quincy and Adams County, Illinois, recalls the events leading to the enforcement of the Volstead Act in the town of Quincy. It states that Quincy residents greeted prohibition by stocking up on alcohol and congregating in the town's saloons to celebrate the "death of John Barleycorn," a term of endearment for beer. The society claims that most of the town's saloons had shut down by July 1, 1919, proof that the war effort helped to advance the temperance movement.

T he Volstead Act of November 21, 1918, stated that "after June 30, 1919, until the conclusion of the present war and thereafter until the termination of demobilization, the date of which shall be determined and proclaimed by the President of the United States, it shall be unlawful to sell for beverage purposes, any distilled spirits."[1]

It had been done. True, some states were dry, but few thought it ever possible that the entire country would be this way. How

1. Reference to barley, which is brewed to produce beer.

could a man find the "hair of the dog that bit him" (the night before), if he couldn't even find the "dog"!

The Eighteenth Amendment became a part of the Constitution on January 16, 1920, but actual prohibition came through the enforcement of the wartime emergency act more than seven months after the war's end, or on July 1, 1919.

Here in Quincy, Mayor P.J. O'Brien said, "There will be no dram shops in Quincy because no saloon licenses will be issued and all existing licenses will expire July 1." Chief of Police Thomas Ryan said, "There will be no sale of intoxicants after midnight, Monday, June 30." The state's attorney, J. LeRoy Adair, and his assistant, Arthur R. Roy, said, "The law will be rigidly enforced."

Up to eight o'clock Saturday evening, June 28, there was hope that President Woodrow Wilson would act to keep the country from going dry. Then the newspapers posted bulletins saying that the president stated he would not interfere with the wartime prohibition, and all hope faded. The attorney general had advised Wilson that he had no legal power on the ban of liquor. Until demobilization was terminated, Wilson could not act.

The defeat of the Kaiser [German Emperor Wilhelm II] was soon forgotten in the death of King Barleycorn.[1] After July 1 the licenses would be issued by the federal government, not for the sale of the "good stuff," but for soft drinks and near-beer.

STOCK UP!

There was only one thing to do—stock up! There was an estimated fifty thousand gallons of whiskey in the city's wholesale houses. The wholesale houses, J.H. Duker at 323 Hampshire and Siepker's at 319 Hampshire, caught the rush, as did Urban's at 507 Hampshire. Crowds jammed these wholesale liquor firms until midnight and came back on Monday, the last day before the deadline. Hampshire was jammed with cars. Everyone was very serious about his business—there was no joking. None took chances because of the search and seizure law, and each carried his "treasure" home in a suitcase. There were more suitcases to be seen on Hampshire Street than during an Elk's convention!

Ott Urban sold $5500 worth of whiskey to one local man and had an order for $2500 worth from an out-of-town customer. A man walked into Urban's and asked if they had Hermitage whiskey on hand. Thinking he wanted to buy a bottle, Gus Urban replied that they had it. The man ordered 10 cases at $3.50 a quart. Another customer took five thousand dollars worth of whiskey and another three thousand dollars worth.

Duker's sold one man $1500 in gin at $6.50 a bottle. Siepker's said the poorer grades of whiskey were selling for twenty-six dollars a case and the better brands for forty dollars.

Monday, the last day, was like Saturday. The wholesale houses remained open until midnight, with Siepker's cutting the price of Old Taylor from $2.50 to $2.25. Many hoped for more substantial cuts, which didn't materialize. It was said that the whiskey factories in Peoria had enough of the "golden amber" on hand to float a battleship.

Wholesale dealers here shipped a lot of stuff out too in those last days before prohibition became effective. During the two weeks preceding the deadline, the little stern wheel steamboat Keokuk of the Blair White Collar Line, which hauled freight and passengers between Quincy and Burlington, Iowa, transported liquor and beer upriver to the Illinois and Missouri towns it served (Iowa was already dry). On its last run as a legal "rum runner," it did not lay overnight at Keokuk, as it usually did, but pushed upriver to unload the last of its alcoholic cargo at Nauvoo.

LIKE CHRISTMAS EVE

Saturday night, June 28, was like Christmas Eve in Quincy saloons and, for that matter, in most cities and states in the nation, with the exception of those already dry. Men were crying, "It's a long time between drinks, so let's have another." More than thirty-five thousand dollars worth of liquor was sold here on Saturday and perhaps ten thousand worth went "down the hatch." A big sign on Hampshire Street said "it's bone dry after July 1."

Everybody was stocking up. Quincy basements were reported to be booze parlors, although no names were ever printed in the newspapers. Chief Ryan assigned nine officers, instead of the usual four, to business district to keep order. All saloons were ordered to close at midnight.

The old No. 9 Saloon at 526 Hampshire—opened in 1840 by Peter Sengen, then bought by Carl Peine in 1862 and operated by his sons after his death, where the sandwiches were always famous—planned to close.

Col. Henry Hofer, who started working at the No. 9 (or

Apollo Saloon as it was called at one time) at the age of seventeen in 1872, said he would quit bartending. Louis Nebe, who first worked for Gus Roth in the basement saloon on Fifth between Maine and Hampshire and in 1919 worked for Fink's at Sixth and Maine, also announced his plan to quit. He had had it!

Dick's Brewery ran out of beer early in the rush and let their drivers help Ruff. Manny Dick said plans were indefinite for their brewery. It was an orderly crowd for the most part, although as the time to close drew near, the police did get calls to pick up stragglers, which kept the paddy wagons busy. One fight between four men had to be broken up by the arrival of the blue coats in front of the Whig Office.

A touring car was seen near the Hotel Quincy with seventy dozen bottles of beer in the back compartment, plus miscellaneous quarts and gallon jugs. The Golden Gate Saloon of Fred Bickelhaupt, at 116 North Fifth, was the first to run out of liquid refreshments and closed at 10:30 on Monday night. This establishment would remain closed, for the building was to be converted into the Odell Edison Gramophone Store.

When the time came to close the doors at midnight, the White Mule had lost its kick. Some, like Fred Smith, anticipated a good soft drink trade. Al Grimm would run the St. James Bar on Sixth Street. The Hotels of Quincy and Newcomb had ordered fountains and would serve soft drinks.

HERE LIES JOHN BARLEYCORN

Art Hageman's Doc's Place would stay open. Steve Malone of the S & S Bar would try near-beer, as would the Franking House. Charlie Lutenberg, at Sixth and Maine, said he was closing. The next day a sign in a Maine Street drugstore read as follows: "Here lies John Barleycorn. Born B.C. 50,000,000 and died July 1, A.D., 1919." Urban's didn't open until noon, and a sign on the front door of Hagan and Rundle said, "Gone on vacation." The Duker and Siepker wholesale houses were deserted on that first day of prohibition. The blinds were drawn on the windows and a sign said "Dead."

The old No. 9 was empty. Down on the levee all was gloom. The Hasse Bar was open and Harry Woods was working. Both Ruff's and Dick's were working full force, producing beer with 2.75 percent alcoholic content. Only a handful of the 123 saloons in Quincy opened their doors that day. The enthusiasm of the war effort had succeeded in accomplishing what the temperance workers could not. Had this come at a different time, the result might have been a different matter. But in the gigantic effort to control and ration grain during the war, the legislation went through the Congress and was ratified by the states in short order. It would take a depression to rescind it.

THE 1919 WORLD SERIES: BASEBALL'S MOST FAMOUS SCANDAL

CHICAGO HISTORICAL SOCIETY

The upset of the Chicago White Sox against the Cincinnati Reds in the 1919 World Series went down as one of the sport's most famous scandals. Rumors that eight White Sox players had made a deal with a gambler in which they would receive $100,000 if the Sox purposefully lost the series rang true. In the following selection, the Chicago Historical Society (CHS) suggests that troubles within the White Sox franchise contributed to the scheme. The fact that they were poorly paid and divided by jealousies, the society contends, may have compelled the White Sox to fix the 1919 World Series for financial gain. The CHS is a privately endowed, independent institution devoted to collecting, interpreting, and presenting the history of Chicago and Illinois.

The 1919 World Series resulted in the most famous scandal in baseball history. Eight players from the Chicago White Sox (later nicknamed the Black Sox) were accused of throwing the series against the Cincinnati Reds. Details of the scandal and the extent to which each man was involved have always been unclear. It was, however, front-page news across the country and, despite being acquitted of criminal charges, the players were banned from professional baseball for life. The

Excerpted from "The Black Sox," by the Chicago Historical Society, www.chicagohs.org, 1999. Copyright © 1999 by the Chicago Historical Society. Reprinted with permission.

eight men included the great "Shoeless" Joe Jackson; pitchers Eddie Cicotte and Claude "Lefty" Williams; infielders Buck Weaver, Arnold "Chick" Gandil, Fred McMullin, and Charles "Swede" Risberg; and outfielder Oscar "Happy" Felsch.

The White Sox team was formed in 1900 as a franchise of the American League, under the ownership of Charles Comiskey. The Sox were originally called The White Stockings. They shortened the name to White Sox in 1902. In its first year, the team won the league championship. By 1903, the American and National Leagues had agreed to meet in an end-of-the-year play-off, or a "World Series." In 1906, the White Sox won this national championship by defeating the Chicago Cubs four games to two. The next eight years brought a dry spell for the Sox. In many of those years they lost more often than they won.

In 1910, Comiskey built a new ballpark on Chicago's South Side and dedicated himself to building a strong ball club. In 1915, he purchased three star players: outfielder Joe Jackson, second baseman Eddie Collins, and center fielder Happy Felsch. Comiskey, a former first baseman, is also credited with being the first person to train his players to adjust their field positions according to a batter's hitting habits. In 1917, the Sox won the World Series and, managed by William "Kid" Gleason, the 1919 Chicago White Sox had the best record in the American League. Comiskey had succeeded in building one of the most powerful teams in baseball.

AN UNHAPPY TEAM

Despite their many wins on the field, the White Sox were an unhappy team. No club played better in 1919, but few were paid so poorly. Many knowledgeable observers believe that it was Comiskey's stinginess that is largely to blame for the Black Sox scandal: if Comiskey had not grossly underpaid his players and treated them so unfairly, they would never have agreed to throw the Series. Comiskey was able to get away with paying low salaries because of the "reserve clause" in players' contracts. This clause prevented players from changing teams without the permission of the owners. Without a union, the players had no bargaining power.

Comiskey frequently made promises to his players that he had no intention of keeping. He once promised his team a big bonus if they won the pennant. When they did win, the bonus turned out to be a case of cheap champagne. Comiskey even charged his players for laundering their uniforms. In protest, for several weeks the players wore the same increasingly dirty uniforms. Comiskey removed the uniforms from their lockers and fined the players.

To make matters worse, the White Sox players did not get along with each other. Their constant infighting was marked by jealousy and verbal abuse. The team was divided into two cliques, one led by second baseman Eddie Collins and the other by first baseman Chick Gandil. Collins's faction was educated, sophisticated, and able to negotiate salaries as high as $15,000. Gandil's less polished group, who only earned an average of $6,000, bitterly resented the difference.

In 1918, with the country disrupted by World War I, interest in baseball dropped to an all-time low. The 1919 World Series was the first national championship after the war, and baseball and the nation as a whole were back to business as usual. Post-war enthusiasm for baseball took everyone by surprise, and fans eagerly followed the games. National interest in the Series was so high, baseball officials decided to make it a best of nine series, instead of the traditional best of seven.

GAMBLERS

Gamblers were often visibly present at ballparks and the fixing of games had been suspected since the mid-1850s. Rumors circulated that players supplemented their incomes by throwing single games. Several ballplayers had the reputation of working closely with gamblers. A small-time gambler, Joseph Sullivan, allegedly made money on inside tips from Chicago's Chick Gandil. Sullivan's bets were safer when he knew a pitcher or hitter was sick, hurt, or having an off week.

Although gambling was intertwined with baseball long before the eight White Sox were accused of fixing the Series, the number of gamblers at ballparks had dramatically increased by 1919. Ironically, Comiskey posted signs throughout the park declaring, "No Betting Allowed In This Park." Unfortunately for Comiskey, the signs were not enough. Player resentment was high and gamblers' offers, which were sometimes several times a ballplayer's salary, were too tempting to refuse.

THE FIX

While the facts surrounding the throwing of the Series are confusing, people familiar with the case agree Gandil was the ringleader. A few weeks before the 1919 World Series, Gandil approached Sullivan about fixing the Series. He told Sullivan that for $100,000, Gandil and several of his teammates would make sure the White Sox would lose. Gandil was known as a rough character and, at the age of thirty-three, he was getting ready to retire. Before his career ended, he had one last shot to make big money. While Sullivan started raising money, Gandil went to work getting the cooperation of his teammates.

If the gamblers were going to put up $100,000, Gandil needed to ensure that a sufficient number of players were willing to go along with the fix. Two of Chicago's pitchers, Cicotte and Williams (some stories say Williams acted as the liaison between the players and the gamblers), had won fifty-two games between them that season. If he was going to succeed, Gandil needed their participation. Cicotte had his own special grudge against Comiskey and was ready to get even. Comiskey had once promised Cicotte that if he won thirty games, he would receive a $10,000 bonus. When Cicotte won twenty-nine games, Comiskey benched him with the excuse that Cicotte should rest up for the pennant games. Comiskey never gave him the money since he had won only twenty-nine games. Cicotte's personal request, regarding the fix, was $10,000 up front. Williams and Risberg were interested and utility-man McMullin, who overheard Gandil talking to shortstop Risberg, demanded a piece of the action.

Jackson and Weaver are the two players whose involvement in the fix is most disputed. According to Jackson, when Gandil offered him $10,000 for his help in throwing the Series, Jackson turned him down. When Gandil upped the amount to $20,000, Jackson again refused. Gandil supposedly told Jackson he could take it or leave it, because the fix was going to happen as long as the gamblers came up with the money. Jackson's refusal could have been a problem, because he was the star of the team and the gamblers wanted him involved. Many believed Gandil simply lied and said Jackson was part of the scheme. Weaver attended several of the meetings of the player-conspirators, but he apparently also refused to be a part of the plot.

Sullivan did not have the resources to come up with the $100,000 Gandil wanted, so he involved several infamous gamblers in the plot: Abe Attell, a former featherweight boxing champion; ex-White Sox pitcher "Sleepy Bill" Burns, and New York Giant first baseman Hall Chase. Arnold Rothstein, however, was the man who provided most of the cash. He was known throughout New York City as a gambler who would bet on anything he could fix.

FAVORED FIVE TO ONE

Matched against the Cincinnati Reds, the Chicago White Sox were favored to win the World Series. They were almost the same team that won the 1917 championship and the 1919 Series looked to be no contest. It was said that people came not to see if the Sox won, but how they won. Early gamblers' odds favored them 5 to 1. The day before the Series opened in Cincinnati rumors of the fix were everywhere. As quickly as big bills started changing hands, the odds began to shift toward Cincinnati. That night Cicotte found $10,000 in his hotel room.

Chicago lost the first game 9-1, but the players didn't receive the $20,000 in cash Gandil had been promised for losing that game. They were willing to lose game two as long as the money came by the end of the next day. Chicago lost 4-2. The Sox players not involved in the fix were beginning to get suspicious. Catcher Ray Schalk knew something was wrong with the pitching. He and manager Kid Gleason reportedly got into fights with Gandil and Williams over their poor performances. After the game, Gandil looked up Abe Attell to collect the $40,000 owed him and his teammates for throwing two games. He received only $10,000. The players were upset and began to have second thoughts about continuing to lose.

Chicago won the third game and many of the gamblers betting on individual games lost a great deal of money. It was Attell's turn to feel betrayed and he refused to pay any more. Sullivan came up with $20,000 before the fourth game and at least some of the traitors were still willing to lose. Cicotte made several errors, and the Reds won 2-0. Chicago lost game five, as well, with a final score of 5-0.

By now the gamblers had missed another payment, and the players had decided there was no reason to lose. At least if they won the Series, they would collect $5,000 each. Chicago won the sixth game 5-4 and the seventh 4-1. The players all seemed to play to the best of their abilities, and the national championship was within their grasp. Unfortunately, any chance of winning was ruined by Arnold Rothstein. Instead of betting individual games, he had bet on Cincinnati to win the series. With his investment at risk, Rothstein sent one of his henchman to visit

Williams, who was pitching in the eighth game. He explained to Williams that Rothstein wanted the Series to end the next day. He threatened Williams and his wife. Chicago lost 10-5. In the end, one scared man handed Cincinnati the World Series. . . .

Throughout the Series, Hugh Fullerton, a sports writer for the *Chicago Herald* and *Examiner*, had been paying close attention to the rumors of a fix: He hinted about the selling of the Series in his newspaper columns and urged club owners to do something about gamblers' involvement in baseball. Most people didn't believe fixing the World Series was possible. Club owners, who knew better, were afraid the public would turn their backs on baseball if they admitted any wrongdoing, and refused to acknowledge a problem. The entire controversy might have blown over if the problem had not continued to grow. During the 1920 season, players on other teams began to take advantage of gamblers' offers. Widespread rumors surfaced about games being thrown by players from the New York Giants, New York Yankees, Atlanta Braves, and Cleveland Indians.

THE GRAND JURY HEARINGS

In September 1920, a Cook County, Illinois, grand jury convened to look into allegations that the Chicago White Sox had thrown games against the Philadelphia Phillies. The investigation soon extended to the 1919 World Series and baseball gambling in general. The White Sox were enjoying a good season when the grand jury began calling players, owners, managers, writers, and gamblers to testify about what had happened the previous year. At the urging of Comiskey, who was trying to cover up his own knowledge of the conspiracy, Jackson and Cicotte were the first to admit everything they knew about the fix.

When the grand jury finally concluded its investigation, indictments were handed down against the eight White Sox players, as well as Hal Chase, Abe Attell, Joe Sullivan, Bill Burns, and several of Arnold Rothstein's henchmen. Rothstein, who allegedly made $270,000 on the 1919 Series, was not indicted by the grand jury. Rothstein moved on to bootlegging, drug dealing, and labor racketeering. He was eventually murdered by a rival gambler whom he had accused of fixing a poker game. The indicted players, however, faced a trial.

The trial of the accused White Sox players, who had been suspended for the remainder of the 1920 season, began in June of 1921. The grand jury records, however, including the confessions of Jackson, Cicotte, and Williams, were reported missing (they turned up four years later in the hands of Comiskey's lawyer, George Hudnall, who never explained their reappearance). After a month of hearing testimony, it took the jury just two hours and forty-seven minutes to acquit all defendants. Lack of evidence and the missing confessions resulted in the not-guilty verdict. In the end, the trial did not answer many questions. The facts, never clear cut to begin with, continued to be manipulated, distorted, and subject to outright lies.

CLEANING UP THEIR ACT

After the 1920 season, fearing baseball might not survive the gambling scandal, club owners decided to clean up their act. The three-man national commission, headed by Ban Johnson, was replaced by a single, independent commissioner with dictatorial power over baseball. Federal Judge Kenesaw Mountain Landis was appointed commissioner, and he acted quickly to restore the public's faith in baseball. Immediately after they were acquitted of any criminal charges, Landis banned all eight players from the game. Landis said, "regardless of the verdict of the juries, no player who throws a ball game, no player who undertakes or promises to throw a ball game, no player who sits in confidence with a bunch of crooked players and does not promptly tell his club about it, will ever play professional baseball." True to his word, Landis never allowed any of the eight White Sox to play professional ball again.

CHRONOLOGY

1896

January 4—Utah becomes the forty-fifth state.

May 18—In the *Plessy v. Ferguson* case, the U.S. Supreme Court rules that the "separate-but-equal" policy of racial segregation is constitutional.

May 27—A tornado strikes St. Louis, Missouri, killing 255 and leaving thousands homeless.

November 3—William McKinley is elected as the twenty-fifth president.

November 14—A power plant at Niagara Falls begins operation.

December 25—John Philip Sousa writes "Stars and Stripes Forever."

1897

January 11—M.H. Cannon of Utah becomes the first female U.S. senator.

February 17—The National Congress of Parents and Teachers (PTA) organizes in Washington, D.C.

April 19—The first American marathon is held in Boston, Massachusetts; John J. McDermott wins in two hours, fifty-five minutes, and ten seconds.

November 25—Spain grants Puerto Rico autonomy.

1898

February 15—The U.S.S. *Maine* explodes off the coast of Havana, Cuba; two hundred fifty-eight American personnel on board are killed.

April 25—The United States declares war on Spain.

May 12—Louisiana adds a grandfather clause to its constitution with the intention to eliminate black voters; only voters whose fathers were registered to vote by 1867—the year before blacks were granted suffrage—were permitted to vote.

June 12—Philippine nationalists declare independence from Spain.

July 1—Assistant secretary of the U.S. Navy, Theodore Roosevelt, leads his "Rough Riders" up San Juan Hill in Cuba.

July 7—The United States annexes Hawaii.

July 17—Spain surrenders to the United States at Santiago, Cuba.

December 10—The Spanish-American War ends; the United States acquires the Philippines, Puerto Rico, and Guam.

1899

January 17—The United States takes possession of Wake Island in the Pacific Ocean.

February 4—Philippine rebels revolt against American occupation of the Philippines.

March 3—George Dewey becomes the first admiral of the U.S. Navy.

December 2—The United States and Germany agree to divide Samoa between them.

1900

March 25—The U.S. Socialist Party is formed at Indianapolis, Indiana.

August 14—International forces, including U.S. marines, enter Beijing to end the Boxer Rebellion, which was aimed at expelling foreigners from China.

September 8—The most deadly hurricane and tidal wave in American history hits Galveston, Texas; six thousand people are killed.

November 6—President William McKinley is reelected for a second term.

1901

February 5—Financier J.P. Morgan forms the U.S. Steel Corporation.

May 23—American forces capture the leader of the Philippine rebels, Emilio Aguinaldo.

September 6—President McKinley is shot at the Pan-American Exposition in Buffalo, New York, and dies eight days later; Vice President Theodore Roosevelt succeeds him, becoming the twenty-sixth president of the United States.

1902

March 4—The American Automobile Association is founded in Chicago, Illinois.

April 2—The first motion-picture theater opens in Los Angeles, California.

December 28—A trans-Pacific cable links the United States to Hawaii.

1903

January 19—The first regular transatlantic radio broadcast between the United States and England takes place.

February 14—The U.S. Department of Commerce and Labor is established.

February 24—The United States acquires a naval station at Guantanamo Bay, Cuba.

June 16—Automobile manufacturer Henry Ford forms Ford Motors.

October 20—The United States wins the disputed boundary between the District of Alaska and Canada.

November 3—Colombia grants Panama independence.

November 18—The Hay-Bunau-Varilla Treaty gives the United States exclusive rights to the Panama Canal project.

December 1—The film *The Great Train Robbery* is released.

December 17—Orville and Wilbur Wright's biplane achieves the first heavier-than-air flight at Kitty Hawk, North Carolina.

1904

February 5—American occupation of Cuba ceases.

February 6—The Russo-Japanese War begins.

May 14—The first Olympics in the United States are held in St. Louis, Missouri.

May 15—Coney Island reopens.

November 6—President Theodore Roosevelt is reelected for a second term.

December 6—The Roosevelt Corollary is added to the Monroe Doctrine of 1823—which declared the territories in the Western Hemisphere free from future colonization by any European power—justifying American intervention as foreign policy in Latin America.

1905

April 29—The Socialist weekly *Appeal to Reason* begins publishing Upton Sinclair's controversial book on the meat packing industry, *The Jungle.*

September 5—The Treaty of Portsmouth, signed at Portsmouth, New Hampshire, ends the Russo-Japanese War; Russia is

forced to abandon its expansionist policy in Asia; President
Roosevelt serves as the mediator.

December 28—The Intercollegiate Athletic Association of the
United States is founded. (It becomes the National College
Athletic Association in 1910.)

1906

April 18—The most deadly earthquake in American history hits
San Francisco; more than three thousand people are killed,
and fires ravage the city.

June 29—The Hepburn Act is passed, giving the federal government more power over railroad companies.

June 30—The first Pure Food and Drug Act and Meat Inspection Act are passed.

December 10—President Roosevelt becomes the first American
to be awarded the Nobel Peace Prize in recognition of mediating the Russo-Japanese War peace conference.

1907

March 21—U.S. marines land in Honduras to intervene in a
revolution.

November 16—Oklahoma becomes the forty-sixth state.

December 6—Coal mine explosions in Monongah, West Virginia, kill 361 people.

December 31—The first ball drops at Times Square in New York
City to ring in a new year.

1908

April 12—A fire in Chelsea, Massachusetts, leaves seventeen
thousand people homeless.

July 26—The Federal Bureau of Investigation is established.

August 14—A race riot erupts in Springfield, Illinois, killing two
blacks and five whites; property damages exceed two hundred thousand dollars.

October 1—Automobile manufacturer Henry Ford introduces
"the universal cheap car," the Model T.

November 3—William Howard Taft is elected as the twenty-seventh president.

1909

February 12—The National Association for the Advancement
of Colored People is founded.

February 22—The first U.S. fleet to circle the globe, the Great
White Fleet, returns to Virginia.

July 12—The Sixteenth Amendment is approved, giving the federal government the power to collect income taxes.

December 16—Under pressure from the United States, Nicaraguan president José Santos Zelaya leaves office.

1910

January 19—The National Institute of Arts and Letters is established by Congress.

February 8—The Boy Scouts of America is incorporated.

November 8—The first election in which women may vote is held in Washington State.

1911

February 8—The United States helps to overthrow the president of Honduras, Miguel Dávila.

March 25—One hundred and forty-eight workers are killed in the Triangle Shirtwaist Factory fire in New York City.

May 15—The U.S. Supreme Court orders the dissolution of the Standard Oil Company because it is in violation of the Sherman Antitrust Act.

1912

January 6—New Mexico becomes the forty-seventh state.

January 12—Ten thousand textile workers go on strike in Lawrence, Massachusetts; by February, thirty thousand workers are on strike.

April 15—The luxury ocean liner *Titanic* sinks after striking an iceberg off the coast of Halifax, Nova Scotia; 1,503 of the 2,200 passengers onboard die.

May 13—The Seventeenth Amendment, which requires the direct election of senators, is passed.

August 24—The United States passes the Anti-Gag Law, giving federal employees the right to petition the government.

November 5—Woodrow Wilson is elected as the twenty-eighth president.

1913

February 17—The first minimum wage law in the United States is enforced in Oregon; progressive artists open the highly influential Armory Art Show in New York City.

March 3—Suffragists march for women's suffrage in Washington, D.C.

December 6—The U.S. Congress passes a bill authorizing the damming of Hetch Hetchy Valley in Yosemite National Park.

December 23—The Federal Reserve System, which serves as America's central bank, is established.

1914

February 7—Entertainer Charlie Chaplin's character "the Tramp" makes its first appearance in *Kid Auto Races at Venice.*

May 7—The U.S. Congress establishes Mother's Day.

June 28—The archduke of Austria-Este, Franz Ferdinand, and his wife, Sophia, are assassinated in Sarajevo by Serbian nationalist Gavrilo Princip.

August 1—Germany declares war on Russia in World War I.

August 3—Germany declares war on France and invades Belgium.

August 4—Germany declares war on Belgium; Great Britain declares war on Germany.

August 15—The Panama Canal opens.

August 19—President Woodrow Wilson issues the U.S. Proclamation of Neutrality.

September 26—The Federal Trade Commission is established to regulate interstate commerce.

1915

February 8—The film *The Clansman,* later titled *The Birth of a Nation,* debuts.

February 18—Germany begins its naval blockade of Great Britain.

February 22—Germany commences "unrestricted" submarine war.

May 7—The British ocean liner *Lusitania* is sunk by a German submarine; 1,198 lives are lost, including 128 Americans.

1916

February 21—The Battle of Verdun (World War I) begins.

October 16—Margaret Sanger opens the first birth control clinic in Brooklyn, New York.

November 7—Jeannette Rankin of Montana becomes the first female U.S. representative; President Wilson is reelected for a second term.

1917

February 3—The American ocean liner *Housatonic* is sunk by a German submarine; the United States ends diplomatic relations with Germany.

March 31—The United States purchases the West Indies from Denmark for $25 million and renames them the Virgin Islands.

April 2—President Wilson delivers his war message to Congress.

April 6—The United States declares war on Germany and enters World War I.

June 5—Ten million American men begin registering for the World War I draft.

June 26—The first American Expeditionary Force arrives in France.

November 2—The first American soldiers are killed in combat.

1918

January 8—Mississippi becomes the first state to prohibit alcohol.

March 11—The first wave of the influenza epidemic in the United States hits Fort Riley, Kansas.

June 5—The United States wins its first World War I victory at the Battle of Belleau Wood in France.

June 16—Socialist Eugene Debs gives his antiwar speech in Canton, Ohio.

July 18—American and French forces open their Aisne-Marne offensive in France.

September 29—The Allied forces successfully break through the Hindenburg Line, Germany's central trench system.

November 11—Armistice Day; the fighting of World War I ends at 11:00 A.M.; Germany surrenders.

November 21—The Volstead Act is passed, stating that until the conclusion of World War I, it would be illegal to manufacture, transport, and sell alcoholic beverages after June 30, 1919.

December 4—President Wilson departs for the Versailles Peace Conference in France, becoming the first American president to travel outside of the United States while in office.

1919

January 18—The World War I peace conference opens in Versailles.

January 25—The League of Nations is founded.

January 29—The U.S. secretary of state proclaims the Eighteenth Amendment (Prohibition).

June 4—The U.S. Congress passes the Women's Suffrage bill.

June 28—The Treaty of Versailles is signed, ending World War I.

July 10—President Wilson delivers the Treaty of Versailles to the U.S. Senate.

July 27—The Chicago race riots occur; fifteen whites and twenty-three blacks are killed.

October 1—The World Series—in which the Chicago White Sox intentionally lose to the Cincinatti Reds—begins.

November 19—The U.S. Senate rejects (55 to 39) the Treaty of Versailles and the League of Nations.

December 22—The United States deports 250 alien radicals, including American anarchist Emma Goldman.

FOR FURTHER RESEARCH

Judith Icke Anderson, *William Howard Taft: An Intimate History.* New York: W.W. Norton, 1981.

Robert B. Asprey, *At Belleau Wood.* New York: Putnam, 1965.

Thomas A. Bailey and Paul B. Ryan, *The Lusitania Disaster.* New York: Free Press, 1975.

John Marshall Barker, *The Saloon Problem and Social Reform.* Boston: Everett Press, 1905.

Robert Beisner, *Twelve Against the Empire: The Anti-Imperialists, 1898–1900.* New York: McGraw-Hill, 1968.

Edward A. Berlin, *Ragtime: A Musical and Cultural History.* Berkeley: University of California Press, 1980.

Richard Dodgson Bowman, *Charlie Chaplin: His Life and Art.* New York: Haskell House, 1974.

Thomas Brook, ed., *Plessy v. Ferguson: A Brief History with Documents.* Boston: Bedford Books, 1997.

Milton W. Brown, *The Story of the Armory Art Show.* New York: Abbeville Press, 1988.

David Mark Chalmers, *The Social and Political Ideas of the Muckrakers.* New York: Citadel Press, 1964.

Ellen Chesler, *Woman of Valor: Margaret Sanger and the Birth Control Movement in America.* New York: Simon and Schuster, 1992.

Rose Cohen, *Out of the Shadow.* New York: George H. Doran, 1918.

Nancy F. Cott, ed., *Woman Suffrage.* New Providence, NJ: K.G. Saur, 1994.

John E. DiMeglio, *Vaudeville U.S.A.* OH: Bowling Green University Popular Press, 1973.

John W. Dodds, *Everyday Life in Twentieth Century America*. New York: G.P. Putnam's Sons, 1965.

Melvyn Dubofsky, *Industrialism and the American Worker, 1865–1920*. Wheeling, IL: Harlan Davidson, 1996.

Foster Rhea Dulles, *20th Century America*. New York: Houghton Mifflin, 1945.

Robert F. Durden, *The Climax of Populism: The Election of 1896*. Lexington: University of Kentucky Press, 1965.

Edward Robb Ellis, *Echoes of Distant Thunder: Life in the United States 1914–1918*. New York: Coward, McCann & Geoghegan, 1975.

David S. Foglesong, *America's Secret War Against Bolshevism: U.S. Intervention in the Russian Civil War, 1917–1920*. Chapel Hill: University of North Carolina Press, 1995.

Lettie Gavin, *American Women in World War I: They Also Served*. Niwot: University Press of Colorado, 1997.

Meirion Harries and Susie Harries, *The Last Days of Innocence: America at War, 1917–1918*. New York: Random House, 1997.

A.A. Hoehling, *The Great Epidemic*. Boston: Little, Brown, 1961.

Jerry Israel, *Progressivism and the Open Door: America and China, 1905–1921*. Pittsburgh: University of Pittsburgh Press, 1971.

John F. Kasson, *Amusing the Million: Coney Island at the Turn of the Century*. New York: Hill & Wang, 1978.

John Keegan, *The First World War*. New York: Alfred A. Knopf, 1999.

Charles Flint Kellogg, *A History of the National Association for the Advancement of Colored People. 1909–1920*. Vol. 1. Baltimore: Johns Hopkins University Press, 1967.

Gina Kolata, *Flu: The Story of the Great Influenza Pandemic of 1918 and the Search for the Virus That Caused It*. New York: Farrar, Straus, and Giroux.

Alan M. Kraut, *The Huddled Masses: The Immigrant in American Society, 1880–1921*. Arlington Heights, IL: Harlan Davidson, 1982.

Robert Lang, ed., *The Birth of a Nation: D.W. Griffith, Director.* New Brunswick, NJ: Rutgers University Press, 1994.

Arthur S. Link, *Woodrow Wilson and the Progressive Era, 1910–1917.* New York: Harper & Row, 1954.

Arthur S. Link, William A. Link, and William B. Catton, *American Epoch: A History of the United States Since 1900.* Vol. 1. New York: Alfred A. Knopf, 1987.

Arthur S. Link and Richard L. McCormick, *Progressivism.* Arlington Heights, IL: Harlan Davidson, 1983.

Frederick C. Luebke, *Bonds of Loyalty: German-Americans and World War I.* Dekalb: Northern Illinois University Press, 1974.

Albert Marrin, *The Yanks Are Coming: The United States in the First World War.* New York: Antheneum, 1986.

David McCollough, *The Path Between the Seas: The Creation of the Panama Canal 1870–1914.* New York: Simon and Schuster, 1977.

Nathan Miller, *Theodore Roosevelt: A Life.* New York: William & Morrow, 1992.

H. Wayne Morgan, *William McKinley and His America.* NY: Syracuse University Press, 1963.

Elting E. Morison, *Admiral Sims and the Modern American Navy.* Boston: Houghton Mifflin, 1942.

John Muir, *The Yosemite.* New York: Century, 1912.

Dana Gardner Munro, *Intervention and Dollar Diplomacy in the Caribbean, 1900–1921.* NJ: Princeton University Press, 1964.

Charles Musser, *The Emergence of Cinema: The American Screen to 1907.* Berkeley: University of California Press, 1994.

Allan Nevins and Frank Ernest Hill, *Ford: Expansion and Challenge, 1915–1933.* New York: Charles Scribner's Sons, 1957.

Thomas C. Reeves, *Twentieth-Century America: A Brief History.* New York: Oxford University Press, 2000.

Edward V. Rickenbacker, *Fighting the Flying Circus.* New York: Frederick A. Stokes, 1919.

Donald Smythe, *Pershing, General of the Armies.* Bloomington: Indiana University Press, 1986.

Martha Solomon, *Emma Goldman.* Boston: Twayne, 1987.

Allan H. Spear, *Black Chicago: The Making of a Negro Ghetto, 1890–1920.* Chicago: University of Chicago Press, 1967.

Leon Stein, *The Triangle Fire.* Ithaca, NY: Cornell University Press, 2001.

Mark Sullivan, *Our Times: The United States 1900–1925.* New York: Charles Scribner's Sons, 1935.

Henry Watterson, *The History of the Spanish-American War.* New York: Werner, 1898.

Adna Ferrin Weber, *The Growth of Cities in the Nineteenth Century.* New York: Macmillan, 1899.

C. Vann Woodward, *Origins of the New South, 1877–1913.* Baton Rouge: Louisiana State University, 1951.

Larzer Ziff, *The American 1890s: Life and Times of a Lost Generation.* New York: Viking Press, 1966.

INDEX